Frommer's™

Salzburg
day BY day™

1st Edition

by

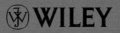

WILEY

A John Wiley and Sons, Ltd, Publication

Contents

UK Publisher: Sally Smith
Production Manager: Daniel Mersey
Commissioning Editor: Fiona Quinn
Development Editor: Fiona Quinn
Content Editor: Erica Peters
Photo Research: David Cottingham/Jill Emeny
Cartography: Simonetta Giori

Wiley also publishes its books in a variety of electronic formats. Some
content that appears in print may not be available in electronic books.

British Library Cataloguing in Publication Data
A catalogue record for this book is available from the British Library

ISBN: 978-0-470-72119-3 (paperback)
ISBN: 978-0-470-66587-9 (ebk)

Typeset by Wiley Indianapolis Composition Services
Printed and bound in China by RR Donnelley

5 4 3 2 1

A Note from the Editorial Director

Organizing your time. That's what this guide is all about.

Other guides give you long lists of things to see and do and then expect you to fit the pieces together. The Day by Day guides are different. These guides tell you the best of everything, and then they show you how to see it *in the smartest, most time-efficient way*. Our authors have designed detailed itineraries organized by time, neighborhood, or special interest. And each tour comes with a bulleted map that takes you from stop to stop.

Hoping to follow in the footsteps of Mozart, listening to exquisite music? Hoping to climb every mountain from *The Sound of Music* while sampling the sensational skiing? Or simply soak up the atmosphere of Europe's finest baroque city? Whatever your interest or schedule, the Day by Days give you the smartest routes to follow. Not only do we take you to the top attractions, hotels, and restaurants, but we also help you access those special moments that locals get to experience—those "finds" that turn tourists into travelers.

The Day by Days are also your top choice if you're looking for one complete guide for all your travel needs. The best hotels and restaurants for every budget, the greatest shopping values, the wildest nightlife—it's all here.

Why should you trust our judgment? Because our authors personally visit each place they write about. They're an independent lot who say what they think and would never include places they wouldn't recommend to their best friends. They're also open to suggestions from readers. If you'd like to contact them, please send your comments our way at feedback@frommers.com, and we'll pass them on.

Enjoy your Day by Day guide—the most helpful travel companion you can buy. And have the trip of a lifetime.

Warm regards,

Kelly Regan

Kelly Regan, Editorial Director
Frommer's Travel Guides

About the Author

Nick Dalton is a freelance travel writer based in London. He writes regularly in the *Daily Telegraph* and has written for *The Times, The Independent* and *The Daily Express* as well as countless magazines. He has covered mountain destinations around the world, from the Rockies to South Korea, and is a leading ski journalist who loves using his trips to the slopes as a way to explore their surroundings . . . Salzburg in particular. He has also written travel guides for Colorado, Canada, Tennessee and other destinations. He is the co-author of *Frommer's Wales with Your Family*.

Acknowledgments

Thanks to Maria Altendorfer and Andrea Heitzer at Salzburg Tourism, Sabine Arnold at Ski Amadé, Doris Thurnhofer at Salzburgerland Tourism, and Karoline Scheiber and everyone at the Austrian Tourist Office in London. A big thank you to Deborah Stone for helping with the photography. This book is dedicated to Deborah, Georgia and Henry, who make the family research such fun.

An Additional Note

Please be advised that travel information is subject to change at any time—and this is especially true of prices. We therefore suggest that you write or call ahead for confirmation when making your travel plans. The authors, editors, and publisher cannot be held responsible for the experiences of readers while traveling. Your safety is important to us, however, so we encourage you to stay alert and be aware of your surroundings.

Star Ratings, Icons & Abbreviations

Every hotel, restaurant, and attraction listing in this guide has been ranked for quality, value, service, amenities, and special features using a **star-rating system.** Hotels, restaurants, attractions, shopping, and nightlife are rated on a scale of zero stars (recommended) to three stars (exceptional). In addition to the star-rating system, we also use a **kids icon** to point out the best bets for families. Within each tour, we recommend cafes, bars, or restaurants where you can take a break. Each of these stops appears in a shaded box marked with a coffee-cup-shaped bullet ☕ .

The following **abbreviations** are used for credit cards:

AE	American Express	DISC	Discover	V	Visa
DC	Diners Club	MC	MasterCard		

Travel Resources at Frommers.com

Frommer's travel resources don't end with this guide. Frommer's website, **www.frommers.com,** has travel information on more than 4,000 destinations. We update features regularly, giving you access to the most current trip-planning information and the best airfare, lodging, and car-rental bargains. You can also listen to podcasts, connect with other Frommers.com members through our active-reader forums, share your travel photos, read blogs from guidebook editors and fellow travelers, and much more.

A Note on Prices

In the "Take a Break" and "Best Bets" sections of this book, we have used a system of dollar signs to show a range of costs for 1 night in a hotel (the price of a double-occupancy room) or the cost of an entree (main course) at a restaurant. Use the following table to decipher the dollar signs:

Cost	Hotels	Restaurants
$	under $100	under $10
$$	$100–$200	$10–$20
$$$	$200–$300	$20–$30
$$$$	$300–$400	$30–$40
$$$$$	over $400	over $40

How to Contact Us

In researching this book, we discovered many wonderful places—hotels, restaurants, shops, and more. We're sure you'll find others. Please tell us about them, so we can share the information with your fellow travelers in upcoming editions. If you were disappointed with a recommendation, we'd love to know that, too. Please write to:

Frommer's Salzburg Day by Day, 1st Edition
Wiley UK

15 Favorite
Moments

15 Favorite **Moments**

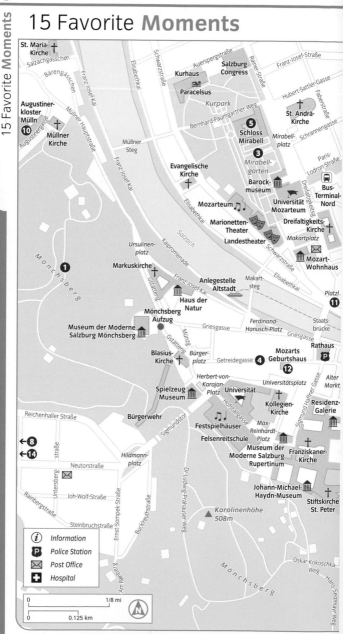

St. Maria-Kirche
Salzachgässchen
Bärengässchen
Elisabethkai
Schwarzstraße
Auerspergstraße
Rainer-Straße
Franz-Josef-Straße

Kurhaus
Salzburg Congress
Paracelsus

Hubert-Sattler-Gasse
Faberstraße
St. Andrä-Kirche
Schrannengasse

Augustiner-kloster Mülln **10**
Augustinergasse
Müllner Hauptstraße
Müllner Kirche

Kurpark
Bernhard-Paumgartner-Weg

Schloss Mirabell **5**
Mirabell-platz
Paris-Lodron-Straße

Müllner Steg
Müllner Steg

Franz-Josef-Kai

Evangelische Kirche

Mirabell-garten **3**

Barock-museum

Dreifaltigkeitsgasse
Bus-Terminal-Nord

Elisabethkai
Salzach

Mozarteum 🎵

Universität Mozarteum

Dreifaltigkeits-Kirche

Kapromenade

Ursulinen-platz

Marionetten-Theater

Makartplatz

M ö n c h s b e r g **1**

Markuskirche
Gstättengasse
Franz-Josef-Kai

Landestheater

Schwarzstraße

Mozart-Wohnhaus

Elisabethkai

Makart-steg

Anlegestelle Altstadt

Haus der Natur

Mönchsberg Aufzug

Museum der Moderne Salzburg Mönchsberg

Ferdinand-Hanusch-Platz
Griesgasse

Platzl **11**

Staats-brücke

Griesgasse

Rathaus 🅿

Alter Markt

Blasius-Kirche
Gstättengasse
Münzg.
Bürger-platz
Getreidegasse **4**
Mozarts Geburtshaus **12**

Spielzeug Museum

Herbert-von-Karajan-Platz
Universität
Universitätsplatz

Sigmund Haffner Gasse

Kollegien-Kirche
Residenz-Galerie

Bürgerwehr

Reichenhaller Straße

Hofstallgasse

Festspielhäuser 🎵

Max-Reinhardt-Platz

Felsenreitschule

Museum der Moderne Salzburg Rupertinum

Franziskaner-Kirche

←**8**
←**14**
straße
Neutorstraße
Hildmann-platz

Joh.-Wolf-Straße

Untersberg
Rainbergstraße

Steinbruchstraße

Dr.-Ludwig-Prähauser-Weg

Johann-Michael-Haydn-Museum

Stiftskirche St. Peter

Karolinenhöhe 508m

M ö n c h s b e r g

Oskar-Kokoschka-Weg

Hans-Sedlmayr-Weg

Ernst-Sompek-Straße
Buolkreuthstraße
Am Kapl

ⓘ Information
🅿 Police Station
✉ Post Office
✚ Hospital

| 0 | 1/8 mi |
| 0 | 0.125 km |

Previous page: Winter view of Salzburg.

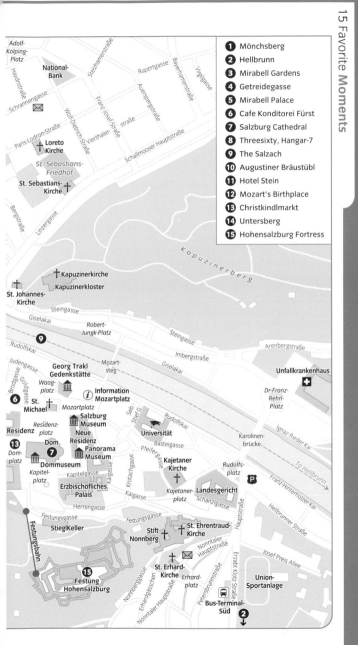

1 Mönchsberg
2 Hellbrunn
3 Mirabell Gardens
4 Getreidegasse
5 Mirabell Palace
6 Cafe Konditorei Fürst
7 Salzburg Cathedral
8 Threesixty, Hangar-7
9 The Salzach
10 Augustiner Bräustübl
11 Hotel Stein
12 Mozart's Birthplace
13 Christkindlmarkt
14 Untersberg
15 Hohensalzburg Fortress

Adolf-Kolping-Platz

Haydnstraße
National-Bank
Schrannengasse
Stelzhamerstraße
Rupertgasse
Bayerhamerstraße
Vigiligasse
Auerspergstraße
Franz-Josef-Straße
Wolf-Dietrich-Straße
Vierthaler-Straße
Schallmooser Hauptstraße

Paris-Lodron-Straße
Loreto Kirche
St. Sebastians-Friedhof
St. Sebastians-Kirche
Bergstraße
Linzergasse

St. Johannes-Kirche
Kapuzinerkirche
Kapuzinerkloster
Kapuzinerberg

Steingasse
Giselakai
Robert-Jungk-Platz
Steingasse
Arenbergstraße

Rudolfskai
9
Judengasse
Brodgasse
Goldgasse
Georg Trakl Gedenkstätte
Waag-platz
Mozart-steg
Imbergstraße
Giselakai
Unfallkrankenhaus
Dr-Franz-Rehrl-Platz

6
St. Michael
Information Mozartplatz
Mozartplatz
Salzburg Museum
Seb. G.
Rudolfskai

Residenz
Residenz-platz
Neue Residenz
Universität
Basteigasse
Karolinen-brücke
Ignaz-Rieder-Kai
To Hellbrunn

13
Dom-platz
Dom
7
Dommuseum
Panorama Museum
Pfeifergasse
Kajetaner Kirche
Rudolfs-platz
P
Franz-Hinterholzer-Kai

Kapitel-platz
Erzbischöfliches Palais
Kapitelgasse
Kaigasse
Krotachgasse
Kajetaner-platz
Landesgericht
Schanzlgasse
Hellbrunner Straße

Herrengasse
Festungsgasse
Festungsgasse
St. Ehrentraud-Kirche
Nonntaler Hauptstraße
Josef Preis Allee

StieglKeller
Stift Nonnberg

Festungsbahn
15
Festung Hohensalzburg
Nonnberggasse
Erhardgässchen
Nonntaler Hauptstraße
St. Erhard-Kirche
Erhard-platz
Petersbrunnstraße
Erzabt Klotz Straße
Union-Sportanlage

Bus-Terminal-Süd
2

Salzburg is a city known for its music and its history. What's surprising to the first-time visitor is how small and walkable the place is, and how many simple pleasures there are to be had. These are just a few of the things that I find special about this gorgeous city on the edge of the mountains.

1 Walking the Mönchsberg. One of a pair of mini-mountains bookending the city, this semi-wild park high above the streets has walks from the ancient Hohensalzburg Fortress to the sleek Museum of Modern Art. There's a real feeling of being behind the tourist scenes as you find hidden paths and discover yet another breathtaking view through the trees. *See p 60.*

2 Taking the children to Hellbrunn. The palace, in its huge park, is an ideal family excursion. Youngsters love getting soaked (and watching adults getting soaked) on the tour of the trick fountains, then running wild in the grounds and at the impressive adventure playground. If you have the energy to take them to the zoo, they'll love you even more. *See p 19.*

Hellbrunn Palace.

3 Singing *The Sound of Music* songs in Mirabell Gardens. Salzburg is full of *The Sound of Music* locations but these ornate gardens sum it all up, a mix of timeless beauty and movie memories. Here, among the fountains, arched hedge, and exquisite flower displays, is where *Do-Re-Mi* was sung. *See p 12.*

4 Wandering the narrow streets. The Getreidegasse and the roads, paths, and alleys that criss-cross the Old Town never fail to entertain. There's something around every corner, on every wall, and down every opening, whether shops with ornate medieval signs, little pieces of history, or cafes. And you can never stray far, with the Mönchsberg on one side and the river on the other. *See p 60.*

5 Listening to a Schlosskonzerte at the Mirabell Palace's Marble Hall. I feel like I've penetrated the inner sanctum of Mozart's city at one of the almost-daily recitals by cool quartets and other small groups in the small, refined setting. No fancy wigs or gold buttons, just black suits and T-shirts, and a friendly makeshift bar. *See p 27.*

6 Popping into Fürst's for a Mozart Ball. It's a childlike treat to have just one of the original, handmade, chocolate-covered marzipan treats. These gobstopper-sized chocs, created in 1890, can't be eaten in one bite, and let me know I'm back in Salzburg, sipping a coffee in one of the handful of Fürst's cafes. *See p 26.*

7 **Being amazed at the Dom.** The Dom is the cathedral, a baroque masterpiece of frescoes, gilt, and carving. The font where Mozart was baptized is here but that's over-shadowed by the sheer Italianate grandeur of the place. It's relaxing when it's quiet, but I love it most when it's packed for Sunday Mass, with organ and choir in full swing. *See p 9.*

8 **Having a glass of bubbly in Threesixty.** No matter how many times I come here, I'm still in awe. Threesixty is a glass-walled, glass-floored pod of a bar hanging from the roof of the modernistic glass-and-steel Hangar-7, where Red Bull drinks baron Dietrich Mateschitz keeps his collection of planes, heli-copters, and cars. I like to take the heady, spiraling walkway and sip champagne just as the sun is slip-ping behind the mountains, turning the world to gold. *See p 113.*

9 **Biking along the river.** The Salzach cuts through the middle of Salzburg. I like to rent a bike for the day on the Old Town's riverbank, and then I follow the flat river path south. If I fancy an easy jaunt, it's down to Hellbrunn and back along the other side; a longer trip and it's

Sunset over the Dom.

as far as the town of Hallein. Either way, it's easy cycling at the foot of the encroaching mountains. *See p 80.*

10 **Sipping a beer in the Augustiner Bräustübl.** This is the beer hall to end beer halls, room after cathedral-like room. Grab a tankard, pay, and have it filled from a single tap. I still haven't worked my way through the corridor of stalls selling all manner of snacks from peppery radishes to spit-roasted

The alleys off Getreidegasse are full of temptations.

The Salzach has bike paths along both sides of the river.

chicken, cured fish to enormous sausages—but I'm trying. *See p 101.*

⑪ **Having an evening cocktail on the Steinterrasse.** The rooftop bar at the Hotel Stein, on the New Town riverbank, has one of the world's most glorious views, straight across from the brilliantly lit Hohensalzburg Fortress and the yellow lights of the narrow streets below. *See p 114.*

⑫ **Standing in the house where Mozart was born.** The uneven stairs, the low ceilings, and the sheer feeling of history are overwhelming in this ancient house where a genius came into the world. The fact that it contains instruments he used to play in his earliest days makes it even more awe-inspiring. *See p 24.*

⑬ **Watching the snow fall at Christmas.** There's nowhere more magical than Salzburg at this time, whether you're browsing in the Christkindlmarkt—the king of Christmas markets—or shopping in the

gaily-lit and decorated streets. Even doing the tourist sites takes on a new dimension, with the sounds and scents of the season all around. *See p 48.*

⑭ **Heading up the Untersberg.** I adore this lonely mountain only a short bus ride from town. The historic cable car up is fun, and then you have serious hikes (I've been to Germany and back) as well as gentle walks with immense views. If the clouds roll in, I just head to one of the cafes. *See p 84.*

⑮ **And finally . . . just standing outside the Hohensalzburg Fortress and gazing.** The city spreads out below, a mass of tumbling roofs and soaring spires, and the mountains rise up a few miles away. It truly is a beautiful place, somewhere that has the benefits of a city, but with the joys of a small town— and somewhere that when you've been once you'll always want to come again. *See p 9.* ●

The Best **in One Day**

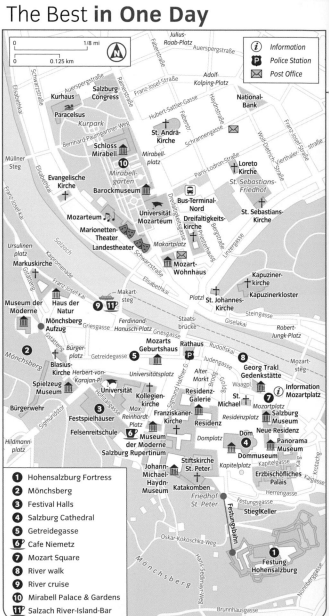

i	Information
P	Police Station
$\boxtimes$	Post Office

1 Hohensalzburg Fortress
2 Mönchsberg
3 Festival Halls
4 Salzburg Cathedral
5 Getreidegasse
6 Cafe Niemetz
7 Mozart Square
8 River walk
9 River cruise
10 Mirabell Palace & Gardens
11 Salzach River-Island-Bar

Previous page: The domes of the cathedral and Kollegienkirche line up.

With just a day, you simply want to go and explore Salzburg, and there's no easier city to come to grips with; a compact place and simple to get around. Soak up the history, take in the views, try the food, and cruise down the river. Be prepared for a decent amount of walking, because that's the only way to see Salzburg properly. START: **Hohensalzburg funicular.**

① ★★★ **Hohensalzburg Fortress (Festung Hohensalzburg).** The fortress that sits on a rocky plateau and dominates the city skyline protected church rulers in their lofty perch for centuries. It was built in 1077 by Archbishop Gebhard and considerably enlarged 4 centuries later, and is now the largest, fully preserved fortress in central Europe. This is the place to start any tour of Salzburg. You can take a slow walk up or ride the funicular, which click-clacks almost vertically up the hillside. *See p 10.*

② ★★★ **Mönchsberg.** From the fortress walk along the top of the plateau—this high-level park has treelined paths and a view over the city in one direction and toward the mountains in the other. You can buy a drink from a snack kiosk after a short distance, and benches at every turn will tempt you to chill out in the sun. When you reach the modernistic **Museum der Moderne** (Museum of Modern Art, p 40, ①), take the elevator, which drops through the rock to the streets below. ⏱ *30 min. See p 60 for a full tour of the Mönchsberg.*

③ **Festival Halls (Festspielhäuser).** Walk with the Mönchsberg on your right and you come to the Festival Halls complex, where the world-famous **Salzburg Festival** (p 122) is held. This also contains the **Felsenreitschule** (Rock Riding School, p 33, ⑤), the open-air concert venue made famous in *The Sound of Music* (p 30) that is only visible during a tour of the halls. ⏱ *10 min. See p 43 ⑨.*

④ ★★★ **Salzburg Cathedral (Salzburg Dom).** Rated as the most impressive early baroque edifice on the northern side of the Alps, this really is unmissable. The cathedral *(the Dom)* presents a mighty facade topped with a dome, incredible in itself since the current dome was built after the original was demolished by wartime bombing. The present building dates from 1628, and is the third on the site; the first, from 774, was destroyed by fire and its replacement, itself fire-damaged, was torn down in 1598 by Archbishop Wolf Dietrich, later imprisoned for his actions. Inside, the baroque artwork is some of Europe's best and there's the font in which

The Hohensalzburg Fortress looms over the city.

Hohensalzburg Fortress

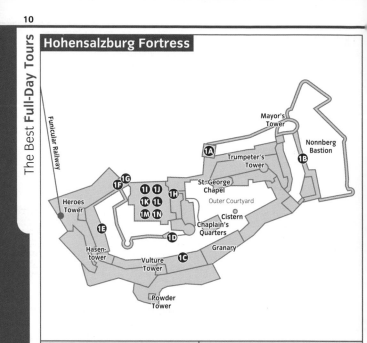

Funicular Railway

Mayor's Tower

Nonnberg Bastion

1A
Trumpeter's Tower

1B

1G
1F

St. George Chapel

Outer Courtyard

11 **1J**
1K **1L**
1M **1N**
1H

Heroes Tower

Cistern

Chaplain's Quarters

1E

1D

Hasen-tower

Granary

Vulture Tower
1C

Powder Tower

From the **1A ticket office,** the steep **1B snake path** curves upward, through the cloistered tunnel. You emerge outside the **1C bar/cafe** with a **1D tower of cannon-balls** opposite. Continue to the **1E stables** where you can join the free audio tour (the only way to get into this area), taking in the **1F torture chamber,** filled with portraits of prince archbishops and models of the fortress down the ages, and out

A carved bench in the Golden Hall.

onto the **1G tower roof** for panoramic views. After the tour, you're free to walk into the **1H Romanesque chapel** with its excavated flooring and uncovered fresco remains. Enter the **1I castle keep** and head up the stone stairs into the **1J old living quarters** where you'll find exhibitions on the history of the fortress and Salzburg, items of warfare right up to the Nazi occupation in World War II, and ecclesiastical treasures. On the top floor, the extravagant **1K archbishops' private quarters** include the **1L Golden Hall** (now used for concerts), the **1M Golden Room** with its fantastically decorated tiled oven, and the **1N bedroom.** ⏱ *2 hr. Mönchsberg 34.* ☎ *0662/84243011. www.salzburg-burgen.at. Admission 10.50€ adults, 6€ children 14 and under, free 5 and under. Daily May–Sept 9am–7pm; Oct–Apr 9:30am–5pm (Easter/Advent weekends 6pm).*

Mozart was christened, an organ surrounded by angels (Mozart was court organist), and carved portals. In late 2009, a 12th-century choir crypt (filled in after the fire and discovered in the 1950s) was transformed into a public space. In it, French artist Christian Boltanski has created a danse macabre shadow play involving flickering candles and metal puppets. The adjoining museum (see p 40, **3**) contains many works of art. ⏱ *1 hr. Domplatz.* ☎ *0662/80477950. www.kirchen.net/dommuseum. Free admission. Daily 6:30am–7pm (5pm winter). Charge for museum, see p 40, **3**. Tours in English from end July to Aug, 2:30pm; rest of year by arrangement. Bus: 1.*

5 ★★★ **Getreidegasse.** Walk across Residenzplatz, then along Alter Markt, and you find yourself at the bustling, picturesque heart of Salzburg, a narrow street running canyon-like through the high, historic buildings on either side. Along with **Mozart's Birthplace** (p 24, **1**), it is packed with shops as well as romantic passageways and courtyards that have been turned into glitzy shopping arcades. As you stroll, gaze up at the metal pictorial shop signs (dating from when few of the populace could read) and smile at the one that signifies a disguised McDonald's. ⏱ *40 min.*

6 *Cafe Niemetz.* Okay, you're not going to experience the Salzburg Festival but you can experience some of the atmosphere at this cafe next to the Festival Halls. The place is full of musical memorabilia and there's every chance you could be sitting next to a world-famous musician. *Herbert-von-Karajan-Platz 11.* ☎ *0622/843367. $$.*

7 ★ **Mozart Square (Mozart-platz).** Walk through the backstreets, this time heading through

St. Peter's Cemetery (p 26, **6**), across Kapitelplatz, to this classical square featuring the statue of Mozart by Ludwig Schwanthaler, unveiled on September 5, 1842, in the presence of Mozart's sons. You'll also find the **Salzburg Museum** (p 41, **6**) occupying one side of the square. ⏱ *20 min.*

8 ★ **River walk.** Head to the riverbank path (taking care to avoid the many carefree cyclists) and stroll along with views across to the Kapuzinerberg, the Hotel Stein (p 68) with its roof terrace, and other grand buildings until you reach the Makartsteg footbridge, where you'll see the river cruise pontoon. ⏱ *10 min.*

9 ★ **River cruise.** The *Amadeus Salzburg* plies the Salzach from mid-April to mid-October, giving views up at the city skyline through its panoramic windows. The cruise is short enough to get a feel for the river and to see things from a different perspective, but there's not much to keep the attention once out of the city—although switching

Salzburg Cathedral.

A glorious winter's day seen from the Makartsteg footbridge.

on the jet overdrive gives a fun turn of speed. This is a good opportunity to relax with a coffee or beer after all that walking. The captain's finale of using the jets to send the boat on a mad waltz accompanied by blaring Mozart music is always a crowd pleaser. The trip heads upriver as far as Hellbrunn, and some cruises include a visit to Hellbrunn Palace (p 19, ❶) with a bus back. ⏱ *35–40 min (standard cruise). Makartsteg footbridge.* ☎ *0622/825858. www. salzburgschifffahrt.at. Standard cruise: 13€ adults, 7€ children 15 and under, free 3 and under. Incl. on Salzburg Card (p 165). Boats leave on the hour, Apr–Oct (between four*

and nine a day depending on season). Advance booking (at the riverside office) is recommended, particularly in summer.

❿ ★★ **Mirabell Palace & Gardens (Schloss Mirabell).** Cross the Makartsteg footbridge and you'll find yourself at the Makartplatz entrance to the gardens. The vast formal gardens are a delight of fountains, sculptures (including original 1689 statues of Roman gods), clipped greenery, and bold flowers, and are rated Europe's most important baroque gardens. On a good weather day, you'll want to wander aimlessly, letting the spray from the

The Salzburg Card

Nowhere does it better—just about everything you would want to do is included on a single micro-chipped card. With the Salzburg Card you can visit all the city's attractions, plus use public transport (including the funicular to the fortress, boat trip along the river, and the Untersberg mountain cable car) for no extra cost other than the price of the card. The Salzburg Card also gives discounts for cultural events as well as many tours and excursions. For full details, see p 165.

fountains wash over you. You can then walk across a footbridge onto old fortifications where there are more gardens, and into the **Kur Gardens,** a more casual park with trees and a small hill topped with rose bushes. In 1606, Prince Archbishop Wolf Dietrich von Raitenau had the palace built for his mistress, merchant's daughter Salome; in return she bore him 15 children, so you can see the attraction. Since then it's had baroque and neoclassical overhauls, been home to the Austrian emperor, and now houses the Salzburg mayor's office. Most of the building isn't open to the public but you can gasp at the mighty marble staircase adorned with marble cherubs, and the ornate **Marble Hall** (*Marmorsaal*), or check it out at one of the nightly concerts by the Salzburger Mozartsolisten (p 27). ⏱ *40 min. Mirabellplatz.* ☎ *0662/80722334. Marble Hall: free admission. Mon, Wed, Thurs 8am–4pm; Tues, Fri: 1–4pm. Gardens daily, unrestricted access. Bus: 1.*

The ornate marble stairwell of the Mirabell Palace.

☕ **Salzach River-Island-Bar.** At the river cruise company base you'll find this floating panoramic bar/restaurant. Open from 7pm it's a popular haunt for locals as the sun goes down, and a great place to relax before considering dinner options. *Makartsteg footbridge.* ☎ *0622/825858. www.salzburg schifffahrt.at. $$.*

The Mirabell Palace & Gardens.

The Best **in Two Days**

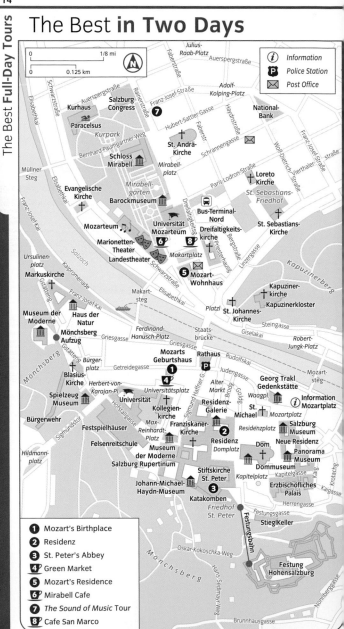

	Information
	Police Station
	Post Office

1. Mozart's Birthplace
2. Residenz
3. St. Peter's Abbey
4. Green Market
5. Mozart's Residence
6. Mirabell Cafe
7. *The Sound of Music* Tour
8. Cafe San Marco

Day two gives you an increasing feel for what makes the city tick, notably Mozart and *The Sound of Music* tour (booking required), while letting you get inside the sublime region surrounding it. First, more of the same: walking and wandering, seeing the city from the tiny, quaint, meandering streets. And then the opportunity to dart out into the countryside. START: **Getreidegasse.**

❶ ★★ Mozart's Birthplace (Mozarts Geburtshaus).

The apartment where the Mozart family lived from 1747 to 1773, and where Wolfgang Amadeus Mozart was born in 1756. Today it has grown from being a quaint, cluttered collection of artifacts such as Mozart's childhood violin and piano to a modern place with a rather avant-garde approach. Some feel it's gone a little too far in this direction with the things that you really want to see playing second fiddle, as it were, to design. Mozart fans would want to spend longer here browsing amongst the exhibits.
🕐 *45 min. See p 24,* ❶.

❷ Residenz.

Now this is what pomp and circumstance is all about . . . a sprawling medieval bishops' residence with 180 rooms, three courtyards, and a wealth of gold and velvet. It was given a baroque appearance at the end of the 16th century and is now mostly used for state functions. However, the part that is open, the **State Rooms,** is big and grand enough so you can live without seeing the rest. You do have to pay attention to the audioguide, though, because there's no other way to work out what you're looking at. The **Residenz Gallery** has a collection of Old Masters including Rubens, Rembrandt, and Breughel.
🕐 *45 min. Residenzplatz 1.* ☎ *0662/ 80422690. www.salzburg-burgen.at. Admission 8.50€ adults, 2.70€ children 14 and under, free 5 and under. Daily 10am–5pm. Audioguide in seven languages. Guided tours by arrangement.*

❸ ★★ St. Peter's Abbey (Stiftskirche St. Peter).

In any normal city this would be the ecclesiastical highlight but, a 2-minute walk from the Dom, it slips into second place. Just. The church is high-Romanesque, but was given a baroque makeover in the 17th century, like many of Salzburg's buildings. One of the chapels in the south aisle contains a memorial for Johann Michael Haydn and a marble plaque for Mozart's sister, Nannerl. The **cemetery** (p 26 ❻) is fascinating and beautiful, pushed up against the Mönchsberg rock, with intricate memorials to a number of well-known locals, including Nannerl and Haydn's composer brother Michael. Fascinating **catacombs** hewn out of the Mönchsberg rock walls (which only take a few minutes to look at) are thought to be of early Christian origin and are a strange find in a city center. See p 26, ❺ & ❻. 🕐 *30*

Mozart's Birthplace, the heart of Salzburg.

The ceiling of one of the Residenz State Rooms.

min. Erzabtei St. Peter. ☎ 0662/ 844576. www.stift-stpeter.at. *Church: free admission. Daily 8am–noon, 4:30–6:30pm. Catacombs admission 1€ adults, .60€ children 17 and under, free 5 and under. May–Sept 10:30am–5pm; Oct–Apr Wed/Thurs 10:30am–3:30pm, Fri–Sun 10:30am–4 pm. Hours subject to change. Closed 3 weeks in Nov. Bus: 5.*

4̲⃝ Green Market. Salzburg's leading market for local produce with dozens of stalls. It starts on Universitätsplatz, but spills down side streets and reaches the front of the Festival Halls. Even if you're not stocking up, this is a place for window shopping, full of sights and enticing smells. Grab some bread, cheese, ham, fruit, and a bench for a casual, early lunch. *Universitätsplatz. Mon–Fri 7am–7pm, Sat 7am–3pm.*

❺ ★★ Mozart's Residence (Mozart Wohnhaus). Head across the Makartsteg footbridge to the New Town and you'll find yourself on Makartplatz, with the plush Hotel Bristol on one side and the building housing the apartment where Mozart lived on the other. Mozart lived here with his family from 1773–1780, and by this time was now a bit of a celebrity. He wrote a number of works in the big, airy apartment and the place is a fascinating mix of manuscripts and musical instruments. The museum traces Mozart's time here (with multi-lingual audio) and there's a film, *Mozart and Salzburg,* which provides a good overview (using the audioguide headsets). Serious Mozart aficionados will want to spend more time here (see p 27, **⓫**). ⏱ *45 min. Makartplatz 8.* ☎ *0662/8422740.*

The Residenz.

(p 19, ), and Nonnberg Convent (p 32, ❶). The tour is fun whether you're a *Sound of Music* buff or not; pleasantly tongue-in-cheek yet informative with a chance to see both the city and the countryside. It's brought alive by the constant chatter and jokes of a guide who knows his stuff but still sees the funny side. There's an hour or so stop in the lakeside town of Mondsee (p 151, ❿) for the church, or just taking in the scenery. ⏱ *4 hr. Panorama Tours, departs Mirabellplatz (but free pick-up from city hotels). www.panoramatours.com.* ☎ *0662/ 8832110. 37€ adults, 18€ children 12 and under, free 3 and under. Departs 9:30am & 2pm. See p 30 for a full* The Sound of Music *tour.*

St. Peter's Abbey.

www.mozarteum.at. Admission 7€ adults, 3€ children 15–18, 2.50€ 6–14. Daily 9am–5:30pm (8pm July/ Aug). Combined ticket with Mozart's Birthplace (p 24, ❶) 12€/4.50€/ 3.50€.

🍽 **Mirabell Cafe.** On a summer's day, sitting in the Mirabell Gardens is a delight, and this little cafe on the grass and under the trees just inside the Makartplatz gate across from Mozart's Residence has a casual, almost French country feel. The place to relax with coffee and cake. *No phone. $.*

❼ ★★ **The Sound of Music Tour.** A relaxing 4-hour tour (you need to pre-book), with an English-speaking guide, takes you out of the city to see the mountain landscape where the opening scenes of the movie were filmed. It includes the church where Maria and the Baron were married, as well as Salzburg beauty spots Leopoldskron Palace (p 35, ⓰), Hellbrunn Palace

🍽 **Cafe San Marco.** When you've had enough of the tourist trail, disappear into this little bar and pizzeria. There's the public face on the corner of Makartplatz (just along from the Hotel Bristol, with tables on the square), and the lively, divey back bar opening onto the covered walk-through by the Universität Mozarteum bike garage. Here, a pint of Stiegl costs just 2.90€ and a margarita pizza 5.50€. *Makartplatz 5.* ☎ *0662/ 872088. www.cafesanmarco.at. $.*

Mozart's Residence.

The Best **in Three Days**

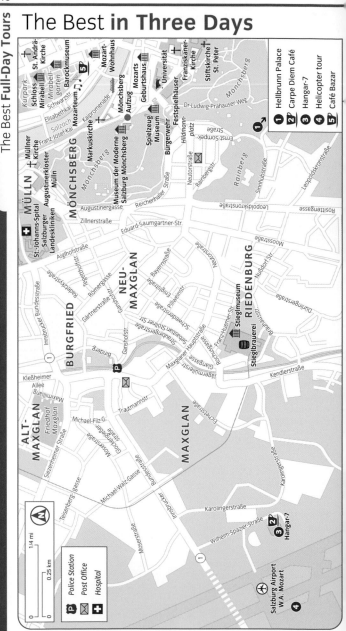

1 Hellbrunn Palace
2 Carpe Diem Café
3 Hangar-7
4 Helicopter tour
5 Café Bazar

Kurpark
Schloss Mirabell
Mirabellgarten
St. Andrä-Kirche
Barockmuseum
Mozart-Wohnhaus
Elisabethkai
Schwarzstr.
Mozarteum
Franz-Josef-Kai
Kaipromenade
Universität
Mozarts Geburtshaus
Franziskaner-Kirche
Stiftskirche St. Peter
Mönchsberg

MÜLLN
Müllner Kirche
AUGUSTINERKLOSTER Mülln
MÖNCHSBERG
Markuskirche
Mönchsberg Aufzug
Festspielhäuser
Dr-Ludwig-Prähauser-Weg

St-Johanns-Spital
Salzburger Landeskliniken
Museum der Moderne Salzburg Mönchsberg
Spielzeug Museum
Bürgerwehr
Hildmannplatz
Ernst-Sompek-Straße
Rainberg
Leopoldskronstraße

Aiglhofstraße
Zillnerstraße
Augustinergasse
Reichenhaller Straße
Neutorstr.
Rainbergstr.
Simmühlstraße
Leopoldskronstraße
Rosittengasse

Eduard-Saumgartner-Str.
Neutorstraße
Moosstraße

Imbstrucker Bundesstraße
BURGFRIED
NEU-MAXGLAN
Radetzkystraße
Römergasse
Gebirgsjägerstraße
Tegetthofstr.
Gärtnerstraße
Gnigler Str.
Bayernstraße
Engelstr.
Pillweinstr.
Schwedenstraße
Sebastian Stoiner Str.
Straßburgerstraße
Stieglbrauerei
Stieglmuseum
Franz-Huemer-Str.
RIEDENBURG
Nußdorfer Str.
Baumgartnerstraße
Türrigerstraße

Kleßheimer Allee
Maximilianstraße
Ganshofstr.
Binderg
Maxglaner Hauptstraße
Rochusgasse
Glangasse
Jägermüllerstr.
Kendlerstraße

ALT-MAXGLAN
Friedhof Maxglan
Siezenheimer Straße
Moserstraße
Glockerstraße
Michael-Filz-G.
Trautmannstr.
MAXGLAN
Eichetstraße
Karolingerstraße

Teisenberg-gasse
Michael-Walz-Gasse
Moserstraße
Imbstrucker Bundesstraße
Karolingerstraße
Wilhelm-Spazier-Straße
Hangar-7
2
3

Salzburg Airport W.A. Mozart
4

N

0   1/4 mi
0   0.25 km

Police Station
Post Office
Hospital

Today, you have the chance to see some out-of-town delights with the ease of public transport, making the day a little more relaxing. You'll combine some of Salzburg's most beautiful spots, the city's most stunning modern attraction, and unforgettable views from the air (advance booking required). START: **Mirabellplatz for bus no. 25 to Hellbrunn.**

❶ ★★ Hellbrunn Palace (Schloss Hellbrunn). The trick fountains here are stupendous, even more so when you learn they were the joke of Prince Archbishop Markus Sittikus (1574–1619), who had this summer palace built 400 years ago. There are dozens of fountains: some which spurt out of pathside rocks, some which form arcs as you walk, and Markus's greatest joke—those which shoot up from stone seats at his outdoor dining table. You can only see the fountains (p 56, **❷**) on a guided tour, which also allows you entry into the palace. The large surrounding park has free entry and is a fine place for walking. If you find yourself with more time, it's also a pleasing hour's walk, much of it along the river, back to town. ⏱ *2 hr (1 hr fountains/palace, 1 hr park). Fürstenweg 37.* ☎ *0662/8203720. www.hellbrunn.at. Palace and fountains: adults 9.50€, children 18 and under 4.50€, children 3 and under* free; students 6€. Late Mar, Apr, Oct daily 9am–4:30pm; May, June, Sept to 5:30pm; July/Aug to 9pm. Grounds: free admission. Apr–Sept daily 6am–9pm; Mar/Oct 6:30am–6pm; Dec–Feb 6:30am–5pm. Bus: 25.

Head back on the bus to Mirabellplatz, and from there take bus no. 2 for the 10-minute ride to Karolingerstrasse.

❷ Carpe Diem Café. Stop for coffee and cake or lunch in this cafe in Hangar-7, right by the collection of planes and cars, in architecturally stunning surroundings. The reputation for fine food at the main restaurant, Ikarus, spills over into this casual spot with everything from Viennese dishes (fried chicken with potato-corn salad, pumpkin seed oil, and cranberries) to a modern take on kebabs. *Wilhelm-Spazier-Strasse 7a.* ☎ *0662/219777. www.hangar-7. com. $$.*

Hellbrunn Palace.

Hangar-7.

❸ ★★★ Hangar-7. An extraordinary place on the opposite side of the runway from Salzburg Airport's terminal. This curving, futuristic, glass-and-steel hangar is the toy of Dietrich Mateschitz, the Red Bull fizzy drink creator, who owns sports teams, not least a successful Formula 1 set-up. Here is his collection of historic planes, from fighter jets to Yugoslav President Tito's Douglas DC-6B state airliner and a North American B-25J Mitchell bomber, along with helicopters and racing cars (including the winner of the 2008 Formula 1 Italian Grand Prix). It's also home to the fleet of the Flying Bulls. It's difficult to know which is the more beautiful: the exhibits or the building that also features the glass-floored **Threesixty bar** (p 113) dangling from the roof. The sun pours through the arching roof and the mountains fill the view in one direction—the place is particularly stunning in the late afternoon light. ⏱ *1 hr. Wilhelm-Spazier-Strasse 7a.* ☎ *0662/21970. www.hangar-7.com. Free admission. Daily 9am–10pm. Bus: 2.*

The airport is only one further stop on bus no. 2, and afterwards you can take the bus straight back to the city.

❹ ★ Helicopter tour. The combination of timeless architecture and the white-tipped mountain backdrop makes Salzburg a wondrous place to see from the air. **Helios flights,** based at Salzburg airport, then take you onward to look at the mighty Hohe Tauern peaks (65 min), the pretty Lake District (30 min) or the greenery of Upper Bavaria (40 min). It's not cheap, but then any helicopter flight is a luxury. ⏱ *30–65 min.* ☎ *0622/32994. www.helios.at. Booking required. From 180€ per person. Bus: 2.*

❺ Café Bazar. After arriving back in town, this is a place to relax, either for late afternoon coffee, an early evening drink, or even dinner. The Bazar is on the river, just along from the Mirabellplatz bus stop, and has a lovely outdoor area. You can order hot and cold food all evening and, with sister hotel the Brandstätter (p 101) owned by the same family having a Michelin star, the quality is guaranteed. *Schwarzstrasse 3.* ☎ *0662/84278. Closed Sun. $$.* ●

2 The Best Special-Interest Tours

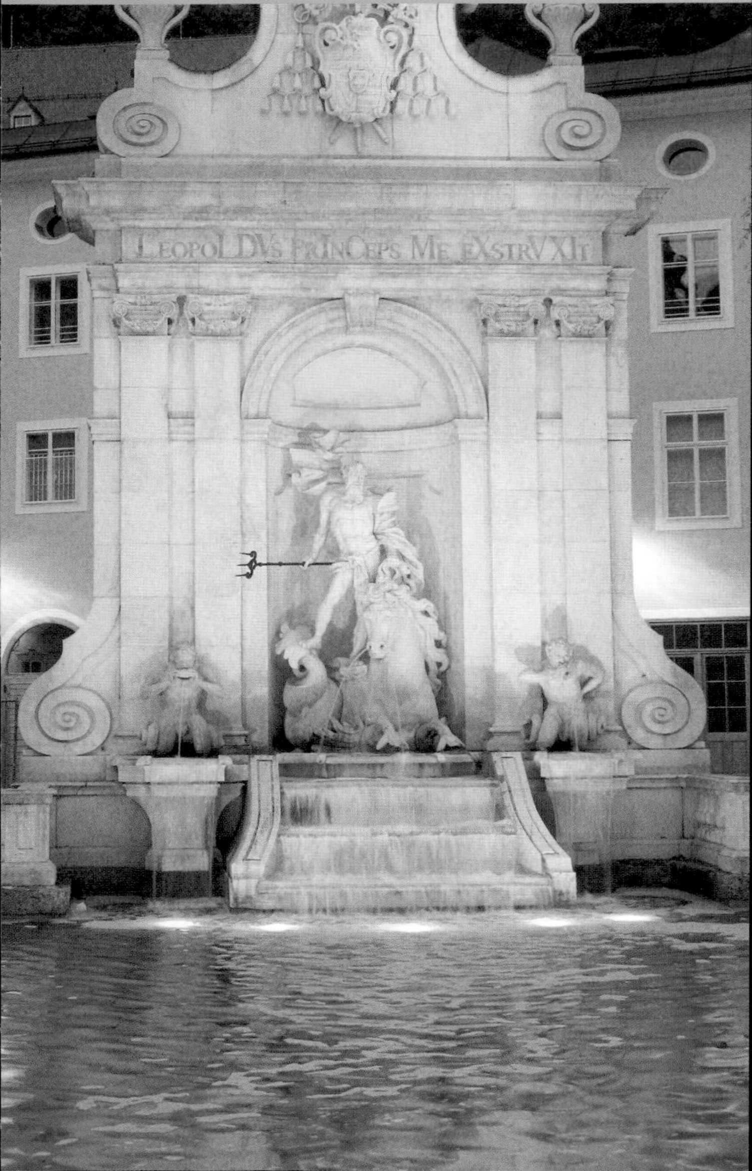

Mozart

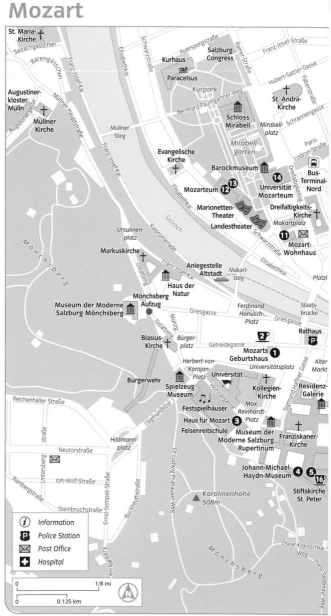

St. Maria-Kirche
Salzachgasschen
Bärengässchen
Schwarzstraße
Auerspergstraße
Rainer-Straße
Franz-Josef-Straße
Kurhaus
Salzburg Congress
Hubert-Sattler-Gasse
Faberstraße
Paracelsus
St. Andrä-Kirche
Augustiner-kloster Mülln
Müllner Kirche
Augustinergasse
Müllner Hauptstraße
Elisabethkai
Kurpark
Bernhard-Paumgartner-Weg
Schrannengasse
Schloss Mirabell
Mirabell-platz
Paris-Lodron-Straße
Franz-Josef-Kai
Müllner Steg
Mirabell-garten
Evangelische Kirche
Barockmuseum
Dreiheiligkeits-
Bus-Terminal-Nord
Mozarteum 12 13
14 Universität Mozarteum
Elisabethstraße
Salzach
Marionetten-Theater
Dreifaltigkeits-Kirche
Ursulinen-platz
Kaipromenade
Landestheater
Makartplatz
Mönchsberg
Markuskirche
Gstättengasse
Franz-Josef-Kai
Schwarzstraße
11 Mozart-Wohnhaus
Elisabethkai
Platzl
Anlegestelle Altstadt
Makart-steg
Haus der Natur
Museum der Moderne Salzburg Mönchsberg
Mönchsberg Aufzug
Münzg.
Griesgasse
Ferdinand-Hanusch-Platz
Staats-brücke
Blasius-Kirche
Gstätteng.
Bürger-platz
Getreidegasse
Griesgasse
Rathaus
Bürgerwehr
Herbert-von-Karajan-Platz
Mozarts Geburtshaus 1
2
Alter Markt
Reichenhaller Straße
Spielzeug Museum
Universität
Hofstallg.
Universitätsplatz
Residenz-Galerie
Sigmund-Haffner-Gasse
Festspielhäuser
Kollegien-Kirche
Max-Reinhardt-Platz
Franziskaner-Kirche
Hildmann-platz
Haus für Mozart 3
Felsenreitschule
Museum der Moderne Salzburg Rupertinum
Neutorstraße
Untersberg
Rainbergstraße
Joh-Wolf-Straße
Ernst-Sompek-Straße
Buckelreuthstraße
Dr-Ludwig-Prähauser-Weg
Johann-Michael-Haydn-Museum 4 5
16
Stiftskirche St. Peter
Steinbruchstraße
Am Rainberg
Karolinenhöhe 508m
Mönchsberg
Oskar-Kokoschka-Weg
Hans-Sedlmayr-Weg

(i) Information
P Police Station
✉ Post Office
✚ Hospital

0   1/8 mi
0   0.125 km
N

Previous page: The Neptune fountain in Kapitelplatz.

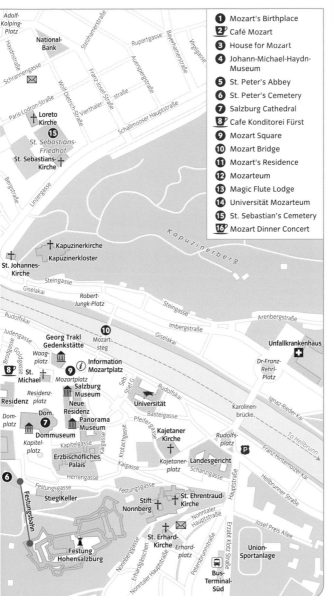

1. Mozart's Birthplace
2. Café Mozart
3. House for Mozart
4. Johann-Michael-Haydn-Museum
5. St. Peter's Abbey
6. St. Peter's Cemetery
7. Salzburg Cathedral
8. Cafe Konditorei Fürst
9. Mozart Square
10. Mozart Bridge
11. Mozart's Residence
12. Mozarteum
13. Magic Flute Lodge
14. Universität Mozarteum
15. St. Sebastian's Cemetery
16. Mozart Dinner Concert

Salzburg is the city of Mozart. The great composer was born here and lived here until well into his 20s. He composed some of his greatest works here and the city is alive with his music in festivals and concerts. You'll find everything in his name from skiing—the nearby region of Ski Amadé is named after him—to chocolates, with the world-famous Mozart Ball. START: **Getreidegasse.**

❶ ★★★ kids
Mozart's Birthplace. Getreidegasse 9, in the heart of the city, is where the Mozart family lived in an apartment from 1747 to 1773. Wolfgang Amadeus Mozart was born here on January 27, 1756, the seventh child of Salzburg royal chamber musician Leopold Mozart. Today it houses Mozart's childhood violin, concert violin, clavichord, and harpsichord, along with portraits and family letters. The top floor is devoted to Mozart and the stage, with intricate models of his sets and music from his operas. It has been a museum since 1880, but recently has annexed an adjoining house and undergone a revamp. It is now a modern, artsy attraction—some may

The unfinished portrait is just one of the delights at Mozart's Birthplace.

say too modern and artsy. ⏱ *1 hr. Getreidegasse 9.* ☎ *0662/844313. www.mozarteum.at. Admission 7€ adults, 3€ children 15–18, 2.50€ 6–14. Daily 9am–5:30pm; July/ Aug until 8pm.*

❷ ★★ Café Mozart.
Only a few steps from where the composer was born. Grab a heady coffee or have a solid start to the day with the Mozart Breakfast Exklusive—smoked salmon with scrambled eggs plus a glass of prosecco and coffee or hot chocolate, rolls, and honey for only 12€. *Getreidegasse 22.* ☎ *0662/843958. www.cafe mozartsalzburg.at. $–$$.*

Café Mozart, across from Mozart's Birthplace.

❸ House for Mozart.
Not a house, but a hall, part of the Festival Halls complex (p 43, ❾), opened in 2006 as part of Mozart Year, the 250th anniversary of Mozart's birth. It was designed by Wilhelm Holzbauer, born in Salzburg in 1930, a student of Clemens Holzmeister, the architect who created the adjoining Large Festival Hall. It cleverly incorporates the foyer from the former Small Festival Hall, preserving the 1926 frescoes by Anton Faistauer. Entry only as part of a Festival Halls guided tour. ⏱ *1 hr. Hofstallgasse 1.*

Mozart—A Life in Music

Wolfgang Amadeus Mozart, born in Salzburg in 1756, was a child prodigy and continued to amaze throughout his short life. He was playing piano at 3, wrote his first tune aged 4, and composed his first symphony at the age of 8. He became a virtuoso pianist, organist, and violinist. Chaperoned by his father, an ambitious musician himself, young Mozart was constantly touring and playing for royalty. Reaching adulthood, his audience became bored and he was forced to get a real job as court organist for the Archbishop of Salzburg. Among his most famous works are *Eine kleine Nacht-musik* (A Little Night Music, 1787) and the operas *Don Giovanni* (1787) and *Die Zauberflöte* (The Magic Flute, 1791). Mozart died from a fever at 35, leaving a legacy of more than 600 works covering opera, symphony, concerto, chamber, choral, instrumental, and vocal music.

☎ *0662/8045500. www.salzburger festspiele.at. Admission 5€ adults, 2.90€ children 17 and under, free 5 and under. Tours daily at 2pm (not July during Festival) with more in summer months. Reservations needed. Bus: 1.*

④ Johann-Michael-Haydn-Museum. Haydn followed his friend Mozart as court and cathedral organist in Salzburg in 1781. This small museum combines original sheet music, letters, and modern listening stations as well as instruments from the period in an historic setting in the courtyard of St. Peter's Abbey. There are also summer music recitals late afternoon. ⏲ *20 min. Courtyard, Erzabtei St. Peter.* ☎ *0662/84457619. www.concerts-at-five.com. Admission 2€ adults, 1€ children 17 and under, free 5 and under. May, June, Oct 2–5pm; July–Sept 12:30–5pm; closed Wed.*

The House for Mozart.

Listen to the Music

Mozart's music is performed almost non-stop in Mozart Week, the last week in January. It's a stirring celebration of Mozart and more, with concerts by leading orchestras and ensembles. The **Salzburg Festival** (p 122) is the world's most famed celebration of classical music (late July–end Aug), with plenty of Mozart but open to other composers. There are music festivals throughout the year that feature Mozart, and you'd feel hard done by if you arrived in the city and there wasn't a concert while you were there.

⑤ ★★ St. Peter's Abbey (Stiftskirche St. Peter).

Mozart was associated with the beautiful church from an early age. Aged just 13, he composed *Dominicus Mass* in 1769 for his boyhood friend, Kajetan Rupert Hagenauer, abbot from 1786 to 1811, conducted his famous *Mass in C minor* in the church in 1783, and another Mass, uncompleted, was first performed on October 26, 1783. Mozart conducted and his wife, Constanze, sang the soprano part. One of the chapels in the south aisle contains a memorial to Johann-Michael Haydn and a marble plaque for Mozart's sister, Nannerl. ⏲ *45 min. See p 15,* ❸.

⑥ ★★ kids St. Peter's Cemetery.

With its unique backdrop of St. Peter's, this is one of the oldest and most charming cemeteries in the world. While Mozart himself rests in Vienna, here lie his sister Nannerl, Lorenz Hagenauer (family friend and landlord), Sigmund Haffner (mayor and Mozart benefactor, immortalized in Mozart's *Haffner Serenade* and *Haffner Symphony*), not to mention Michael Haydn (composer and Joseph Haydn's younger brother), opera singer Richard Mayr, and many others from musicians to World War II heroes. ⏲ *30 min. See p 32,* ❸.

⑦ ★★ Salzburg Cathedral.

This baroque masterpiece is where Mozart played as court organist (1773–77), and for which he composed most of his sacred music. Turn a sharp left inside the main door and you'll come to the medieval font in which he was christened. His parents were also married here in 1747. ⏲ *30 min. See p 9,* ❹.

⑧ ★★ Cafe Konditorei Fürst.

Take a breather at the first Fürst. This is where confectioner Paul Fürst started making Mozart Balls (as a tribute to the composer) back in 1890. Stock up on the moreish chocs with the composer's face staring out from the silver wrapper, or relax with coffee and cakes. *Alter Markt, Brodgasse 13.* ☎ *0662/ 8437590. www.original-mozartkugel. com. $–$$. See p 46,* ❾.

⑨ Mozart Square (Mozartplatz).

A classical square that is dominated by the statue of Mozart dating back to 1842. Not a terribly good likeness by all accounts, and clutching a pencil rather than the appropriate quill, but it's all the more interesting because of it. You have the chance to buy a tacky souvenir at **Zum Mozart** (p 77). ⏲ *5 min. See p 11,* ❼.

⑩ ★★ Mozart Bridge. Not a bridge that Mozart ever had the chance to use, but this delicate Art Nouveau pedestrian river crossing was named after him. Find it just off one end of Mozartplatz and use it to get to the New Town. A short river-bank stroll gets you to Mozart's Residence. ⏱ *5 min.*

⑪ ★★★ Mozart's Residence. Mozart's family moved to this spacious eight-room apartment (Austrian signs call it the *Mozart-Wohnhaus*) in 1773, in what is now Makartplatz. Young Mozart stayed until 1780 and composed many works here, including countless symphonies, serenades, divertimenti, and five concerts for violin and piano. The museum—actually more satisfying than his Birthplace (p 24, ❶)—has a wealth of original manuscripts and instruments. The exhibition, with excellent free audioguide, traces Mozart's time here, and his many tours around Europe, including London. The building also contains the **Mozart Sound and Film Collection,** the world's largest audiovisual collection of Mozart-related works that visitors can watch on a collection of screens. ⏱ *1½ hr. See p 16,* ❺.

The cathedral, along with most of Salzburg's architectural delights, can best be seen from the Mönchsberg.

⑫ ★★ Mozarteum. The international foundation oversees all things Mozart, from the Birthplace and Residence museums to the **Bibliotheca Mozartiana,** a library containing 35,000 items from manuscripts to books. Entry to the library is free, but it's a place for scholars, largely German-speaking ones.

The Best of the Best

The most impressive concerts in the city on an almost daily basis (more than 300 a year) are the **Salzburger Schlosskonzertes** by the Salzburger Mozartsolisten in the Mirabell Palace's beautiful Marble Hall (*Marmorsaal*). No costume drama, just small ensembles of slightly dissolute chaps (and the occasional beautiful woman) in black suits play to several dozen people, with *Eine kleine Nachtmusik*, the equivalent of a rock 'n' roll band finishing with a Chuck Berry number. Another tip is to visit the cathedral for 10am Sunday Mass. It varies, but can well be a Mozart Mass, involving a massive organ, choir, and strings creating an emotional sound. Moreover, it's free—just arrive at least 20 minutes early as it fills up.

The impressive entrance to Mozart's Residence.

There is also a major concert hall where top names appear during the Mozarteum's Mozart Festival (p 121) each January. You may find the foyer open for ticket sales at certain times so you can get a feel for the place. ⏱ *10 min. Schwarzstrasse 26.*

The Mozart Bridge.

☎ *0662/8894013. www.mozarteum. at. Library: free admission. Mon, Tues, Fri 9am–1pm; Wed/Thurs 1am–5pm.*

⓭ ★★ **Magic Flute Lodge.** The Lodge (the *Zauberflötenhäuschen*) is in the **Bastion Garden** outside the Mozarteum's Large Hall, and can be visited, free, but only during concerts. The small wooden building is where Mozart supposedly composed elements of his *Magic Flute* masterpiece. He met singers here for rehearsals and is said to have been locked in by his librettist, Emanuel Schikaneder, to ensure he completed the work on time. ⏱ *10 min. Free admission during concerts only.*

⓮ **Universität Mozarteum.** Salzburg's revered music school is surrounded by students with bicycles and instrument cases. It's not a place to visit, but students put on daily (usually free) recitals in its small studios. Look for the unassuming poster in the window for a heady array of bargain performances here, along with a list of larger concerts by the students at other venues. ⏱ *5 min.*

Buy the Music

There's no shortage of Mozart music on CD. The gift shops at both Mozart's Birthplace (p 24, **1**) and Residence (p 27, **11**) have a good selection, as does the shop at the Festival Halls (p 43, **9**). The shop at the Salzburg Museum (p 41, **6**) also has a music section, and gift shops at other attractions generally have some. Realistically, though, there's little that qualifies as a real souvenir, or that you can't find cheaper on the Internet. A good keepsake, and something you won't find elsewhere, is the album on sale at the Mozart Dinner Concert (below, **16**).

Mirabellplatz 1. ☎ *0662/61983125. www.moz.ac.at. Recitals daily; prices vary but usually free.*

15 ★ **St. Sebastian's Cemetery (Friedhof St. Sebastian).** This beautifully tranquil spot hidden away off the traffic-free street in the oldest part of the New Town is a bit of a treasure trove for Mozart completists. The grave of Mozart's father, Leopold, is the one most people come to see (it's rather unassuming, near the gate), but you'll also find Mozart's wife Constanze, her second husband and her aunt, Mozart's grandmother, and his sister Nannerl's first daughter. ⏱ *15 min. Linzergasse.* ☎ *0662/84457687. www. stift-stpeter.at. Free admission. Daily 8am–6pm (winter hours may vary).*

16 ★ **Mozart Dinner Concert.** There are various dinner concert options around the city, but this is the one you should start with in the charming candlelit setting of the Baroque Hall in what is accepted as the oldest restaurant in central Europe, first mentioned in the year 803 when Charlemagne dropped by. Mozart classics, both musical pieces and opera excerpts, are performed on piano and stringed instruments and by singers all kitted out in lavish

period clothing; while the food is a modern take on an historic menu— breast of roasted capon on truffled cream of sage with polenta, potato-stuffed pear, and vegetables. ⏱ *3 hr. Reservations recommended. See p 122.*

Mozart's father Leopold is buried in St. Sebastian's Cemetery.

The Sound of Music

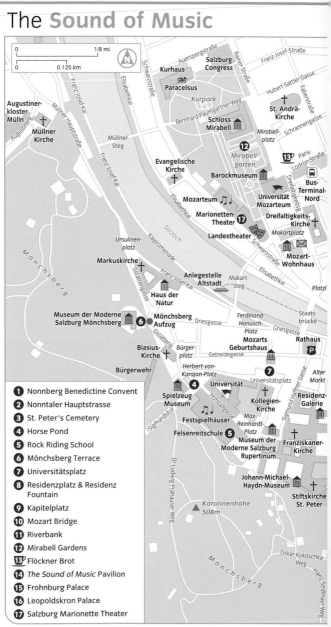

1	Nonnberg Benedictine Convent
2	Nonntaler Hauptstrasse
3	St. Peter's Cemetery
4	Horse Pond
5	Rock Riding School
6	Mönchsberg Terrace
7	Universitätsplatz
8	Residenzplatz & Residenz Fountain
9	Kapitelplatz
10	Mozart Bridge
11	Riverbank
12	Mirabell Gardens
13	Flöckner Brot
14	*The Sound of Music* Pavilion
15	Frohnburg Palace
16	Leopoldskron Palace
17	Salzburg Marionette Theater

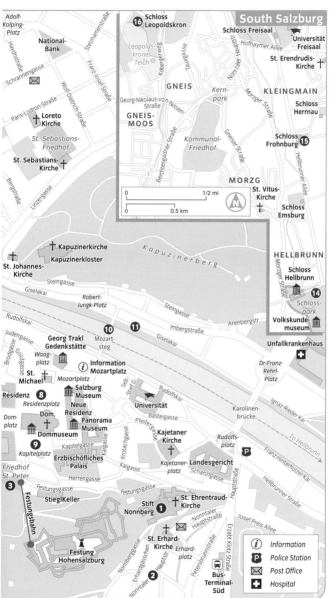

South Salzburg

16 Schloss Leopoldskron
Schloss Freisaal
Universität Freisaal
St. Erendrudis-Kirche
National-Bank
Adolf-Kolping-Platz

Leopolds-kroner Teich
Hofhaymer Allee

GNEIS
Kern-park
KLEINGMAIN
Schloss Herrnau

Georg-Nikolaus-von-Straße
GNEIS-MOOS
Kommunal-Friedhof
Schloss Frohnburg 15

Loreto Kirche
St. Sebastians-Friedhof
St. Sebastians-Kirche

MORZG
St. Vitus-Kirche
Schloss Emsburg

0   1/2 mi
0   0.5 km

Kapuzinerkirche
Kapuzinerkloster
Kapuzinerberg

HELLBRUNN
Schloss Hellbrunn 14
Schloss-park
Volkskunde-museum

St. Johannes-Kirche

Steingasse
Robert-Jungk-Platz
Steingasse
Imbergstraße
Arenbergstr.

Unfallkrankenhaus

Giselakai

Rudolfskai
Judengasse
Brodgasse
Goldgasse

Georg Trakl Gedenkstätte
Waag-platz
10 11
Mozart-steg
Giselakai

Dr-Franz-Rehrl-Platz

Information Mozartplatz
St. Michael
Mozartplatz
Salzburg Museum
Residenz
Residenzplatz
Neue Residenz
Panorama Museum
Universität
Basteigasse
Seb. Stief G.
Rudolfskai

Karolinen-brücke.
Ignaz-Rieder-Kai
To Hellbrunn

Dom-platz
Dom
Dommuseum
9
Kapitelgasse
Kapitelplatz
Erzbischöfliches Palais
Pfeifergasse
Krotachgasse
Kajetaner Kirche
Kajetaner-platz
Landesgericht
Schanzlgasse

Rudolfs-platz
P
Franz-Hinterholzer-Kai

Friedhof St. Peter
3
StieglKeller
Festungsgasse
Herrengasse
Festungsgasse
Kaigasse
Stift Nonnberg 1
St. Ehrentraud-Kirche
Nonntaler Hauptstraße

Hellbrunner Straße

Festungsbahn
Festung Hohensalzburg
Nonnbergasse
Nonntaler Hauptstr.
St. Erhard-Kirche
Erhard-platz
2
Peterbrunnstraße
Erzabt Klotz Straße
Bus-Terminal-Süd
Josef Preis Allee

i   Information
P   Police Station
⊠   Post Office
✚   Hospital

The **Hills Are Alive**

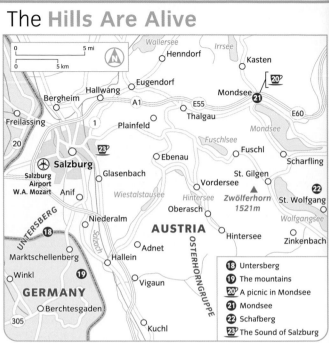

0 — 5 mi
0 — 5 km

Wallersee   Irrsee
Henndorf   Kasten
Eugendorf   **20**
Hallwang   Mondsee   **21**
Bergheim   A1   E55
Freilassing   Thalgau   E60
1   Plainfeld
20   Mondsee
Salzburg   **23**   Fuschlsee
Salzburg   Ebenau   Fuschl
Airport   Glasenbach   Scharfling
W.A. Mozart   Anif   St. Gilgen
Wiestalstausee   Vordersee   **22**
Hintersee   Zwölferhorn   St. Wolfgang
Niederalm   Oberasch   1521m
AUSTRIA   Wolfgangsee
18   UNTERSBERG   Adnet   Hintersee   Zinkenbach
Marktschellenberg   Hallein   OSTERHORNGRUPPE
Winkl   **19**   Vigaun
GERMANY
Berchtesgaden
305   Kuchl

18	Untersberg
19	The mountains
20	A picnic in Mondsee
21	Mondsee
22	Schafberg
23	The Sound of Salzburg

I t was an unlikely movie hit: a true love story amid the tale of an Austrian family troupe hounded by Nazis as World War II nears. Yet the Rodgers and Hammerstein songs and music were outstanding and had already made it a Broadway hit. Interest is higher than ever, with plenty of timeless settings to see. START: **Nonnberg Benedictine Convent.** TRIP LENGTH: **1 or 2 days.**

❶ ★★ Nonnberg Benedictine Convent. It's here, on the edge of the Mönchsberg, that Maria was late for Mass, and where the nuns sung *How Do You Solve a Problem Like Maria?*. The gates are seen as German troops storm in. In real life, this is where Maria and the Baron were married in 1927. The 15th-century Gothic building on 11th-century Romanesque foundations contains a wealth of beautiful works including Romanesque frescoes and the late-Gothic winged altar with a shrine adorned by a Madonna between

St. Rupert and St. Virgil. ⏱ *20 min. Nonnberggasse 2.* ☎ *0662/841607. www.benediktinerinnen.de. Free admission. Daily 7am–dusk, closed during Mass.*

❷ Nonntaler Hauptstrasse. This is the street near the convent where Maria and the children were seen riding in a horse-drawn carriage on their tour of the city. ⏱ *5 min.*

❸ St. Peter's Cemetery. A short walk through the Old Town and you arrive at the ancient cemetery with its wrought-iron gates

The Sound of Music Story

The movie of *The Sound of Music* was released in 1965. It won five Oscars, including Best Picture and Best Director (Robert Wise). There were a further 10 nominations, including one for Julie Andrews who leapt to stardom in her role as Maria. It also won two Golden Globes and a host of other awards. The film, which also starred Christopher Plummer as Captain von Trapp, was based on the successful stage musical inspired by Maria von Trapp's autobiography *The Story of the Trapp Family Singers*. After the Trapps fled Austria—recounted in the movie's gripping finale—they settled in the U.S. where the Trapp Family Lodge is still one of the leading hotels in the Vermont ski resort of Stowe.

where the Trapp family tried to hide as they fled from the approaching Nazi troops. It was here that Liesl's boyfriend, Rolf, glimpsed them, but allowed them to make their escape. 🕐 *15 min. See p 26,* ❻.

❹ **kids Horse Pond (Pferdeschwemme).** This large pond is where Maria and the singing, dancing children stopped to look at the large statue of a groom trying to rein in a horse as they excitedly explored the city. 🕐 *5 min. Herbert-von-Karajan-Platz.*

❺ **Rock Riding School.** Here, in the open-air Felsenreitschule, the Trapp family performed their farewell song and Baron von Trapp sang *Edelweiss* before slipping away into the night and confounding the Nazis. Now an open-air theater and part of the Festival Halls complex, it is only accessible as part of a guided tour. 🕐 *1 hr.*

❻ **kids Mönchsberg Terrace.** Now the terrace of the **Museum der Moderne** (Museum of Modern Art, p 40, ❶) this is the spot where the children sang *Do-Re-Mi* as they enjoyed the panoramic views of the city. 🕐 *10 min.*

❼ **Universitätsplatz.** This is the square housing the market (now the Green Market, p 77) where Maria and her charges played with the fruit and veg, and little Gretl dropped a ripe tomato. 🕐 *5 min.*

❽ **kids Residenzplatz & Residenz Fountain.** Maria strolls into the square at the side of the cathedral through one of the imposing arches dividing it from Domplatz (Cathedral Square) to catch a bus on her way from the Nonnberg Convent to the Trapp Villa. She passes the elegant fountain, and splashes the water, singing *I Have Confidence in Me.* The Residenz is also seen ominously covered in Nazi flags towards the end of the movie. 🕐 *15 min.*

❾ **Kapitelplatz.** This is the square, on the other side of the cathedral, where Maria is seen boarding her bus, with views of the small Horse Pond in the background. 🕐 *5 min.*

❿ **kids Mozart Bridge.** After walking across Mozart Square, you'll find this Art Nouveau footbridge across the river—a pretty, iron affair—where Maria and the children were seen cavorting. 🕐 *5 min.*

The Sound of Music *Tour makes a stop at Wolfgangsee.*

⑪ Riverbank. The grassy banks on the New Town side are where Maria and the children ran in single file as they sang, with little Gretl falling then picking herself up and catching up with the others. ⏱ *5 min.*

⑫ ★★★ kids Mirabell Gardens. Perhaps the most iconic spot for *The Sound of Music* fans, as here you'll find the steps where the children sang *Do-Re-Mi*. They marched around the Pegasus Fountain and cavorted in front of the grand fountain. Maria and the children also danced down the hedge-covered arch, and the youngsters imitated the dramatic poses of the statues of fighting men. Another statue, of a bespectacled dwarf, received a pat on the head. The glorious gardens combine the city's beauty with the movie's upbeat joy. ⏱ *30 min. See p 12, ⑩.*

⑬ Flöckner Brot. Just across the road from the Mirabell Gardens is this little bakery, part of a small chain that was born in 1837. They sell a wide range of (mostly organic) breads, pastries, cookies, pretzels, and cakes for a picnic, or you can eat in the small cafe area and garden. *Mirabellplatz 7.* ☎ *0662/871438.* *www.floeckner.at. $.*

Take bus no. 25 for 15 minutes to Hellbrunn.

⑭ *The Sound of Music* Pavilion. Hellbrunn Palace (p 19, ❶) is famed for its dancing fountains (for which there is a charge) but the expansive grounds are free. Just inside the gate, you'll find the gazebo where Liesl and Rolf sang *16 Going on 17* and Maria and the Captain sang *Something Good*. At the time, the pavilion was at the Leopoldskron Palace but was moved when the palace owners became tired of fans climbing over their wall to get at it. There's little to see (it's rather like a small conservatory, and it's locked) but you can relax in the park happy in the knowledge that you've seen it. A brief visit covers the movie setting, but if you take in the gardens, fountains, and zoo you could easily spend longer here. ⏱ *25 min. See p 19, ❶.*

⑮ Frohnburg Palace. A pleasing stroll along the treelined Hellbrunner Allee brings you to this palace, which served as the von Trapp residence in the movie. You might find yourself confused at first as the front was filmed as the back of the Trapp home (overlooking the lake, which isn't here) and the rear was seen as the front of the house. Maria jumped off the bus in the

Allee when she arrived at the gates for her job with the Trapp family. There's no entry as it's private (part of the **Mozarteum** music school) but you can take a walk around the outside, peeking through the gates and railings. ⏱ *20 min. See p. 27,* **⑫**.

Grab bus no. 25 back and jump off at Sinnhubstrasse. Walk 10 minutes through green and pleasant backstreets to:

⑯ Leopoldskron Palace. A private educational institution, Leopoldskron is only viewable from across the lake (unless you're staying in one of the exclusive hotel rooms). This was where Maria and the children fell from their boat, although the palace's ornate waterside gardens were off-limits even then and the outdoor scenes were filmed outside the adjoining **Meierhof building** (now part of the Leopoldskron campus) with the famed lakeside horse statues re-creations of the original a few yards away. Winter is particularly nice, with the lake used for **ice skating.** The Venetian Room was recreated in the studios in larger form for the ballroom scenes. Retrace your steps to the bus stop—although you can continue

The children danced around the Pegasus Fountain in Mirabel Gardens.

on foot, a pleasing walk under the Mönchsberg (p 9, **②**), with views up to the convent (p 32, **①**). The only way you can get in and see all the sights is by renting one of the hotel rooms. ⏱ *15 min. See p 139.*

⑰ kids Salzburg Marionette Theater. The puppet theater that featured in the movie (lonely goatherds et al) now turns full circle with its own 90-minute tribute *The Sound of Music* performance. Jerky, *Thunderbirds*-like puppets combine with the Rodgers and Hammerstein soundtrack in English, especially

The Mirabell Gardens steps made famous in The Sound of Music.

The Sound of Music *Pavilion*.

recorded in the United States. It's a bizarrely riveting spectacle, particularly the appearance of the giant, human chief nun. It alternates with other shows, but a 5:30pm performance (it's also on at 2pm and 7:30pm) doesn't take over your evening. ⏱ *1¾ hr. See p 121.*

Day Two

TRAVEL TIP

You can take in a number of spots with movie connections in the area surrounding Salzburg. Various companies run bus tours but they don't cover all the bases as the places are widely spread. Hire a car and you can nip around them all—although just about everyone you meet will have a different story about where the mountain scenes were really filmed.

Take the riverside Rudolfskai south from the Old Town. It quickly becomes the busy Alpenstrasse, which passes under the A10 *autobahn* and heads into the village of St. Leonhard (20 minutes from Salzburg) and its cable car. Alternatively, bus no. 25 takes you to the bottom of the cable car.

⑱ **Untersberg.** Take the cable car up the top of this mountain. This is where the Trapp family was seen pretending to be hiking as they fled the Nazis. *See p 85.*

Take the A10 south for around 20 minutes for the scenery, until you reach Hallein.

⑲ **The mountains.** Many of the movie's opening scenes—including Maria singing *The Hills Are Alive*) were filmed by helicopters above the peaks to the south of Salzburg. The spots are all but impossible to get to even if you could identify them, but you can get the feel by driving around.

At the town of Hallein, turn around and head back up the A10 past the city. Turn right onto the A1, which takes you all the way to Mondsee, an hour's journey.

20 A picnic in Mondsee. The simple, grassy waterfront park in Mondsee, on the lake of the same name, isn't a place that featured in the movie—but the children would have loved to frolic here with Maria. Plan to have brought something with you (the car park's nearby), or take the short stroll into town where there are plenty of delis. *Robert-Baum-Promenade, Mondsee. $.*

21 Mondsee. In the lake district, half an hour east of Salzburg, the town of Mondsee is where you'll find the church where the wedding of Maria and the Baron was filmed. Just outside the town is where Maria and the children were seen on a lakeside bicycle ride—take the lakeside road on the eastern side of the lake and you soon reach the spot where the road hugs the water. *See p 151,* ❿.

Turn back and follow the road around the lake to St. Gilgen. Here the road splits—turn left along Wolfgangsee, circling the bottom of the lake to St. Wolfgang.

22 Schafberg. This bald peak (Sheep Mountain) on the banks of Wolfgangsee is where Maria and her charges were briefly seen on the little, red cog train. The train still runs. *See p 149,* ❸.

Head back to St. Gilgen and turn left, which will take you all the way back into the heart of the city in about 40 minutes.

23 The Sound of Salzburg. Finish the day with this dinner show by the Sound of Music Singers, not quite sing-along-a-Sound-of-Music, but not far off. The show, in period costume, not only includes the big movie numbers, but also the Trapp Family Folk Music Revival. Dinner is what you might expect: roast pork and apple strudel, in a candlelit setting. *Sternbräu Dinner Theater, Griesgasse 23.* ☎ *0662/826617. www.soundofsalzburgshow.com. Nightly 7:30pm. Tickets incl. one drink and three-course dinner. 46€ adults, 37€ children 7–14. $$. See p 123.*

Leopoldskron, where the children fell from their rowing boat.

Art & Architecture

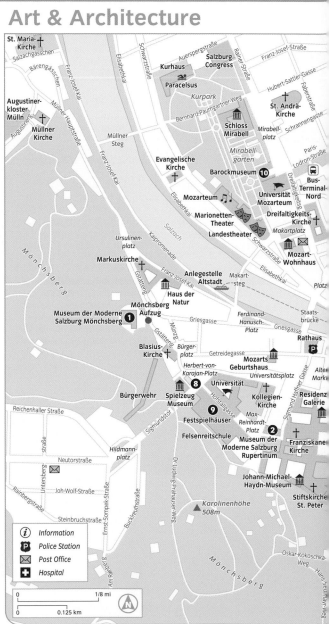

1 Museum der Moderne
2 Museum der Moderne Rupertinum
3 Dommuseum
4 Cathedral Excavations Museum
5 Kapitelplatz Market
6 Salzburg Museum
7 Panorama Museum
8 Karajan-Platz
9 Festival Halls
10 Salzburger Barockmuseum
11 Linzergasse

The buildings of Salzburg tell their own story. The city's baroque architecture is world-famous. One of the best-preserved cities north of the Alps, it was declared a UNESCO World Heritage Site in 1997. Yet it's not just the outside—within are superlative collections of art, from baroque to classical, religious to modern, as well as much hidden history. START: **Mönchsberg elevator.**

❶ ★ Museum der Moderne.

The Museum of Modern Art has, from the streets below, a jokey cliff-top appearance with gaudy lettering and a child-like tower, but close up it's simplistic and exciting. Take the Mönchsberg elevator up through the mountain and you move from the historic streets to the new world. The serious, regularly changing exhibitions can be a little heavy (given the wealth of beauty outside) but the building is worth exploring, and it's free with the Salzburg Card (p 165). From here, you can gaze over the cityscape and marvel at the range of elegant baroque buildings, the twin cathedrals of the Dom and St. Peter's almost next to each other, the narrow, medieval streets, and the Mirabell Palace. ⏱ *30 min. Mönchsberg 32.* ☎ *0662/842220401. www.museumdermoderne.at. Admission 8€ adults, 6€ children 6–15. Tues–Sun 10am–6pm (Wed until 8pm); summer/Easter Mon 10am–6pm.*

❷ Museum der Moderne Rupertinum.

Walk down from the Mönchsberg via the path on the far side of the funicular and you drop into the city streets just around the corner from this sister modern art gallery. There's more of the same, along with collections such as the works of Gustav Klimt, including *Litzlberg am Attersee*, one of the artist's few landscapes, plus the charm of an early baroque 14th-century building that used to be a training hall for priests. ⏱ *30 min. Wiener-Philharmoniker-Gasse 9.* ☎ *0662/842220451. www.museumdermoderne.at. Admission 6€ adults, 4€ children 6–15. Tues–Sun 10am–6pm (Wed until 9pm); summer/Easter Mon 10am–6pm.*

❸ Dommuseum.

The Cathedral Museum, high in the galleries, has a rich, heady collection of artwork from the Archdiocese of Salzburg as well as the cathedral itself. The

Museum of Modern Art.

The Sphaera (or Man on Mozartkugel) in Kapitelplatz.

highlight is **St. Rupert's Cross,** the largest surviving metal cross, dating back 1,300 years and which was believed to have been mounted in the first Salzburg cathedral. You'll also be treated to views of the city and cathedral interior. 🕐 *30 min. Domplatz 1a. www.kirchen.net/ dommuseum. Admission 5€ adults, 1.50€ children 15 and under. Mon–Sat 10am–5pm, Sun/Festival 11am–6pm.*

❹ **Cathedral Excavations Museum.** This is a dark, evocative time capsule under two squares, Residenzplatz and Domplatz. There are the remains of a Roman villa (including mosaics, walls, and sewer), and foundations and wall fragments of the Romanesque cathedral that was demolished in 1598 after a fire. 🕐 *1 hr. Residenzplatz.* 📞 *0662/620808131. www. salzburgmuseum.at. Admission*

2.50€ adults, 1€ children 6–15. July– Aug daily 9am–5pm; rest of year by appointment.

❺ ★★ **Kapitelplatz Market.** The square next to the cathedral has a number of stalls, some of them selling trinkets and souvenirs, some of them selling snacks. Grab a giant pretzel, sit on a bench, and enjoy the contrasting styles—the Dom's Italianate towers on one side, the looming Hohensalzburg Fortress on the other, with altogether more delicate buildings in between. *Kapitelplatz. $.*

❻ ★★ **kids Salzburg Museum.** This is your chance to get inside the **Neue Residenz** with its courtyard, in a museum that only opened in 2007, yet which won European Museum of the Year 2009. Contemporary and historic art, special exhibitions, and more than a touch of city history are all the more interesting and state-of-the-art than one might expect. In one of the towers, and visible from the courtyard, is a clockwork **glockenspiel** that has been

Salzburg Museum.

The ornate Horse Pond in Karajan-Platz.

⑦ ★ Panorama Museum. In the Salzburg Museum's basement is the awesome panorama of Salzburg by Johann Michael Sattler painted between 1826 and 1829. It's a clever circular painting, more than 25m (80 ft.) in circumference, in which you stand in the middle, getting views of the city and the surrounding countryside. A Time Telescope allows comparison between the present and the eerily accurate snap of the past. 🕐 *15 min. Mozartplatz 1.* ☎ *0662/620808-730. www.salzburgmuseum.at. Admission 2€ adults, 1€ children 15 and under. Daily 9am–5pm (Thurs until 8pm).*

⑧ Karajan-Platz. This is a superb square dedicated to world-famous conductor Herbert von Karajan (1908–89), who ousted Archbishop Sigismund Christian Schrattenbach from the name plaques. The classic marble architecture butts up against the Mönchsberg, right by the tunnel out of the Old Town, the oldest road tunnel in Austria. In the middle, you'll see the wonderful, ornate Horse Pond (p 33, ④) with mighty central statue, *The Horse Tamer,* one of Salzburg's best, dating back

playing music since 1704, and the repertoire includes pieces by Haydn and Mozart. 🕐 *1 hr. Mozartplatz 1.* ☎ *0662/620808700. www.salzburg museum.at. Admission 7€ adults, 3€ children 15 and under. Daily 9am–5pm (Thurs until 8pm); closed Mon Sept–Nov, Jan–June.*

City of Churches

Salzburg has more than 20 churches and cathedrals, most in the heart of the city or within a short stroll, with a wealth of variety, from baroque to Gothic, Romanesque to medieval. If you've already done the Dom and St. Peter's, next on your list should be the **Franziskanerkirche**—the Franciscan church (Siegmund Haffner-Gasse, www.kirchen.net/franziskanerkirche/geschichte2.htm) with its Gothic choir, delicate pillars, and ribbed ceiling. **St. Andrew's (Andräkirche),** on Mirabellplatz, is generally passed by in a rush but it is worth a look for its blend of late 19th-century Gothic and modern simplicity due to much of it being destroyed in World War II. The website www.salzburg.info has a good section on all the churches.

to the 17th century when the royal stables were nearby. ⏱ *10 min.*

⑨ Festival Halls. The complex that's at the heart of the Salzburg Festival (p 122) is worth a look even when there's nothing going on. The Large Festival Hall, House for Mozart (p 24, **③**), and the Rock Riding School (p 33, **⑤**) can be admired during a guided tour in English. ⏱ *1 hr. Hofstallgasse 1.* ☎ *0662/ 8045500. www.salzburgfestival.at. Tours 5€ adults, 2.90€ children 11 and under. Daily 2pm (not July), with additional tours in high season.*

⑩ ★ Salzburger Barockmuseum. Head across the Makartsteg bridge into the Mirabell Gardens (p 12, **⑩**) and you find an impressive art hoard tucked away in a former orangery. The collection

Linzergasse, with a view of St. Sebastian's Church.

The Salzburger Barockmuseum is discreet but packed with astonishing works.

focuses on the early days of baroque art, the drawings and preparatory oils from which extravagant masterpieces by the likes of Rubens evolve. To the untrained eye many look perfect—it's difficult to believe they were only the starting point for greater works. ⏱ *30 min. Orangerie des Mirabellgartens.* ☎ *0662/87743217. www.barock museum.at. Admission 4.50€ adults, 3.70€ children 15 and under. Wed– Sun 10am–5pm; Tues–Sun July–Aug.*

⑪ ★ Linzergasse. This picturesque street, from the Staatsbrücke bridge into the oldest part of the New Town, is subtly different to the Old Town. The latter became filled with elegant shops while here were merchants and services such as gunsmiths, coopers, and chemists. In fact no. 3 is where famed scientist **Paracelsus** lived from 1540 to 1541. The architecture is less grand than across the river but every bit as interesting. ⏱ *20 min.*

Gourmet Salzburg

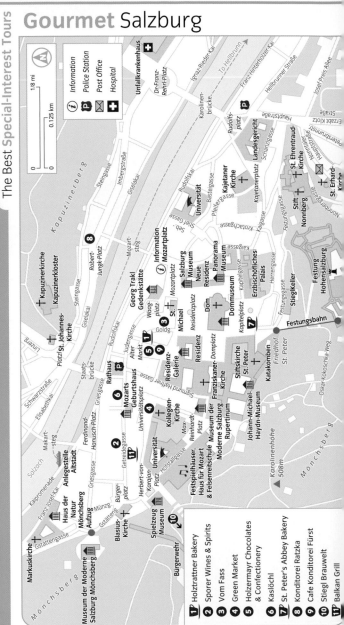

Legend:
- (i) Information
- P Police Station
- ✉ Post Office
- ✚ Hospital

1/8 mi
0.125 km

N

Map labels:
Markuskirche, Museum der Moderne Salzburg Mönchsberg, Haus der Natur, Anlegestelle Altstadt, Aufzug, Blasius-Kirche, Spielzeug Museum, Bürgerwehr, Kapuzinerkirche, Kapuzinerkloster, St. Johannes-Kirche, Rathaus, Mozarts Geburtshaus, Universität, Kollegien-Kirche, Festspielhäuser, Haus für Mozart & Felsenreitschule, Museum der Moderne Salzburg Rupertinum, Franziskaner-Kirche, Stiftskirche St. Peter, Johann-Michael-Haydn-Museum, Katakomben, Friedhof St. Peter, Karolinenhöhe 508m, Georg Trakl Gedenkstätte, Information Mozartplatz, Salzburg Museum, Neue Residenz, Panorama Museum, Residenz-Galerie, Residenz, St. Michael, Dom, Dommuseum, Erzbischöfliches Palais, Kapitelplatz, Stieglkeller, Festung Hohensalzburg, Festungsbahn, St. Peter, Universität, Kajetaner Kirche, Landesgericht, St. Ehrentraud Kirche, Stift Nonnberg, St. Erhard-Kirche, Unfallkrankenhaus

Street labels:
Solzach, Franz-Josef-Kai, Kaipromenade, Schwarzstraße, Elisabethkai, Makartsteg, Ferdinand-Hanusch-Platz, Griesgasse, Gstättengasse, Mönchsberg, Münzgasse, Bürger-platz, Herbert-von-Karajan Platz, Hofstallgasse, Max-Reinhardt-Platz, Sigmund Haffner Gasse, Getreidegasse, Universitätsplatz, Goldg., Alter Markt, Judengasse, Rudolfskai, Staats-brücke, Giselakai, Imbergstraße, Steingasse, Kapuzinerberg, Rudolf-kai, Seb.-Stief Gasse, Mozart-steg, Robert-Jungk-Platz, Mozartplatz, Pfeifergasse, Bastei-gasse, Kaigasse, Krotachgasse, Kapitelgasse, Herrengasse, Festungsgasse, Nonnberg-gasse, Brunnhausgasse, Nonntaler Hauptstraße, Kajetanerplatz, Oskar-Kokoschka-Weg, Karolinen-brucke, Ignaz-Rieder-Kai, Rudolfs-platz, Dr-Franz-Rehrl-Platz, Hellbrunner Straße, Franz-Hinterholzer-Kai, Josef Preis Allee, Hauptstraße, Erzabt Klotz Straße, Petersbrunnstr., Nonntaler Hauptstr., Schanzlgasse

To Hellbrunn

Legend — Gourmet Salzburg listings:
1. Holztrattner Bakery
2. Sporer Wines & Spirits
3. Vom Fass
4. Green Market
5. Holzermayr Chocolates & Confectionery
6. Kaslöchl
7. St. Peter's Abbey Bakery
8. Konditorei Ratzka
9. Cafe Konditorei Fürst
10. Stiegl Brauwelt
11. Balkan Grill

Austrian food isn't just pork and sauerkraut; today's Austria is a gastronomic destination with a commitment to local, organic food. In Salzburg, modern cuisine pays homage to hearty mountain fare, with traditional dishes, coffee houses, farm produce, and chocolate treats. Salzburg is also Austria's beer capital with frothy Märzen brewed since 1492. START: **Kapitelplatz.**

1 ★ **Holztrattner Bakery.** Not just a bakery—40 different types of dough turn out a phantasmagorical variety of bread along with fruit loaf, Danish pastries, and grissini to die for. Take out a bundle or try for one of the three tables where everyone from students to businessmen choose homemade lunch from a daily changing menu. *Brodgasse 9.* ☎ *0662/841682. $.*

2 ★★ **Sporer Wines & Spirits.** The narrowest building in this historical street dates back to 1407. It's an Aladdin's cave stocked with fine liqueurs, punches, and schnapps in 100-year-old casks lining the walls. Distilling goes on upstairs, with tastings in the vaults. Try the orange punch, made from the same recipe since 1927. Lots of Austrian (and very local) wines too. ⏱ *20 min. Getreidegasse 39.* ☎ *0662/8454314. www.sporer.at.*

3 ★★ **Vom Fass.** A quaint little place that concentrates on oils, vinegars, and liqueurs. You can find the highly rated Styrian pumpkin seed oil, and a goodly selection of schnapps and vinegars in an extraordinary number of varieties. Take your own bottle, or buy one of the individually labeled ones. ⏱ *20 min. Goldgasse 5.* ☎ *0662/849316.*

4 ★★★ **Green Market.** The city's major market is a beautiful place to stroll among the fresh fruit and vegetables, pungent cheeses, sizzling sausages, and crusty breads. It starts on Universitätsplatz but meanders along paths and roads to the Festival Halls. ⏱ *40 min. Universitätsplatz.*

5 ★ **Holzermayr Chocolates & Confectionery.** Joseph Holzermayr's chocolates were so well regarded that Archduke Franz Ferdinand appointed him as purveyor to the Imperial Court in 1890. The company produces its own *Mozartkugel* (p 76), the famed chocolate-dipped marzipan Mozart Ball, as well as a version for diabetics. The shop is an exercise in nostalgia with sweets and candies, sugared almonds, and much more. ⏱ *15 min. Alter Markt 7.* ☎ *0662/842365. www.en. holzermayr.at.*

6 **Kaslöchl.** The quirky wooden storefront opens onto a tiny space hiding a treasure trove of cheese dating back to 1892 (the shop, not the cheese). There are up to 150 varieties, many organic, almost all

The Green Market has a wealth of local produce.

Buying Time

This isn't a tour you should attempt on a Sunday. Many shops, particularly those which involve cafes or sell souvenirs, are now open on a Sunday, but some aren't, including markets. Salzburg Festival time, however, can bring out the entrepreneur in the most traditional shopkeeper. Most shops are open 10am to 6pm Monday to Friday and 10am to 5pm on Saturday. Bakers may be open from 6:30am, and food shops from around 8am. Some still close for lunch.

Austrian. Try the *Vorarlberger Hochalpkäse*, hard, rich, and Austria's highest mountain cheese aged up to 18 months. Other treats include organic Parma ham and (perhaps an acquired taste) sheep's milk chocolates. ⏰ 30 min. *Hagenauerplatz 2.* ☎ 0662/844100. *www.kasloechl.at.*

7 ★★ **St. Peter's Abbey Bakery.** Salzburg's oldest bakery, mentioned in records dating back to the 12th century, is in a building next to the ancient waterwheel at the foot of the Hohensalzburg Fortress. Original wood-burning ovens give a special finish to the natural sourdough loaves. Bring some cheese and

picnic in the adjoining St. Peter's Cemetery (p 26, **6**), ancient and soothing. *Kapitelplatz 8.* ☎ 0662/434187. *Closed Wed. $.*

8 ★★ **Konditorei Ratzka.** Austria's gourmet guide, the *Gault Millau*, has declared this the country's best cake shop, and it's easy to see why—the display cases are a riot of custard and cream, tarts, and strudels. Choose from 20 options daily, not least the famed apricot *Marillenfleck* and the raspberry-truffle torte. ⏰ 15 min. *Imbergstrasse 45.* ☎ 0662/640024.

9 ★★ **Cafe Konditorei Fürst.** The Holy Grail for those in search of

Holzermayr creates Mozart Balls, a traditional treat of Salzburg.

the Mozart Ball (p 76), that pistachio-marzipan-nougat-chocolate sensation. It was first made here, in this classic coffee house with gardens, in 1890. Creator Paul Fürst's great-grandson Norbert continues the tradition with lots of other chocolatey delights and pastries. There's a further cafe and two shops in the Old Town. 🕐 *15 min. Alter Markt, Brodgasse 13.* ☎ *0662/843759-0. www.original-mozartkugel.com.*

Cross the river, take the no. 1 bus from Mirabellplatz to the Bräuhausstrasse stop.

🔟 ★★ **Stiegl Brauwelt.** Salzburg's iconic beer, Stiegl, dating back to the 15th century, is celebrated in a rather charming museum at the brewery complex near the airport. Entry gets you a beer tasting, and there's a shop to buy beer to take home, and a beer garden, as well as restaurants. 🕐 *1 hr. Bräuhausstrasse 9.* ☎ *0662/83871492. www.brauwelt. at. Museum: admission 9€ adults, 4€ children 6–16, free 5 and under. Daily 10am–5pm (July/Aug 7pm); pub and beer garden daily 10am–midnight; Paracelsus restaurant lunch & dinner Tues–Sat. Bus: 1. See p 106.*

Take the bus back to the Old Town.

Cafe Konditorei Fürst, home of the first Mozart Ball.

11️⃣ ★★★ **Balkan Grill.** Well, yes, it is a hotdog stand but one that's taken on iconic status. It serves the Bosna, what was originally a Bulgarian staple that is now a Salzburg tradition as everyone from gastronomes to local workers cluster around the unassuming window. And what for? A grilled pork bratwurst, with onions, fresh parsley, and a secret blend of spices. Plus many variations on a theme. *Getreidegasse 33.* ☎ *0662/ 841483. $.*

Organic Delights

Austria has been hailed for its 'aristocratic' green sensibility, and you'll rarely find food with less of a carbon footprint. Long before it was trendy, locally produced food from farms using natural methods has been the way of life. Now it is even more so. In 1993, the Austria Bio Garantie (ABG) was founded, the first certification body for organic products in Austria. Today the group (www. abg.at) carries out inspections down every link of the food chain, and involves 10,700 organic farmers and 900 processors. Finding organic produce in restaurants is the norm rather than exception, yet little fuss is made as it's what's been expected for generations.

The Magic of Christmas

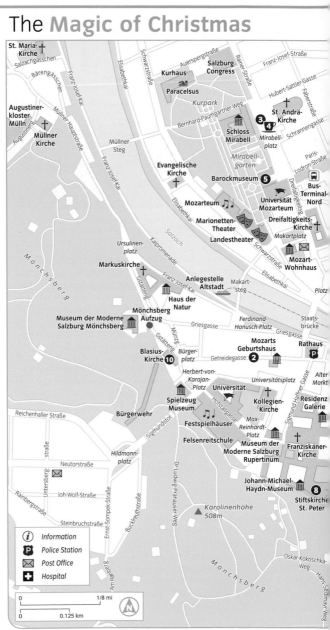

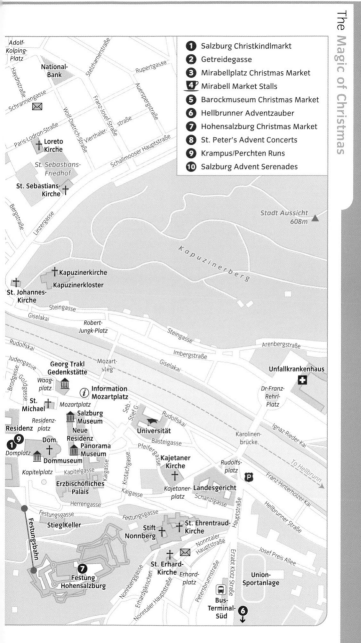

1. Salzburg Christkindlmarkt
2. Getreidegasse
3. Mirabellplatz Christmas Market
4. Mirabell Market Stalls
5. Barockmuseum Christmas Market
6. Hellbrunner Adventzauber
7. Hohensalzburg Christmas Market
8. St. Peter's Advent Concerts
9. Krampus/Perchten Runs
10. Salzburg Advent Serenades

While Salzburg is beautiful at any time of year, it is made for Christmas. The ancient streets are usually covered with a soft veneer of snow, the historic buildings are awash with twinkling lights, the scent of cinnamon and grilling sausages wafts from just about every street corner, and carols fill the air. New Year is also a treat (see 'Entertainment,' p 117). START: **Domplatz, from end of November to Christmas.**

Christkindlmarkt, Domplatz.

❶ ★★★ kids **Salzburg Christkindlmarkt.** The main Christmas market in Salzburg, and also one of the best in the Alps. The twinkling lights and candles in front of the cathedral and the drifting scents of roasted almonds, hot chestnuts, and mulled wine create a magical ambiance that neither Disney nor Coca-Cola could hope to match. The dozens of traditional booths sell handicrafts, cakes, and gingerbread men, aromatic tree ornaments, and other delicate decorations. There are performances by traditional Salzburg choirs and children's school groups to add to the allure. The market is opened by the archbishop on the first Saturday in Advent (late November) after the blessing of the Advent wreaths. ⏱ *1hr. Domplatz/*

Residenzplatz. www.christkindl-markt. co.at. Advent–December 26 (incl. Christmas day) 10am–8pm Mon–Thurs, 10am–9pm Sun, 9am–Sat, 9am–8:30pm.

❷ ★★ **Getreidegasse.** Before you cross the river for the New Town take a stroll down Salzburg's historic main street—always special, it takes on a different quality at Christmas with extravagant displays in the upmarket shop windows and the narrow alleyways are a riot of seasonal gifts and decorations. ⏱ *20 min.*

❸ ★★ kids **Mirabellplatz Christmas Market.** With its setting on Mirabell Square in front of the Mirabell Palace, this market has its own charms, with plenty of stalls. The Mirabell Gardens are a lovely place to stroll (particularly if the snow is falling) or stop for a steaming hot chocolate and a rich cake from one of the many stands as seasonal music from brass ensembles and choirs fills the air. ⏱ *30 min. Mirabellplatz. www.weihnachtsmarkt-salzburg.at. Advent–Christmas Eve, 10am–8pm Mon–Wed & Fri, 9am–8pm Thurs, 10am–9pm Sat, 10am–8:30pm Sun; 10am–3pm Christmas Eve.*

❹ **Mirabell Market Stalls.** For a quick, atmospheric lunch pop back to the Christmas Market where the stalls offer a wealth of choices—soft pretzels, veal sausages in seeded rolls, gingerbread, and more. *Mirabellplatz. $.*

Christmas Doesn't Come But Once...

Christmas doesn't come just one day a year in Salzburg, it's around for a number of weeks. There are more Christmas markets than listed here on a regular (and irregular) basis in and around Salzburg, from the stalls outside the station to the Waldklang, where the work of dozens of artists vies with DJs, VJs, rock bands, and choirs at the Waldbad Anif swimming lake on the city's outskirts, to those in outlying villages. There are exquisite mangers on display in churches, advent concerts in churches and in the streets, and music and decorations everywhere. The most comprehensive and up-to-the-minute information is found on the official Salzburg website, www.salzburg.info, from sometime in November.

5 ★★ Barockmuseum Christmas Market. Now this is a nice one, the passion and pomp of the baroque way of life transformed into Christmas trinkets and presents with an artiness and style not seen elsewhere. The setting outside the museum in the Mirabell Gardens is special too, even though the gardens are less showy at this time of year. ⏲ *30 min. Mirabell Gardens. From early Dec. Museum hours. See p 43,* **10**.

6 ★★★ kids Hellbrunner Adventzauber. It's worth taking the bus (no. 25, from Mirabellplatz, about 20 min) out to Hellbrunn Palace for this exceptional event in a magical setting. The palace's romantic courtyard (which is free to enter) and a giant Advent calendar form a backdrop to the usual food and fun. A real reindeer pulls sleigh rides, there are real livestock such as sheep and goats, and plenty of entertainment, plus Hellbrunn's usual delights. ⏲ *30 min. www.hellbrunner adventzauber.at. Advent to Christmas Eve Wed–Fri 1–8pm, Sat–Sun 10am–8pm; Christmas Eve 10am–2pm. See p 19,* **1**.

Mirabell Gardens in winter.

Hellbrunn Adventzauber.

❼ ★★ kids Hohensalzburg Christmas Market. Back in town, and it's time to head high above the rooftops to the courtyard of the Hohensalzburg Fortress. This is Christmas sightseeing at its finest, especially when the city's lights really start to sparkle in the late afternoon. Plenty of stalls selling decorations and culinary delights combine with brass bands, choirs, and dancers to create all-round entertainment. Children get to make their own fun—apple-men, straw stars, ice flowers, angels, gift tags, and much more. ⏱ *1 hr. Hohensalzburg. www.salzburg-burgen.at. See p 9, ❶, normal admission charges apply. Weekends from Advent until Christmas, times vary.*

❽ ★★ St. Peter's Advent Concerts. The vaulted Romanesque Hall of St. Peter's Abbey, a short walk

'Twas The Night Before Christmas

The many traditions of Christmas in Salzburg come to a head on Christmas Eve, at which point it is time to take a short break from the fun and remember the importance of the time in a beautiful fashion that is only possible in this city. Each year there is the noon **Christmas and Christ Child salute,** followed by the 2pm **Christmas service** in St. George's Chapel at the Hohensalzburg Fortress. It's unlikely that you'll manage to get in to this, as it gets packed, but you can stay on high and enjoy the 5:30pm **open-air Christmas brass concert** from the Mönchsberg. Later in the evening there is a **Christmas Mass** at the Franciscan Church, with the day culminating in a **Midnight Mass** at the cathedral.

After a pleasantly sedate few days things come alive on New Year's Eve when there is a late-afternoon gun salute from the Mönchsberg, with end-of-year services at St. Peter's and the cathedral.

Magic of the Markets

Christmas markets make a holiday in themselves—and many people come here for several days just to experience them. They generally run from Advent (the last weekend in November) through to Christmas Eve, although some run through to December 26. It's a fairy-tale experience, as warming for adults as it is for children. You'll find all sorts of presents to buy, from gingerbread treats to carved Christmas tree decorations, foodie specials to handicrafts. And you don't need to search out a place for lunch—food is everywhere, with mulled wine to wash it down as snow drifts from the sky.

from the bottom of the Mönchsberg, is a perfect setting for Advent and Christmas songs as well as chamber music by Mozart. The late-afternoon performance sets you up nicely for a stroll among the stalls of a Christmas market in the evening air. ⏱ *1½ hr. St. Peter's Abbey.* ☎ *0662/823788. www.nachmittagskonzerte.at. Admission 22€ adults, 15€ children 17 and under, free 5 and under. Daily at 4pm from late Nov.*

⑨ Krampus/Perchten Runs. Grim-looking demons dash about protecting the populace from evil spirits in this Pagan tradition. The characters in hideous wooden masks run through the city, flailing with rods and cows' tails—anyone hit is said to be blessed. Runs, which are a riot of laughter and fancy-dress, take place regularly (but at no specific time) from late November in late afternoon/early evening and often involve the Christkindlmarkt. ⏱ *30 min. www.salzburg.info. Late Nov late afternoon/early evening.*

⑩ ★★ Salzburg Advent Serenades. A combination of seasonal and other folk and classical music, and poetry by candlelight in the evocative setting of the Gothic Hall at St. Blasius Church in the romantic heart of the Old Town. It's also possible to have a special dinner (an extra 26€) at the Goldener Hirsch hotel (p 136) around the corner, although you'll also find many restaurants offering a celebration menu. ⏱ *1½ hr (not incl. dinner). Gothic Hall, Gstättengasse.* ☎ *0662/436870. www.adventserenaden.at. Admission 26–33€ adults, 10€ children 9 and under. From late Nov varied days at 7:30pm & 4pm Sat.*

Christmas cherubs.

Salzburg with Kids

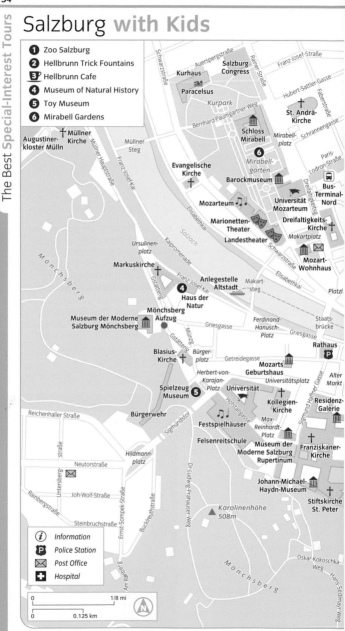

1. Zoo Salzburg
2. Hellbrunn Trick Fountains
3. Hellbrunn Cafe
4. Museum of Natural History
5. Toy Museum
6. Mirabell Gardens

Schwarzstraße
Auersbergstraße
Rainer-Straße
Franz-Josef-Straße

Kurhaus
Salzburg Congress
Paracelsus

Kurpark
Hubert-Sattler-Gasse
Faberstraße

St. Andrä-Kirche
Schrannengasse

Bernhard-Paumgartner-Weg

Schloss Mirabell
Mirabell-platz

Augustiner-kloster Mülln
Müllner Kirche
Müllner Steg
Müllner Hauptstraße

6 Mirabell-garten

Pans-Lodron-Straße

Evangelische Kirche

Barockmuseum

Bus-Terminal-Nord

Franz-Josef-Kai

Mozarteum
Universität Mozarteum

Dreifaltigkeitsweg

Elisabethkai
Solzach

Marionetten-Theater
Landestheater
Dreifaltigkeits-Kirche

Makartplatz

Ursulinen-platz

Kaipromenade

Mozart-Wohnhaus

Mönchsberg

Markuskirche

Franz-Josef-Kai

Anlegestelle Altstadt
Makart-steg

Makartplatz

Elisabethkai

Platzl

Gstätteng.

4 Haus der Natur

Museum der Moderne Salzburg Mönchsberg
Mönchsberg Aufzug

Münzg.

Griesgasse

Ferdinand-Hanusch-Platz

Staats-brücke

Gstätteng.

Griesgasse
Griesgasse

Blasius-Kirche
Bürger-platz

Getreidegasse

Rathaus

Reichenhaller Straße

Spielzeug 5 Museum
Bürgerwehr

Herbert-von-Karajan-Platz

Mozarts Geburtshaus

Universitätsplatz

Alter Markt

Residenz-Galerie

Universität
Kollegien-Kirche

Sigmund Haffner Gasse

straße

Sigmundstor

Festspielhäuser

Max-Reinhardt-Platz

Felsenreitschule
Museum der Moderne Salzburg Rupertinum

Franziskaner-Kirche

Neutorstraße
Hildmann-platz

Untersberg

Johann-Michael-Haydn-Museum

Rainbergstraße
Joh-Wolf-Straße

Stiftskirche St. Peter

Ernst-Sompek-Straße

Buckreuhstraße

Dr.-Ludwig-Prähauser-Weg

Steinbruchstraße

Karolinenhöhe 508m

Am Rainberg

Oskar-Kokoschka-Weg

Mönchsberg

Hans-Sedlmayr-Weg

ⓘ Information
🅿 Police Station
✉ Post Office
✚ Hospital

0 ——— 1/8 mi
0 ——— 0.125 km

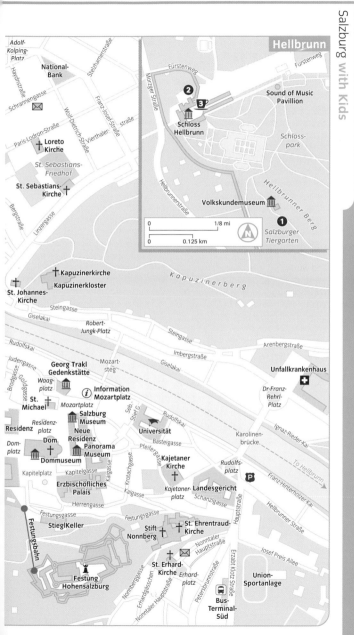

Hellbrunn

Adolf-Kolping-Platz

National-Bank

Loreto Kirche

St. Sebastians-Friedhof

St. Sebastians-Kirche

Fürstenweg

Fürstenweg

Mörzger Straße

Sound of Music Pavillion

Schloss Hellbrunn

Schloss-park

Hellbrunnerstraße

Hellbrunner Berg

Volkskundemuseum

0   1/8 mi
0   0.125 km

Salzburger Tiergarten

Hardtstraße
Schrannengasse
Sterzhamerstraße
Paris-Lodron-Straße
Wolf-Dietrich-Straße
Franz-Josef-Straße
Vierthaler-Straße
Bergstraße
Linzergasse

Kapuzinerkirche
Kapuzinerkloster

St. Johannes-Kirche

Steingasse

Kapuzinerberg

Giselakai

Robert-Jungk-Platz

Steingasse

Imbergstraße

Arenbergstraße

Rudolfskai

Judengasse
Brodgasse
Goldgasse

Georg Trakl Gedenkstätte

Mozart-steg

Giselakai

Unfallkrankenhaus

Waag-platz

Information Mozartplatz

Dr-Franz-Rehrl-Platz

St. Michael

Mozartplatz

Salzburg Museum

Seb. Stift G.

Rudolfskai

Residenz

Residenz-platz

Neue Residenz

Universität

Basteigasse

Karolinen-brücke

To Hellbrunn

Dom-platz

Dom

Panorama Museum

Pfeifergasse

Kajetaner Kirche

Ignaz-Rieder-Kai

Dommuseum

Kapitelgasse

Krotachgasse
Kaigasse

Kajetaner-platz

Landesgericht

Rudolfs-platz

Franz-Hinterholzer-Kai

Kapitelplatz

Erzbischöfliches Palais

Kaigasse

Schanzlgasse

Hauptstraße

Herrengasse

Festungsgasse

Festungsgasse

Hellbrunner Straße

StieglKeller

Stift Nonnberg

St. Ehrentraud-Kirche

Festungsbahn

Nonntaler Hauptstraße

Josef Preis Allee

Nonnbergasse

St. Erhard-Kirche

Erhard-platz

Erhardgässchen

Nonntaler Hauptstraße

Petersbrunnstraße

Erzabt Klotz Straße

Festung Hohensalzburg

Union-Sportanlage

Bus-Terminal-Süd

Salzburg might be a place of culture but it's also a place for family fun and the perfect city to introduce your children to city breaks, being small and walkable with safe, traffic-free streets. There's a river, bridges, hills, and castles. Youngsters can appreciate the Mozart heritage while other attractions are made especially for them. START: **Bus no. 25 from Mirabellplatz to Hellbrunn.**

1 ★★ kids **Zoo Salzburg.** A likeable and relaxedly small zoo that has been an animal park since 1619, when Archbishop Marcus Sittikus had it created along with the adjoining gardens and Hellbrunn Palace. The animals live in natural enclosures among the trees on the gentle slopes of a small mountain. Children love the wild feel of the place, which manages to feature more than 400 animals from lions, cheetahs, white rhinos, and monkeys to marmots and wolves. ⏱ *1 hr. Anifer Landesstrasse 1.* ☎ *0662/8201760. www.salzburg-zoo.at. Admission 9€ adults, 4€ children 4–14, 7€ students. Combined zoo & Hellbrunn Palace ticket. See below. Daily 9am–4pm; later in summer. Bus: 25.*

2 ★★★ kids **Hellbrunn Trick Fountains.** Before lining up for the tour (the only way you can get in to see them), my children believed they would only see a few jets of water, but by the time they'd been round they were soaked and laughing. As you walk through grotto-like gardens, water spurts from statues, chairs, crevasses, and even regular fountains, all dating from the early 17th century. Everyone joins in the fun, with the guide/operator delighting in catching youngsters (and adults) unawares. Best on a very hot day when everyone can dry off on the bus back to town. The ticket includes entry to the palace but it's not something you really need to bother with. Instead take them into the sweeping grounds where there's a great adventure playground, lots of logs and swings—and you can laze on the lawns. ⏱ *40 min. Best on a very hot day when everyone can dry off on the bus back to town. See p 19,* **1**.

Hellbrunn's trick fountains.

The playground next to the Mirabell Gardens.

3 **Hellbrunn Cafe.** While there is a restaurant-like affair at Hellbrunn, this glorified snack bar is all you need for a break. It's in the palace courtyard, next to the gardens, with shaded seats and tables, and sells ice cream, sandwiches, potato chips, drinks, and cakes. *Hellbrunn Palace courtyard. No phone. $.*

4 ★★★ kids **Museum of Natural History.** This already-impressive museum (signposted Haus der Natur) underwent a rebirth in summer 2009 with sweeping new frontage and exhibition halls. It's not what you'd expect of a natural history museum in the mountains, with its large aquarium, space hall (including a moon landing re-creation), and animatronic dinosaurs, plus a cutting-edge, interactive look at the Salzach river and a homage to Salzburg physicist Christian (Doppler Effect) Doppler. ⏱ *1 hr. Museumsplatz 5.* ☎ *0662/8426530. www.salzburg-zoo.at. Admission 6€ adults, 4€ children 4–14 and students. Daily 9am–5pm.*

5 **Toy Museum.** The biggest collection of European toys in Austria—not that that means much to youngsters, although they will find

Young Explorers

Most museums and galleries provide special facilities for children. The Museum der Moderne Salzburg Rupertinum (p 40, **2**) features workshops in English for youngsters called *Every Picture Tells a Story,* and there are also special tours of the museum's sister facility on the Mönchsberg (p 9, **2**). In fact, most places in Salzburg are great for children, whether it is a stroll across the Mönchsberg, a wilder walk up the Kapuzinerberg, pottering about by the river, darting into chocolate shops, looking at the planes in Hangar-7 (p 20, **3**), or seeing where Mozart was born (p 24, **1**). Cycling is good and safe by the river.

Salzburg's attractions are mostly clustered together, connected by fascinating narrow streets, alleyways, courtyards, squares, and riverside paths. And most attractions a bit farther afield are accessible on the impressive bus service.

Head for the Park & Pool

With the mountains on its doorstep and the Mönchsberg and Kapuzinerberg as places to walk, Salzburg seems to have never fully embraced (or needed to embrace) the idea of the park. Best place for a breath of fresh air and a kick-around is **Franz-Josef Park,** on the banks of the Salzach, just out past the Kapuzinerberg (bus nos. 6, 7, or 20). There's a lake, gardens, sculptures, and plenty of grass. In the adjoining **Volksgarten** is a large open-air swimming pool (**Freibad Volksgarten**), mini-golf, and ice rink. There is also an excellent open-air swimming pool with slides and stuff as well as mini-golf down by the lake at Leopoldskron (bus no. 25), and another on Alpenstrasse. They all open on May 1 each year. There are two swimming lakes near the city, the **Waldbad** in Anif and the **Salzach Lake** north of the city. The **Paracelsus indoor pool,** adjoining the Mirabell Gardens, is open all year.

something they like amongst the dolls, teddy bears, and railways. Children can join in games and crafts, and there's a Punch and Judy show each Tuesday and Wednesday (3pm, not summer/Christmas holidays). The setting, in an historic hospital on a renaissance square, enchants parents and offspring alike. ⏱ 40 min. Bürgerspitalgasse 2. ☎ 0662/620808300. www.salzburg museum.at. Admission 3€ adults, 1€ children 6–15. Tues–Sun 9am–5pm; also Mon July, Aug, Dec.

6 ★★★ kids **Mirabell Gardens.** The gardens themselves offer a perfect space to run around and let off energy, with spraying fountains to cool off. But there is also a free adventure playground on the riverside (through a tunnel at the back of the hedge-covered walkway) amid the old city fortifications. This is a good place to wind down in the shade of towering trees, especially for younger children. There's an excellent climbing tower with a big slide and chute as well as all the usual play equipment. ⏱ 1 hr. See p 12, **10**. ●

The **Mönchsberg**

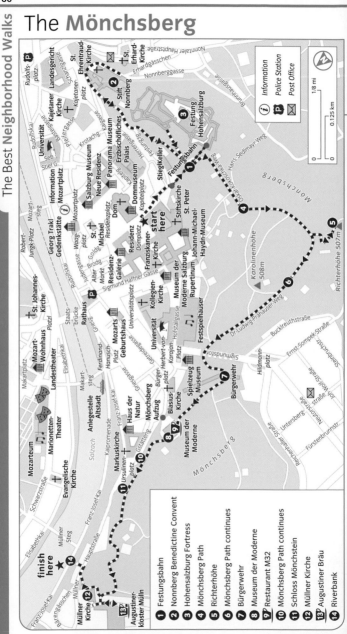

Key
- ⓘ Information
- 🄿 Police Station
- ⌧ Post Office

1 Festungsbahn
2 Nonnberg Benedictine Convent
3 Hohensalzburg Fortress
4 Mönchsberg Path
5 Richterhöhe
6 Mönchsberg Path continues
7 Bürgerwehr
8 Museum der Moderne
9 Restaurant M32
10 Schloss Mönchstein
11 Mönchsberg Path continues
12 Müllner Kirche
13 Augustiner Bräu
14 Riverbank

Previous page: Mönchsberg view.

T he Mönchsberg is the rocky ridge crowned by the Hohensalzburg Fortress, running almost 1.25km (0.8 miles) the
length of the Old Town and reaching 499m (1,640 ft.). It's the prod-
uct of glacial movement, an island of stuck-together rubble (material
used to front many a building in olden times). Now it's a haven from
the crowds and perfect for a relaxed walk. START: **Salzburg Cathedral.**
TIME: **2½–3 hr, longer if you stop for lunch.**

❶ Festungsbahn. Across Kapitelplatz from the cathedral, the
bright red funicular beckons. However, instead take a photograph of it
climbing up the almost-sheer cliff,
and head past the entrance, con-
tinuing along (and up) Festungsgasse. You can take some steep
steps directly upward, but the narrow street offers a seductive,
changing view across the city as you
rise before turning a sharp right
onto the path that hugs the rock.
🕐 *15 min. Festungsgasse 4.*

**❷ Nonnberg Benedictine
Convent.** Before turning right,
take a quick detour straight along
the road. Just as you round the
bend at the very tip of the Mönchsberg, you'll find the Nonnberg, the
abbey from *The Sound of Music*, facing south over the mountains. Turn
back and head up toward the fortress. *See p 32,* **❶**.

❸ Hohensalzburg Fortress.
Obviously a place to visit, but not
during a full exploration of the
Mönchsberg. If you haven't done it
already (and it should be top of
your list), save it for later. Instead of
turning left into the gateway, marvel at the city views and carry on
along the footpath that runs under
the Festungsbahn. 🕐 *10 min or
longer if you want to explore. See
p 9,* **❶**.

❹ Mönchsberg Path. From the
forbidding fortress surrounds,
you're suddenly in the sun-dappled
trees. There are views to the left
(south) to the mountains, and
there's a small hut selling coffees
and soft drinks. You can turn right
for a swift descent to the Old Town,
left for the valley floor, or take one
of several wooded paths across the
summit. 🕐 *15 min.*

A winter view from the far end of the Mönchsberg.

The Festungsbahn on its near-vertical climb up the Mönchsberg.

5 Richterhöhe. Off and up to the left are the ruins of this castle-like lookout post that gave early warning of anyone approaching from the south. The trees have thinned and walkers take the opportunity to sit in the sun on one of a number of benches that face the mountains.

6 Mönchsberg Path continues. Past the Richterhöhe the main path veers around and follows the western ridge, giving views over the Rainberg—another, smaller rock outcrop—and across to the airport and the mountains beyond. The path continues over the narrowest part of the ridge, under which the road runs into the Old Town.

7 Bürgerwehr. These fortifications are part of the ancient city walls. They date from the 13th century, before artillery, and were built with small stones. The building, with its huge walls and five towers, became obsolete when explosives started to be used, as the small stones used in the construction did not stand up to cannon fire. Information boards tell the tale and show where further walls were. There are enchanting views over to both sides and you can walk on the ruins for

free. Follow the path curving behind the fortifications. If you fancy a longer walk, you can take a left and stick to the western ridge that takes you out and past the **Johannes-schlossl,** another old lookout point, or branch off through the wooded area. It's equally tempting to carry straight on toward the Museum der Moderne (Museum of Modern Art). ⏱ *30 min.*

8 Museum der Moderne. You emerge from the ancient forest and, on the city side, find this starkly modern building, yet the startling simplicity somehow fits into the serenity of the lofty setting. There's modern sculpture outside (not least Henry Moore's 1960s' work *Locking Piece*) and generally something interesting to see inside with regularly changing exhibitions. But this is the time to sample its other attraction—the cafe and restaurant, M32. Should you want to curtail your tour you can jump into the **Mönchsberg Elevator,** which takes you straight down through the mountain to the city streets below. ⏱ *20 min. See* *p 40,* **1**.

Path leading to the Hohensalzburg Fortress.

The Hohensalzburg Fortress.

9 Restaurant M32. Stop at the museum's cafe and restaurant, with city views from the ceiling-high windows. It may be you're tempted by a posh lunch, but I'd recommend grabbing a coffee and cake and relaxing on the large terrace. Aside from the views, this is a place to people watch—the tourists, hikers, and arty types all coming together. *Mönchsberg 32.* ☎ *0662/841000. Closed Mon.*

10 Mönchsberg Path continues. The path now starts to meander gently downward with a fantastic viewpoint over the river and city. You are still among the trees, including many beech and rowan (which are as pretty when bare during the winter as during the summer) but there's a feeling of approaching civilization.

11 Schloss Mönchstein. Voted the best five-star hotel in Austria, this fairy-tale castle looming over the city is worth popping in for a look, and is another option for a sophisticated lunch. Even if you're not stopping, poke your head inside the door for a peek. *See p 139.*

12 Müllner Kirche. Just as you're winding your way downward, you

come across this church—unimposing on the outside, splendid within. The Gothic-turned-baroque interior is home to a red marble altar and a late medieval masterpiece—a statue of the Madonna with Child from 1460. ⏰ *15 min. Augustinergasse 4.* ☎ *0662/432671. www.kirchen.net.*

13 Augustiner Bräu. Opposite the Müllner Kirche, as you head down at the end of the Mönchsberg, you find this stone building where monks were brewing beer back in 1621, and where the Bräustübl Tavern is one of Salzburg's leading beer halls with its shady beer garden. This is a great place to finish the walk with a late afternoon beer and something to nibble from the food hall, which has kiosks selling sausages, smoked fish, and much more. *Augustinergasse 4.* ☎ *0662/431246. www.augustiner bier.at. $.*

14 Riverbank. Having wound your way down, you're just a wide stone staircase away from the river and a few minutes' walk from the heart of the city. If you've stumbled from the Augustiner Bräu, pay attention to the bikes racing along as you emerge onto the river path.

The **Kapuzinerberg**

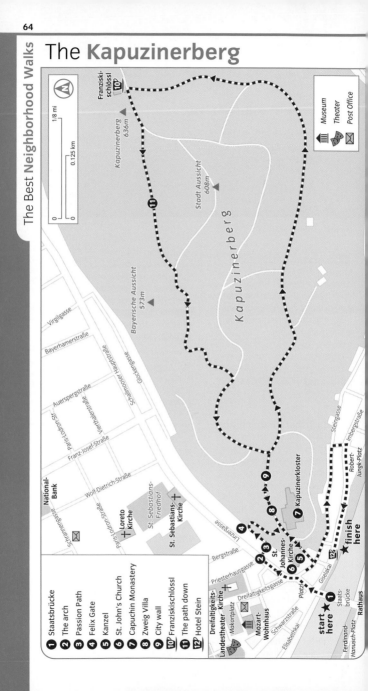

1 Staatsbrücke
2 The arch
3 Passion Path
4 Felix Gate
5 Kanzel
6 St. John's Church
7 Capuchin Monastery
8 Zweig Villa
9 City wall
10 Franziskischlössl
11 The path down
12 Hotel Stein

Museum
Theater
Post Office

start here

finish here

Franziski-schlössl

Kapuzinerberg 636m

Stadt Aussicht 608m

Bayerische Aussicht 573m

Kapuzinerberg

Kapuzinerkloster

Zwettlgasse

Steingasse

Imbergstraße

Robert-Jungk-Platz

Giselakai

Rathaus

Staats-brücke

Ferdinand-Hanusch-Platz

Elisabethkai

Schwarzstraße

Mozart-Wohnhaus

Makartplatz

Dreifaltigkeitsgasse

Landestheater

Dreifaltigkeits-Kirche

Priesterhausgasse

Bergstraße

Linzergasse

St. Johannes-Kirche

St. Sebastians-Kirche

St. Sebastians-Friedhof

Loreto Kirche

National-Bank

Wolf-Dietrich-Straße

Paris-Lodron-Straße

Franz-Josef-Straße

Auerspergstraße

Bayerhamerstraße

Virgilgasse

Glockengasse

Schallmooser Hauptstraße

Paris-Lodron-Str.

Vierthalerstraße

Schrannengasse

1/8 mi

0.125 km

The small mountain, at 635m (2,086 ft.), is Salzburg's highest point on the New Town side. It's steep with upward and downward hiking trails, steps through dense beech trees, and exceptional views. It's most beautiful in late afternoon when the sun starts dropping over the Old Town and the golden rays flicker through the branches. START: **Staatsbrücke bridge**. TIME: **2 hr.**

❶ **Staatsbrücke.** Stand on the bridge and gaze up at the wild Kapuzinerberg, which rises up from the very back of the shops and restaurants on car-free Linzergasse. Walk up Linzergasse and the immensity of this huge rock becomes more and more apparent. It's only a short walk (passing the Restaurant Wasserfall, (p 106), which incorporates a small, real Kapuzinerberg waterfall in its interior) until you find an arch which leads to the mountain.

❷ **The arch.** Not notable in itself but interesting as it is a cut between two buildings, so discreet you could walk past without noticing. Peer through, under the dark upper floors that form the arch, and you just get the idea there might be a path. *Linzergasse 14.*

❸ **Passion Path.** The path is so-called because, after walking through the archway under the historic buildings, you find yourself passing six baroque Stations of the Cross, built by various Salzburg artists between 1736 and 1744. The graphic scenes and figures in the little Passion Chapel document Christ's Passion, culminating in a powerful crucifixion scene on the mound. The path follows parts of the old city walls and has views over the plains to the north before a hairpin turn back toward the river.

❹ **Felix Gate.** Commissioned by Prince Archbishop Paris Lodron in 1632, the huge stone gateway in the city walls frames the city in a perfect view.

❺ **Kanzel.** 'The pulpit' is a magnificent viewpoint on the mountain's edge with benches where you can sit for hours looking over the Old Town (and over to Bavaria), and along the river in either direction. It's a place of calm, and a meeting place for hikers, dog walkers, and tourists. At this point, another path takes you down to Steingasse via the **Imbergstiege** stairs.

Kapuzinerberg view.

Even on a winter's afternoon the Kapuz-inerberg is a lovely place to stroll.

⑥ St. John's Church (Johan-niskirche). Follow this path for a short way and you soon find the pretty, pink little St. John's Church that dates back to at least 1319, but which received a drastic makeover in 1681 thanks to Prince Archbishop Max Gandolf. The main arch still bears his coat of arms. It is said that young Mozart and his sister Nannerl loved the place and played here, but the enchanting story is regarded as more fable than fact. *Information as Kapuzinerkloster, below.*

⑦ Capuchin Monastery (Kapuzinerkloster). Dating back to the end of the 16th century, the

simple but imposing Capuchin Mon-astery and its classic church, the Kapuzinerkirche, which give their name to the mountain, loom over the river beneath a towering cross. The abbey's inner portal frames an exquisite late-Gothic oak door, believed to have come from the original Salzburg cathedral. The main altar dates from the early 18th century, and the central altar paint-ing, depicting the *Adoration of the Magi by the Shepherds*, was painted in 1602. The interior of the church, mostly from the 17th and 18th cen-turies, is simple in accordance with the rules of the order and provides a haven for meditation, a far cry from World War II when the monks were evicted by the Nazis who planned (but failed) to turn it into an imposing HQ. *Kapuzinerberg 6. ☎ 0662/8735630. www.kapuziner. at/nordtirol/sbg/kloster_sbg.html. Free admission. Mon–Sat 6am–6pm (8pm summer), Sun 8am–6pm (8pm summer). No visits during Mass.*

⑧ Zweig Villa. This is a late 17th-century house built onto the old city walls which is now known as the one-time home of famed Austrian writer Stefan Zweig. Zweig was known for his short stories, biographies, and essays, and in the 1930s was one of the world's most translated writers. Zweig bought the villa in 1919 and stayed there until he emigrated to

Up & Over

The Kapuzinerberg is darker and somehow more remote than the Mönchsberg. And whereas the Mönchsberg is mostly easy-going walking on the summit, this involves steepish paths or climb-ing through the trees, perhaps glimpsing the odd chamois and deer (the badgers and martins are harder to spot). The most direct route to the top, called the Stefan-Zweig-Weg, is about 1.6km (1 mile), but take some of the routes that zigzag across it and the distance can easily double.

Beneath These Walls

The oldest parts of the city walls on the Kapuzinerberg date back to the 13th century. The ruins of the medieval Trompeterschlössl Castle were the base for the Kapuzinerkloster, and walls extended down the mountain to the Steingasse. On the other side, they crept down to a house at 12 Linzergasse, next to the footpath, which is long gone. The walls appeared impregnable but failed to fully protect the city during the Thirty Years War, at which point Prince Archbishop Paris Lodron made the decision to include all of the Kapuzinerberg into Salzburg's fortifications. Between 1629 and 1632, work went on to heavily fortify the southern side while the northern side was naturally protected by its steep rock walls and cliffs.

England in 1934. Pacifist Zweig became a British citizen in 1938 but committed suicide in Argentina in 1942 when he thought the world was falling to Nazi rule. There is a bust of Zweig next to the abbey but the house is privately owned and is not open to the public. *Kapuzinerberg 5.*

9 City wall. The ancient wall goes all the way from the Felix Gate, encompassing the Kapuzinerkloster, and runs along the entire western, southern, and eastern mountain slope, following the forbidding contours of the terrain. There are various paths over the Kapuzinerberg, some easy and some barely discernible amongst the trees. If you take the lowest, most southerly track, you not only get intriguing views along the river but eventually find yourself climbing steep steps cut into the mountain in the shadow of the wall (with barred windows and occasional small towers) until it emerges beneath Franziskischlössl.

The Franziskischlössl on a cold winter's day.

10 **Franziskischlössl.** Designed in 1629 by Salzburg Cathedral architect Santino Solari, this heavily fortified watchtower at the northern end of the wall has views of the city and the flatlands. With its white-painted walls it looks like a mini Hohensalzburg Fortress. A tavern opened in 1849 and it is still a place for daytime drinks and snacks. Cozy up under low, white, vaulted ceilings or sit on the terrace with sausages, strudel, beer, and other Austrian fare—for which you'll have worked up an appetite as the only way here is on foot. *Kapuzinerberg 9.* ☎ *0662/87295. www.franziskischloessl.com. $.*

11 **The path down.** This is quite gorgeous, if only because you're facing the Old Town the whole way. It's easy enough to vary your route, but the main path is simplest and gives you most chance to soak up the views. Pass through the Felix Gate but instead of heading back down to Linzergasse, keep to the left. The path curves around the Kanzel, heads down the stone **Imbergstiege** steps and through the **Steintor** (an ancient city gate) and finishes on Steingasse, the little medieval street that manages to squeeze its way along between the rock and the busy Giselakai riverfront road. Walk along the road, with the mountain on your left, for a short distance to get a feel for the treelined slopes, and for the Kapuzinerkloster high above you, before taking one of the side streets across to Giselakai and doubling back to the Hotel Stein.

12 **Hotel Stein.** Finish your walk on the Steinterrasse, the cafe-bar, on the roof of this smart hotel. It's known for its views across the river, but turn around and you can appreciate where you've just come from. *Giselakai 3–5.* ☎ *0662/8743460. www.hotelstein.at. $$.* ●

Kapuzinerberg from the Mönchsberg.

Shopping Best Bets

The crowds gather to window shop on Getreidegasse.

Best **Leather Goods**
Jann-Markl, *Residenzplatz 3 (p 77)*

Tackiest **Souvenirs**
Zum Mozart, *Mozartplatz 5 (p 77)*

Poshest **Keepsakes**
Lobmeyr, *Schwarzstrasse 20 (p 73)*

Best **Gourmet Food**
★★★ RF Azwanger, *Getreidegasse 15 (p 75)*

Best **Chocolate Delight**
★★★ Cafe Konditorei Fürst, *Alter Markt, Brodgasse 13 (p 75)*

Best for **Fresh Produce**
★★★ Green Market, *Universitätsplatz (p 77)*

Best **Classical Records**
★★ Salzburg Festival Shop, *Hofstallgasse 1 (p 78)*

Best **Men's Shirts**
★★ Hemden Babitsch, *Wold-Dietrich-Strasse 15 (p 74)*

Best **Hip Menswear**
★★ Wanger, *Getreidegasse 2 (p 75)*

Best **Designer Womenswear**
Betty Barclay, *Judengasse 9 (p 74)*

Best **Handicrafts**
★★ Salzburger Heimatwerk, *Residenzplatz 9 (p 76)*

Chicest **Jewelry**
★★ Atelier 4, *Münzgasse 1 (p 77)*

Shopping Hours

Most shops are open 10am to 6pm Monday to Friday and 10am to 5pm on Saturday. You'll find some bakers open from 6:30am, and food shops from around 8am. Some still close for a 1- or 2-hour lunch break. Many shops, particularly those selling souvenirs, open on Sunday, although others still observe religious traditions and stay shut. For information on sales tax and related rebates for non-E.U. residents, see p 166.

Previous page: Getreidegasse, Salzburg's main street.

Old Town Shopping

Alte f.e. Hofapotheke 21
Atelier 4 4
Augarten Porcelain 17
Betty Barclay 23
Billa 6
Cafe Konditorei Fürst 22
Cobra Couture 12
Designer Outlet Salzburg 1
Europark 2
Gerhard Swarovski Rosentury 18
Green Market 10
Hermès 20
Jann-Markl 26
Katholnigg House of Music 11
Kirchtag 5
Knopflmayer 14
Madl 9
Max Mara 25
Museumshop 3
Nomination 19
RF Azwanger 8
Salzburg Festival Shop 7
Salzburg Museum 28
Salzburger Heimatwerk 24
Schatz Confectionery 13
Wanger 15
Wolford 16
Zum Mozart 27

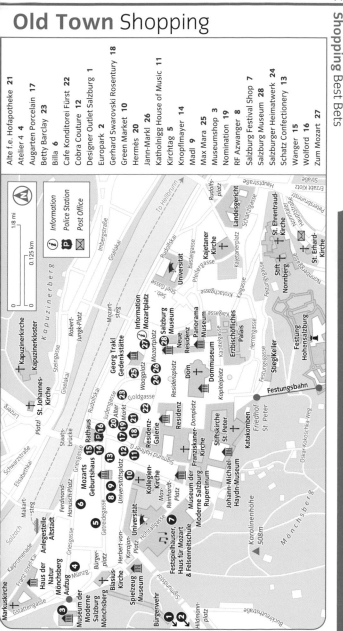

New Town Shopping

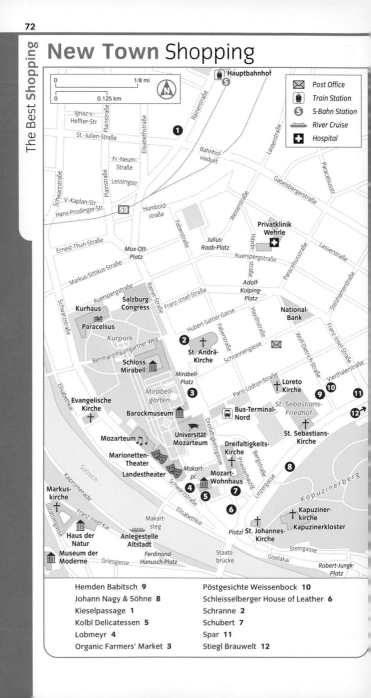

⊠	Post Office
🚉	Train Station
Ⓢ	S-Bahn Station
🚢	River Cruise
✚	Hospital

Hemden Babitsch **9**

Johann Nagy & Söhne **8**

Kieselpassage **1**

Kolbl Delicatessen **5**

Lobmeyr **4**

Organic Farmers' Market **3**

Pöstgesichte Weissenbock **10**

Schleisselberger House of Leather **6**

Schranne **2**

Schubert **7**

Spar **11**

Stiegl Brauwelt **12**

Salzburg Shopping **A to Z**

Art & Design

Augarten Porcelain OLD TOWN
The fabled Augarten white porcelain, made in Vienna since 1718, is sold here along with extravagant hand-painted designs, much with gold embellishment. The shop is worth seeing in itself, dating back to 1325 with an alleyway through the building and entrances featuring Untersberg marble. *Alter Markt 11.* ☎ *0662/840714. www.augarten.at. AE, MC, V. Map p 71.*

★ **Lobmeyr** NEW TOWN   The Viennese glassmaker was supplying the Imperial Court as far back as 1835. This showroom, in a former prison, showcases hand-blown one-of-a-kind pieces, along with less individual (but more affordable) items. *Schwarzstrasse 20.* ☎ *0662/873181. www.lobmeyr.com. AE, MC, V. Bus: 3, 5, 6. Map p 72.*

★★ **Museumshop** OLD TOWN
The shop at the Museum of Modern Art (Museum der Moderne) (p 40, ❶), high above the city on

the Mönchsberg, is packed with arty goods including books, posters, and posh souvenirs such as coffee sets and table lamps. *Mönchsberg 32.* ☎ *0662/842220401. www.museum dermoderne.at. AE, MC, V. Map p 71.*

Pöstgesichte Weissenbock
NEW TOWN   A cute shop selling antique postcards with views of the city and most other places in Austria, starting from around 1.50€, plus lots of artier, rarer works, including Bauhaus designs, which are often sold at auction. *Wolf Dietrich Strasse 6a.* ☎ *0662/8822531. www.wiener-werkstaette-postkarten.com. MC, V. Map p 72.*

Designer Home Goods
★ **Gerhard Swarovski Rosentury** OLD TOWN   Extravagant creations are made from real roses—the flowers are freeze-dried and turned into huge arrangements or delicate sprays. There are also candles and other more manageable gifts. Pop in

Where to Shop

Shopping may not be the main reason to come to Salzburg, but it is a stylish city and, as such, has stylish shops. The **Getreidegasse** might seem to be the tourist heart of the city, yet despite most camera-clutching visitors gazing up at the historic architecture, street level offers a high density of fascinating shops, including many upmarket boutiques. In the surrounding streets and down the many alleyways that connect them there are many more places, although most are esoteric and sell things you really don't need. For more conventional shopping, you need to head to the rather more ordinary streets near the station, which resemble many a city center across Europe. And if you really must have international chain stores, then **Europark** (p 78) is the answer, on the edge of town (but easily accessible by bus).

Cafe Konditorei Fürst.

even if just to sample the heady scent. *Churfürststrasse 4.* ☎ *0662/ 842037. www.swarovski-rosentury. com. AE, MC, V. Map p 71.*

Fashion & Accessories

★★ Betty Barclay OLD TOWN From casual gear to party frocks, outdoor wear to business suits, this is the stylish flagship store of the top Austrian label. *Judengasse 9.* ☎ *0662/840100. www.bettybarclay. de. AE, MC, V. Map p 71.*

★ Cobra Couture OLD TOWN Head here for designer chic, both classic and modern, from designer Katharina Kaesbach. Discuss styles and fabrics before your choice is made up by local seamstresses. *Sigmund Haffner Gasse 14.* ☎ *0662/ 84014. Also Nonntaler Hauptstrasse 18. www.cobra-couture.at. AE, MC, V. Map p 71.*

Hemden Babitsch NEW TOWN Men's shirts are handmade from a selection of fine cloth on the premises of this smart shop. The small team of women tailors can add monograms and do repairs. There is also a small selection of ties, polo shirts, and other accessories. *Wolf-Dietrich-Strasse 15.* ☎ *0662/883852. AE, MC, V. Map p 72.*

Hermès OLD TOWN This stylish emporium is packed with Parisian fashions for men and women along with leather goods, jewelry, watches, blankets, towels, and table linen. *Alter Markt 1.* ☎ *0662/ 84662126. www.hermes.com. AE, MC, V. Map p 71.*

Kirchtag OLD TOWN A century-old umbrella maker, using ebony, maple, cherry, and other wood along with a wealth of fabrics to create the sort of umbrella for men and women that's hard to resist. There's also a selection of luggage and leather goods. *Getreidegasse 22.* ☎ *0662/841310. www.kirchtag. com. AE, MC, V. Map p 71.*

Knopflmayer OLD TOWN A button shop, but a button shop that has been plying its trade in determinedly old-school fashion for 250 years. Thousands of varieties are all neatly stacked in boxes, from chunky traditional varieties to great ones for children to the stylishly modern. They also sell a few handicraft materials. *Rathausplatz 1.* ☎ *0662/842263. MC, V. Map p 71.*

Madl OLD TOWN You can order custom-made pieces for men and women from this exclusive fashion shop. Items are made from local linen, and cashmere or silk from France and Italy. Accessories include pashminas, scarves, hats, belts, bags, and purses. *Getreidegasse 13.* 📞 *0662/845457. www.madlsalzburg. at. AE, MC, V. Map p 71.*

Max Mara OLD TOWN The famed Italian fashion label stocks an exquisite collection of womenswear and accessories. *Waagplatz 5.* 📞 *0662/843534. www.maxmarafashion group.com. AE, MC, V. Map p 71.*

Schubert NEW TOWN Men's shirts from London, Italy, and top labels elsewhere, plus jumpers, ties, and posh pajamas. *Dreifaltigkeitsgasse 8.* 📞 *0662/874411. www.schubert-hemden.com. AE, MC, V. Map p 72.*

Wanger OLD TOWN Men's fashion emporium featuring Dolce & Gabbana, Gucci, and Boss. *Getreidegasse 2.* 📞 *0662/840161. www.wanger.at. AE, MC, V. Map p 71.*

Wolford OLD TOWN Salzburg seems to have a lingerie shop in every street, but Wolford stands out as an Austrian label with its own collection. There's an understated clothing range and swimwear. You'll also find a branch at Europark (p 78). *Kranzlmarkt 5.* 📞 *0662/875442. www.wolford.com. AE, MC, V. Map p 71.*

Food Shops

★★★ Cafe Konditorei Fürst

OLD TOWN The home of the first and best Mozart Ball (p 76), made here since 1890. There are Mozart Balls in every conceivable fashion, from singles to elaborate gift packs. *Alter Markt, Brodgasse 13.* 📞 *0662/8437590. Other Fürst branches are in Sigmund Haffner Gasse, Getreidegasse (by the Mönchsberg elevator), and Mirabellplatz. www.original-mozartkugel.com. AE, MC, V. Map p 71.*

★★ Kolbl Delicatessen NEW

TOWN Smart deli featuring well-chosen items from across Europe, particularly Austria and Italy. Lunch, from roast meat to sandwiches, is served at standing tables. *Theatergasse 2.* 📞 *0662/872423. www.koelbl-feinkost.at. MC, V. Map p 72.*

★ RF Azwanger OLD TOWN The

ancient wooden shelves in this 1656 grocery store show its history, although it now likes to think of itself as a wine and fancy foods emporium. Posh spirits and champagnes, Austrian wines, hand-dipped chocs, and an esoteric selection of other wines and vinegars. *Getreidegasse 15.* 📞 *0662/8433940. www.azwanger.at. AE, MC, V. Map p 71.*

The Mirabell Mozart Balls are available in many shops and supermarkets.

Schatz Confectionery

OLD TOWN   This tiny chocolate and cake shop sells specialties such as chocolate poppy cake and mini meringues, and you can sit and enjoy them with a coffee at one of the tables. *Getreidegasse 3.* ☎ *0662/842792. MC, V. Map p 71.*

Gifts

Johann Nagy & Söhne

NEW TOWN   This shop opened as a chandler and gingerbread maker in 1879. It still sells 40 types of honey gingerbread (with seasonal specials from Easter bunnies to Christmas Krampen figures) along with countless varieties of handmade candles. *Linzergasse 32.* ☎ *0662/882524. www.nagy.at. MC, V. Map p 72.*

Salzburg Museum OLD TOWN   The museum's impressive shop sells a wide range of intelligent items, from the usual pencils, pads, and

A Salzburg souvenir.

books to local beer, salt, and food. *Mozartplatz 1.* ☎ *0662/620808700. MC, V. Map p 71.*

Salzburger Heimatwerk OLD TOWN   Rustic handicrafts, pewter, ceramics, handmade Christmas tree decorations, and carved Nativity scenes. *Residenzplatz 9.* ☎ *0662/844110. MC, V. Map p 71.*

Stiegl Brauwelt OUTSKIRTS   This beer museum, bar, and restaurant has a great gift shop. Clothing such as fleeces is well-designed if a little bright in the company's traditional bright red, but there are also glasses, jugs, and, of course, bottles of beer. *Bräuhausstrasse 9.* ☎ *0662/83871492. www.brauwelt.at. AE, MC, V. Map p 72.*

Mozart Balls—the Real Story

The true Mozart Ball—Mozartkugel—is a blob of green pistachio marzipan coated in a layer of nougat then dunked in chocolate. It was created in 1890 in Salzburg by confectioner Paul Fürst, and named after the local musical hero. It was handmade then, and still is, with more than 1.5 million a year produced in the original Alter Markt premises by Fürst's great-grandson Norbert and his small team. Only these can be called **Salzburg Mozartkugeln,** and they are only available from here, Fürst's three other city stores, and its website (www.original-mozartkugel.com). Other manufacturers have their own versions; Holzermayr has been making its own fine version from almost the beginning. The ones you'll see in most places are from the Mirabell company, which makes around 90 million a year. They're perfectly fine, but are smaller, glossier, like chocs from a box, rather than Fürst's king-size treats, which have a just-the-one air. You'll come across various others, all of which lay claim to some form of originality.

Zum Mozart OLD TOWN Tat and then some, all in a glorious fun lack of taste. A great place to browse among the Hohensalzburg snow-globes, Mozart statuettes, and hundreds of T-shirts. *Mozartplatz 5. MC, V. Map p 71.*

Grocery Stores

Billa OLD TOWN Salzburg's most central grocery store, and hardly huge, serves its purpose in the midst of the tourist streets. There are other branches near the main station and in various suburbs. *Griesgasse 19–21. www.billa.at. MC, V. Map p 71.*

Spar NEW TOWN I like this place, on the corner of Linzergasse; it's handy for bargain local cheeses, dark breads, and potato chips for a picnic lunch, plus Austrian wine at several euros a bottle for a pre-dinner quaff. *Franz-Josef Strasse 34. MC, V. Map p 72.*

Jewelry

Atelier 4 OLD TOWN Modern works—rings, necklaces, etc—in gold and platinum by local designer Birgit Radlke, along with other innovative artists, plus top-quality watches. *Münzgasse 1. ☎ 0662/842987. www.atelier4.at. AE, MC, V. Map p 71.*

Nomination OLD TOWN A shop that pays homage to Italian design, including the trendy composable bracelet made up of letters and symbols of your choice. *Alter Markt 15. ☎ 0662/841158. www.nomination.at. MC, V. Map p 71.*

Leather Goods

★★ Jann-Markl OLD TOWN Exclusive leather and suede goods—gloves, belts, hats—from a tanner with 600 years of history. Also hand-woven jackets, socks, and other gear that was taken up by the English hunting classes. *Residenzplatz 3. ☎ 0662/842610. www.wildleder bekleidung.at. AE, MC, V. Map p 71.*

Schleisselberger House of Leather NEW TOWN In 'Tanner Street', this started out as a tannery and has been family owned since 1422. Leather goods, luggage, and just leather—including bargain off-cuts. *Lederergasse 5. ☎ 0662/873182. www.lederhaus.at. MC, V. Map p 72.*

Markets

★★★ Green Market OLD TOWN The massive daily market spreads out from in front of Collegiate Church. Local fruit, veg, cheese, meat, bread, and more along with exotic foods, handicrafts, and plenty of stalls selling sizzling sausages. *Universität-splatz. Mon–Fri 7am–7pm, Sat 7am–3pm. No credit cards. Map p 71.*

★★ Organic Farmers' Market NEW TOWN Excellent selection of local produce straight from farms, some of which are only a couple of miles away. *Mirabellplatz, Thurs 8am–noon; Papagenoplatz, Fri 8am–noon. No credit cards. Map p 72.*

★★ Schranne NEW TOWN A throbbing mass of stalls selling produce, flowers, and handicrafts. There's a social buzz with food stalls dishing up bratwurst, *bauernkrapfen*

Varied produce of the Green Market.

Linzergasse offers quaint shops in a traffic-free setting.

(doughnuts), *buchteln* (baked yeast dumplings), *gebackene mäuse* (fritters), and *pofesen* (toast fried in batter). *St. Andrew's Church. Thurs 5am–1pm. No credit cards. Map p 72.*

Medical
Alte f.e. Hofapotheke OLD TOWN   Salzburg's first pharmacy is a museum-like treasure trove of dark wooden shelves and big glass bottles alongside the usual supplies. *Alter Markt 6.* ☎ *0662/843623. MC, V. Map p 71.*

Music
Katholnigg House of Music OLD TOWN   Since 1847 this vaulted room with stone floors has been a music shop, switching from pianos in 1922. It now sells CDs and DVDs, mostly classical, although drifting into jazz and folk, plus upmarket wines. *Sigmund-Haffner-Gasse 16.* ☎ *0662/841451. www.salzburg-cd. com. AE, MC, V. Map p 71.*

Salzburg Festival Shop OLD TOWN   A box-office store with a wide range of CDs, DVDs, books, and photos. Interestingly different are the bags and briefcases made in the theater workshops from materials used in productions, as well as own-label wine. *Festspielhaus, Hofstallgasse 1.*

☎ *0662/841451. www.salzburg festival.at. MC, V. Map p 71.*

Shopping Malls
Designer Outlet Salzburg OUTSKIRTS   Opened in summer 2009, this grand and rather stylish-looking indoor mall is designed to look like a 1920s shopping arcade. Top labels are on offer at bargain prices, there are cafes and restaurants, and the bus calls here on the way to the airport. *Kasernenstrasse 1.* ☎ *0662/ 854404–14. www.designer-outlet-salzburg.at. AE, DC, MC, V. Bus: 2. Map p 71.*

Europark OUTSKIRTS   A massive shopping center by the *autobahn* that is supposedly Austria's most successful mall with around 130 stores covering everything from fashions to furniture. There's a Spar superstore, IKEA, H&M, C&A, Levi's, and a Salomon ski and sports shop plus restaurants. *Europastrasse 1.* ☎ *0662/4420210. www.europark. at. AE, DC, MC, V. Bus: 1, 20, 28; S-bahn: S3. Map p 71.*

Kieselpassage NEW TOWN   Small mall opposite the station with various clothes and jewelry stores and a couple of cafes. *Rainerstrasse 21.* ☎ *0662/6285100. www.kiesel. at. AE, DC, MC, V. Map p 72.* ●

River Salzach **by Bike**

1 Franz-Josef-Kai
2 River path
3 Golling
4 Torrenerhof
5 Golling Waterfall
6 Hallein
7 Kaffeehäferl
8 Keltenmuseum
9 Silent Night Museum
10 Franz-Josef-Kai

start & finish here

Previous page: Bikes for hire.

Salzburg and bikes would go together like Sachertorte (the local chocolate and apricot delicacy) and chips, you might think, the rocky bits and mountains being a hindrance. Yet where it's flat, it's very flat. For a good day out, the River Salzach is unbeatable. This tour takes you on paved cycle paths south along one bank and back along the other, for around 65km (40 miles). START: **Makartsteg footbridge.**

❶ **Franz-Josef-Kai.** Start on the riverbank on the Old Town side, as this is where you can rent a bike at **Top Bike Salzburg** for around 15€ a day. From here, cross the bridge and turn right, heading south for the mountain. The path takes you under the Staatsbrücke bridge and past the smart chateau-like houses at the foot of the Kapuzinerberg, with wonderful views of the city on the other side of the river. As you leave the city, you pass by the peaceful Franz-Josef Park then continue along the path past treelined suburbs with the river gently flowing to your right. *Top Bike Salzburg.* ☎ *0676/4767259. www.topbike.at.*

❷ **River path.** Keep going amid the greenery of the countryside, with views of the Untersberg off to the right. The path twice dips under the A1 Tauern-Autobahn and passes Hallein, where the river Salzach splits around a natural island. After the village of Puch, the path drifts away from the river before heading into Golling.

❸ **Golling.** A pretty market town on the river, and the farthest point on your tour. The **Heimatmuseum Burg Golling** has a chapel along with fossils and costumes. *Heimatmuseum. Marktplatz 1.* ☎ *06244/4223. www.museumburggolling.at. Admission 5€ adults, 2€ children 6–16. May–Oct Tues–Sun.*

☕ **Torrenerhof.** A pleasingly traditional hotel across the river in Golling with a dark, simple restaurant where you can relax and cool down after your ride, which has so far been around 32km (20 miles). Schnitzel, a good choice of salads, and big, hearty grills if you need—and you probably will. *Torren 24, Golling.* ☎ *0624/5522. www.torrenerhof.com. $–$$.*

Cycling near Salzburg.

Taking It Easy

The journey to Golling by bike is relatively easy as long(ish) bike journeys go, but may still be too far for most children. A good family-friendly alternative would be to start the tour but only go as far as the river bridge near Hellbrunn, which is about 5km (3 miles). Once you're across the river, a country lane takes you onto treelined Hellbrunner Avenue and along to Hellbrunn Palace, which is about 1km (just over half a mile). Here you can rest and play for free in the grounds with their adventure playground, and have a snack at the cafe or a picnic, before heading back to the riverside path and returning to the city. The whole journey is only around 12km (7 miles) and is flat all the way, and almost all traffic-free.

⑤ ★★★ Golling Waterfall. Get onto Wasserfallstrasse and in less than a mile you'll reach this beauty spot (you'll need a bike lock, as it's a 20-minute walk from the car park). The waterfall is the area's major attraction as it crashes 75m (502 ft.) down the rock face. Cool down in the spray then head back to the river and from here take the bike path along the left bank, back in the direction of Salzburg. ⏱ *30 min. Wasserfallstrasse, Golling.* ☎ *06244/4356. www.golling.info. Daily May–Oct. Admission 2.50€ adults, 1.50€ children 14 and under, free 5 and under.*

Golling Waterfall.

⑥ Hallein. At about the halfway stage back to Salzburg, this charming town, sitting on the valley floor with mountainous backdrop, is a good place to stop. Maybe have a wander around the streets with the pretty market square. The town, with a big student population, is surprisingly lively and a good place for cafes. ⏱ *1 hr.*

⑦ Kaffeehäferl. Take a break in this dark and traditional coffee house. Good, strong drinks, and plenty of cakes. *Pflegerplatz 2.* ☎ *06245/783177. $–$$.*

⑧ ★ Keltenmuseum. A smart, modern museum telling the story of local salt mining and the Celtic miners. *See p 144,* ❸.

⑨ Silent Night Museum. The home of Franz Xaver Gruber, composer of the music for the Christmas carol *Silent Night*. He put to music the poem of Josef Mohr in the hours before a service in the nearby village of Oberndorf in 1818. There are signed copies of the music, along with the guitar with which Mohr accompanied the premiere.

Silent Night Museum.

🕐 *15 min. Gruberplatz 1.* ☎ *06245/ 85394. www.stillenachthallein.at. Admission 2€ adults, .70€ children 18 and under, 6 and under free. Daily Jan 7–Advent 3–5pm; Advent–Jan 6, 11am–5pm.*

⑩ ★★ Franz-Josef-Kai. Free-wheel downhill from the museum to the river where the path heads out of town to the left and continues in the shadow of the rocky Little and Great Barmstein peaks. There are views across the river to the path that you came along earlier in the day, as you continue amid farmland and through woods. As you're about to go under the Tauern-Autobahn for the second time you cross Konigseeache, the river which leads to Konigsee near Berchtesgaden. The path straightens out and you head back toward the city—you know you're just about there when you pass under the Hellbrunner Landesstrasse bridge (the road leading to Hellbrunn Palace). The paths gets busier and the views of the Hohensalzburg Fortress atop the Mönchsberg get bigger before you're passing the Old Town on the way to drop off your bike.

Practical Matters—Salzburg by Bike

Before renting a bike check with your hotel—a number have bikes for complimentary use, or let you use them for a very reasonable rate. The city really does go out of its way to make life easy for cyclists: the city itself is rated the most bike-friendly in Austria, with 160km (100 miles) of paths, including 23 scenic routes, plus (and it's a proud boast) more than 900 signs. In addition, there are 5,500 bike parking spaces, and self-service stations with free tools, bike stands, oil, and compressed air. There's a garage for 350 bicycles (including 130 lockable bike boxes) at the Hauptbahnhof, the main railway station. You'll find contra-flow paths on dozens of one-way streets and the riverside paths have underpasses so you can cross the city without stopping. It's also easy to rent a bike, with handy locations in the heart of the historic city. See p 163 for more details of cycle hire shops.

A modern cyclist on the Old Town riverbank.

The **Untersberg**

1. Untersbergbahn
2. Geiereck
3. Schellenberg Ice Cave
4. Hochalm
5. Untersberg Museum
6. Salzburg Open-air Museum
7. Hotel Untersberg

Salzburg

Schloss Mirabell

Festung Hohensalzburg

Salzburg Airport W.A. Mozart

Hangar-7

Gois

Stieglbrauerei

Mauthausen

Schloss Staufeneck

Märzoll

Fürstenbrunn

Schloss Hellbrunn

Salzburger Tiergarten

Anif

Bad Reichenhall

AUSTRIA

Grödig

Großmain

Geiereck 1806m

Niederalm

Schellenberg Ice Cave

Hallthurm

UNTERSBERG

Marktschellenberg

Karkopf 1740m

LATTENGEBIRGE

Berchtesgadner Hochthron 1972m

Winkl

Lopi

GERMANY

Oberau

Bischofswiesen

Berchtesgaden

Schwarzeck

Strub

Place of Interest

Airport

Funicular Railway

0   3 mi

0   3 km

Curiously, **Salzburg isn't in the mountains,** but it's right on the edge, with a sensational backdrop on three sides. Other than the pair of rocks in town—the Mönchsberg and the Kapuzinerberg—this is the nearest mountain, offering year-round activities. It's easy to get to and has all the attractions of the mountains without going that far. START: **Mirabellplatz.**

1 Untersbergbahn. Take bus no. 25 to the village of Grödig/St. Leonhard at the base of the mountain. The bus stops outside the base of the cable car, which is a tourist attraction in itself. It rises serenely from the plain to 1,807m (5,931-ft.) Geiereck, a 2.4km (1½-mile) ride. Should you be feeling energetic you can take the cable car one way, walking down or even walking up. There's a service every half-hour year-round (some closures in Apr/Nov for maintenance), with slightly shorter hours in winter. ⏱ *20 min. www.members. aon.at/untersbergbahn. July–Sept 8:30am–5:50pm; Mar–June, Oct/Nov 8:30am–5pm; Dec–Feb 9am–4pm. Return trip 19€ adults, 9.50€ children 14 and under, free 5 and under. Reductions for ascent or descent only. Bus: 25 (from the city center); 21, 28, 35 from other areas. For mountain info: www.untersberg.net.*

2 Geiereck. You arrive at this point on the massive table mountain, far outpost of the Berchtesgaden Alps. The mountain, which crosses the border into Germany and Bavaria's Berchtesgaden National Park (p 154, **2**), is home to griffon vultures (bred by Salzburg Zoo), golden eagles, and chamois. Although you can bike and climb, most people come for walking and the *Trekking Map Untersberg—Nature and Culture* is available in English at the cable car station (1.50€).

Most people simply wander around, but there are walks to the 1,852m (6,078-ft.) **Salzburger Hochthron** and 2.054m (6,470-ft.) **Berchtesgadener Hochthron** lookouts. Some hikes should only be undertaken with a guide and others only by those with climbing experience. The weather is unpredictable, so protective clothing is a must—this place is much bigger than it

The Untersberg fills the horizon south of the city.

The Great **Outdoors**

The Zeppezauer House restaurant occupies a stunning spot atop the Untersberg.

looks from below. Several huts serve food and drink, including Zeppezauer House (open May–Oct, ☎ 0662/629862), a 20-minute walk down from the cable car, which dates from 1883. 🕐 *1 hr.*

❸ Schellenberg Ice Cave. This is on the German side, at 1,569m (5,150 ft.), a 2-hour walk from the cable car. It's a quite remarkable experience with halls of ice you pass through over walkways, and up and down wooden stairs. The only light comes from eerie gas lamps carried by the guides and volunteer tourists. There are cathedral-like caves with walls of ice, which change year by year. The Schellenberger Eishöhlenhütte serves refreshments and has 18 beds for hikers. This is a long walk and it should only be undertaken by those with extra

clothing and food. 🕐 *1 hr. Eishöhlenhütte.* ☎ *0664/1341690. www.eishoehle.net. Daily from Whitsun to end of Oct, tours hourly 10am–4pm. Admission 5€ adults, 2.50€ children under 14.*

❹ Hochalm. Opened in 1962, shortly after the cable car that is alongside, this cozy restaurant, decorated with mounted animal heads and historic photos, has spectacular views over Salzburg. There's traditional food and weekend barbecues, a couple of lounges, and a big sun deck. This is the place to refuel after a long walk, but if you want to stay, the simple B&B is around 20€, children half price (or you can bring your sleeping bag). ☎ *0662/628674. www.hochalm.net.* $.

Uses of the Untersberg

Untersberg marble—a mottled yellow and pink—has been used for centuries with columns, tombs, urns, and inscription plaques in Salzburg having their origin in Roman times. The rock can be traced through the building and art history of the city, starting with Roman boundary stones all the way to Renaissance and the baroque statues and buildings. The mountain has also been used for farming, with large areas at one time turned into alpine meadows (particularly in the Middle Ages) but now reforested. The mountain also has plenty of underground springs, which to this day provide around 75% of Salzburg's water.

Ski the Untersberg

This isn't a ski area as such, but it is possible to ski top-to-bottom in winter. The 8-km (5-mile) ski run, which drops around 1,400m (4,600 ft.), starts after a 20-minute walk from the cable car. The run is for experts only and gets steep near the bottom, but it is possible to avoid the section by skiing down a mountain road. It is also a popular spot for ski touring (hiking on skis with special skins on so you can walk up slopes, then ski down). During the ski season, a mountain rescue team is stationed at the Schweigmühl Alm where drinks are available. If you like skiing away from the crowds, this is *the* place.

5 **Untersberg Museum.** A small museum in the village of **Fürstenbrunn**, not far from the cable car base station (also reachable by nos. 21 and 35 buses), which tells the story of 2,000 years of quarrying for marble (see 'Uses of the Untersberg,' p 86), with a marble ball grinding mill, fossils, and changing exhibitions. ⏱ *30 min. Ball Mühlweg 4, Grödig.* ☎ *0624/67206. www.museum.untersberg.net. Mar–Dec Sat, Sun & holidays, 1–6pm; Nov, Mar & Apr 1–5pm.*

6 ★★ **kids** **Salzburg Open-air Museum.** This is one of those big places where they collect buildings—there are 70 here, including farms, mills, blacksmiths', and even a brewery, from across 5 centuries. Set at the bottom of the Untersberg mountain, yet just 9.5km (6 miles) from the city, it's a spectacular spot where children can run free. There are tractors to climb on, as well as a real adventure playground, and all sorts of craft demonstrations. ⏱ *1 hr. Hasenweg, Grossgmain.* ☎ *0662/850011. www.freilichtmuseum.com. Admission 8.50€ adults, 4€ children, under 7s free. Bus 25. Apr–Oct Tues–Sun 9am–6pm; Mon July/Aug. Dec 26–Jan 6 daily 10am–4pm.*

7 **Hotel Untersberg.** Right at the bottom of the mountain, this smartly refurbished hotel has a restaurant opening onto a terrace with Untersberg views. A good place for a beer or meal before heading back to the city. *Dr. Friedrich Ödlweg 1, St. Leonhard.* ☎ *06246/72575. www.hoteluntersberg.at. $$.*

Hiking the Untersberg brings you to many viewing spots.

Salzburg **Snow Shuttle**

1 Obertauern
2 Zauchensee
3 Gastein
4 Kitzbühel
5 Schladming
6 Schnepf'n Alm
7 Flachau
8 Leogang
9 Zell am See
10 Breiteckalm
11 Kitzsteinhorn

GERMANY

AUSTRIA

Place of Interest

✈ *Airport*

NATIONALPARK BERCHTESGADEN

OSTERHORNGRUPPE

DACHSTEINGRUPPE

Hoher Dachstein 2995m

Hoher Zinken 1764m

Bleikogel 2412m

Eisriesenwelt Caves

Gollinger Wasserfall

Salzburg Airport W.A. Mozart

Salzburg

Bad Ischl
Bad Aussee
Hallstatt
Obertauern
Bad Goisern
Gosau
Schladming
Radstadt
Wagrain
Lammertal
Abtenau
Golling
Kuchl
Hallein
St. Gilgen
Werfen
Schwarzach
Hüttschlag
Gastein
Muhlbach
Taxenbach
Kitzsteinhorn
Leogang
Zell am See
Saalbach
Uttendorf
Inzell
Bad Reichenhall
Berchtesgaden
Königssee
Ramsau
Reith
Ruhpolding
Marquartstein
Reit im Winkl
Waidring
St. Johann in Tirol
Fieberbrunn
Kitzbühel
Kirchberg
Westondorf
Kufstein

E60
E52
A8
A10
E55

10 mi
10 km

Austria is one of the world's top ski destinations and Salzburg is a major player—dozens of ski areas are less than an hour away. You can enjoy the delights of the city of Salzburg by night while skiing by day. The Salzburg Snow Shuttle is a fabulous daily coach service that connects the city with a different ski resort each day of the week. START: **Mirabellplatz.**

Monday

❶ ★★ Obertauern. A resort built in the early '60s, but with sympathetic architecture rather than the concrete brutality of French developments. The resort found fame when The Beatles capered around on skis for their movie *Help!* (there are still photos on restaurant walls) but it has other attractions. Set at 1,737m (5,700 ft.) and with skiing nearing 2,500m (8,200 ft.), there is guaranteed snow, a long season (Nov–May) and a good day-long ski circuit, the Tauernrunde, circling high above the village. ☎ 06456/7252. www.obertauern.com.

❷ ★ Zauchensee. Sitting above the trees at 1,350m (4,400 ft.) Zauchensee is Ski Amadé's (see p 91) highest village and has some of the loftiest slopes. It is connected to the slopes of Flauchwinkl by a charming tractor and trailer that hauls giggling skiers through a tunnel as trucks thunder north and south on the Tauern-Autobahn overhead. ☎ 06457/72800. www.skiamade.com. Map p 88.

The wide open slopes of Ski Amadé.

Tuesday

❸ ★★ Gastein. The small ski area of **Dorfgastein** (ideal for families) is the nearest to the entrance of the Gastein valley. Just along the road (connected by free ski bus) is the resort town of **Bad Hofgastein** with its sizeable ski area, which connects with the pretty spa town of **Bad Gastein** and the high, open slopes of **Sportgastein.** ☎ 0642/7645550. www.skiamade.com.

Wednesday

❹ ★★★ Kitzbühel. One of Austria's most-famous ski resorts, this walled medieval town is home to the legendary Hahnenkamm race each January. Yet, despite its reputation, the skiing here is mostly easygoing—better skiers have to look to the off-piste. As a day out, the resort itself is a sparkling, upmarket delight (you don't need to ski to have fun) but it is low so can suffer from poor snow, and is often crowded. There are more than 50 mountain restaurants here, from the historic to the Barenbadalm on the Resterhohe with its smart, modern bar with flatscreen TVs and huge sofas. ☎ 05356/777. www.kitzbuehel.com.

Thursday

❺ ★★★ Schladming. One of Austria's liveliest ski towns (including the Hohenhaus Tenne slopeside bar, traditionally Austrian but on a massive scale). Four side-by-side mountains along the valley—Hauser Kaibling (reaching 2,014m/6,610 ft.), Planai, Hochwursen, and Reiteralm—are connected, offering plenty

The Snow Shuttle

The Salzburg Snow Shuttle runs to a different ski resort each day, Monday from Obertauern or Zauchensee, Gastein, Kitzbühel, Schladming, Flachau, Leogang, Zell am See, or Kitzsteinhorn, although destinations are subject to snow conditions. Journey times are 50 to 90 minutes. Reservations must be made by 5pm the evening prior to travel at your hotel, by phone (☎ 0662/871712) or on the Internet with Salzburg Tourism (www.salzburg.info), although there are changing offers, not least free travel Monday to Wednesday if you buy a lift pass. The buses start from the Europark shopping mall (p 78) at 8am, which suits locals, but most visitors will get on at Mirabellplatz at 8:30am (they also call at some hotels). Buses return at 5 or 6pm. The service runs daily from just before Christmas until March. You can buy lift passes as well as organize equipment hire and lessons through on-board multi-lingual guides. The shuttle is also perfect for (and has information on) tobogganing, walking, cross-country skiing, ice skating, and lazing in natural hot spring spas, as well as simply sightseeing.

of varied skiing and views of the impressive Dachstein mountain opposite. ☎ 03687/22042555. www.skiamade.com.

6 ★★ **Schnepf'n Alm.** Cozy, traditional-but-modern restaurant high on Schladming's Reiteralm slopes. It's part of the Almwelt village of luxurious chalets and rooms, and serves classic Austrian cuisine of the Wiener schnitzel variety, the breadcrumbed and fried veal or pork staple. There's also a panoramic spa with saunas and steam room—perfect if the idea of skiing is too daunting after lunch. ☎ 0645/472577. www.almwelt-austria.at. $–$$.

Friday
7 ★★ **Flachau.** A small village that is the gateway to Ski Amadé's largest connected area, the Salzburger Sportswelt. The long, fast, cruising runs chase from here over to Wagrain and, with only a shuttle bus

ride across town, on to Alpendorf. Fast modern lifts mean you can squeeze an awful lot into a day. With the near Flachauwinkl-Zauchensee area, there are 200km (125 miles) of runs that suit those with modest ski talents while being fast fun for better skiers. ☎ 06457/72800. www. skiamade.com.

Saturday
8 ★★★ **Leogang.** A quiet village with a fine beginner area where the long pistes that thunder down through the trees can be a day out in themselves. Yet Leogang is also part of one of Austria's major linked ski areas, the **Saalbach Hinterglemm Leogang Ski Circus,** 200km (125 miles) of connected slopes in pretty surroundings. Once over to Saalbach, you're onto the circular tour (hence Ski Circus) which takes you along the Glemm valley, past Hinterglemm, then back along the other side. It's all perfectly prepared, intermediate runs and a competent skier would be able

to do the circuit in a day (but no long lunch, especially if you're hoping to catch the bus back). ☎ *06582/ 70660. www.leogang-saalfelden.at.*

Sunday

9 ★ Zell am See. A beautiful lakeside town with skiing looking down on the gently lapping waters. The slopes are mostly easy-going and, while not a huge area, it is a great experience to ski here. The stylish town is an interesting place to visit. ☎ *06542/770. www. zellamsee-kaprun.com.*

10 ★★ Breiteckalm. This is what Austrian mountain restaurants are all about—rustic yet bustling with a mammoth sun deck. People quaff *Jagatee* (traditionally a hot concoction of black tea, rum schnapps, and red wine) and mulled wine from old family recipes, and fill up on local dishes involving cheese, noodles, potatoes, and pork. ☎ *06542/ 73419. www.ski-fun.com. $–$$.*

The slopes above Schladming.

11 ★★ Kitzsteinhorn. This alternate destination is the glacier area above the small resort of Kaprun, just along the lakeside from Zell am See. There is a small but decent collection of above-treeline runs with excellent snow thanks to a top height of 3,029m (9,940 ft.). Kaprun itself has its own small ski area, the Maiskogel, but the glacier, reached by its own gondola, is the place to be. There are gorgeous views from the slopes and mountain restaurants. ☎ *06542/770. www. zellamsee-kaprun.com.*

Ski Amadé

Ski Amadé is Salzburg's ski world and the name makes sense if you know it is named after Wolfgang Amadeus Mozart. It offers the most skiing in Austria on one lift pass. Some resorts (Flachau, Gastein, Schladming, and Zauchensee) are served by the Snow Shuttle. There are 860km (540 miles) of piste and 270 lifts spread across 25 resorts and five regions. The slopes reach almost 3,017m (9,900 ft.), offering snowsure skiing while, just to be certain, 80% of pistes have artificial snowmaking. The skiing isn't all connected like major French areas, but there are large, linked areas, as well as small, beautiful villages. The nearest resort is around 45 minutes from Salzburg, with most areas having car parks just off main roads at the lifts. Schladming is also served by trains from Salzburg, which take a little over an hour. The trains also call at little Pichl at the near end of the area—the station is near the base area. Schladming's new multi-story car park is built onto the edge of the mountain, allowing you to ski straight to the door for your level.

Salzburg Area **Skiing**

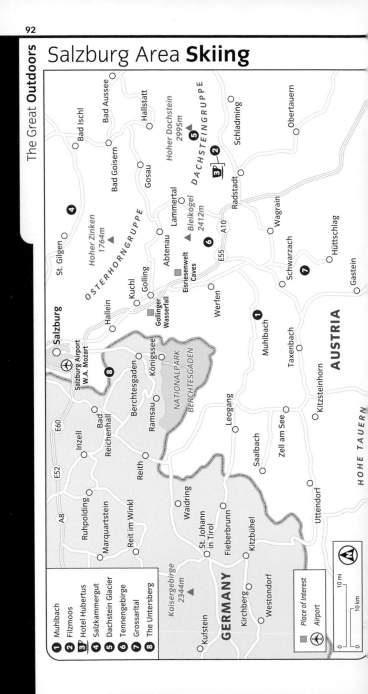

1 Muhlbach
2 Filzmoos
3 Hotel Hubertus
4 Salzkammergut
5 Dachstein Glacier
6 Tennengebirge
7 Grossarltal
8 The Untersberg

Place of Interest
Airport

10 mi
10 km

GERMANY

AUSTRIA

HOHE TAUERN

Kaisergebirge 2344m

Kufstein
Kirchberg
Westondorf
Kitzbühel
Fieberbrunn
St. Johann in Tirol
Waidring
Reit im Winkl
Marquartstein
Ruhpolding
Inzell
Bad Reichenhall
Reith
Ramsau
Berchtesgaden
Königssee

NATIONALPARK BERCHTESGADEN

Leogang
Saalbach
Zell am See
Uttendorf
Kitzsteinhorn
Taxenbach
Muhlbach

A8
E52
E60

Salzburg Airport W.A. Mozart
Salzburg
Hallein
Kuchl
Golling
Gollinger Wasserfall
Eisriesenwelt Caves
Abtenau
Werfen
Schwarzach
Hüttschlag
Gastein

St. Gilgen

Hoher Zinken 1764m

OSTERHORNGRUPPE

Lammertal
Bleikogel 2412m

A10
E55

Radstadt
Wagrain

DACHSTEINGRUPPE

Hoher Dachstein 2995m

Schladming
Obertauern

Gosau
Bad Goisern
Bad Ischl
Bad Aussee
Hallstatt

If you don't take the Snow Shuttle, Salzburg has plenty of other nearby resorts that you can reach easily with a car, safe in the knowledge that you'll be back in the world's most stylish ski town for cocktail hour. Stay in the city for another week and you can explore yet another different resort each day, some of them big, some just fascinating.

Monday

① ★★ **Muhlbach.** Start your trip with this hidden delight, a village that only became a ski area at the tail end of the '80s when its mining operations petered out. It's the nearest entrance to the under-rated (and largely unknown) **Hochkönig** area, and has a car park by the lifts on the valley road. Skiing follows the valley, opposite rugged Hochkönig (High King) mountain, crossing the valley at Dienten, and heading for Hinterthal and the town of Maria Alm. There are plenty of spots for beginners, lots of treelined pistes, and challenging off-piste on the Aberg above Maria Alm. ☎ 06584/7661. www.skiamade.com.

Skiing in Filzmoos.

Tuesday

② ★ **Filzmoos.** A picture-post-card village snuggling between tree-covered slopes with only 13km (8 miles) of runs, but offering a charming experience. It's the place if you fancy a mixture of easy, pretty skiing and a traditional lunch in historic surroundings—with 12 mountain restaurants, it's a pretty good ratio. The annual weeklong balloon festival in mid-January makes you stop and stare into the packed skies as you ski. If you have a car, it's worth staying on into the evening when the streets become a party full of food, drink, and balloons with their burners on. ☎ 06457/2800. www.skiamade.com.

Cross country skiing around the Tennengebirge area.

★★★ Hotel Hubertus. Nowhere does it finer than the Hubertus, home of Austrian celeb chef Johanna Maier. It's open for lunch at weekends, or dinner from 6:30pm Wednesday to Sunday, and the food is exquisite,

A Longer Stay

Salzburg is lovely but in the winter it's tempting to disappear to the slopes for days. Schladming has a wealth of hotels in the busy town. For something quieter I love the large, classy **Pichlmayrgut** (☎ 06454/7305, www.pichlmayrgut.at), which sits on a hillside across the valley from the Hochwursen/Reiteralm lifts (it has a free shuttle bus) with impressive spa and pool. In Hochkönig, the **Über-gossene Alm** (☎ 06461/2300, www.uebergossenealm.at) by the lifts in Dienten is a similar property with excellent spa. In Leogang, the big, stylish **Krallerhof** (☎ 06583/82460, www.krallerhof.com), with its own beginner lift and ski school, is a delight, while over in Hinterglemm the **Theresia** (☎ 06541/74140, www.hotel-theresia. com) is the new face of Austria. Traditional outside, it is cool and white inside with a hip bar (the ironic Cow print on the wall is a signed Andy Warhol), tremendous restaurant, spa, and top-notch children's facilities. Ski Amadé puts together Learn-to-Ski Weeks with hotel, ski hire, ski school, and lift pass with everything but half your accommodation cost refunded if you don't like it.

Summer Skiing

It is possible to ski through the summer on the region's glaciers. The **Kitzsteinhorn,** near Zell am See, and the **Dachstein,** near Schladming, are largely open year-round. There are some spring and early autumn closures, and it is best to check with the resorts before heading out. The snow is best in the morning, with a long lunch, sightseeing, or golf the best options for the afternoon. Conditions improve just before winter and you can often find international ski teams holding a training camp.

dishes such as sweet-sour mushroom soup with crispy fried perch. You can order a la carte, or there's a 170€ five-course gourmet menu with wines. *Dorfplatz 1, Filzmoos.* ☎ *06453/8204. www.hotelhubertus.at. $$$.*

Wednesday
④ ★ Salzkammergut. Salzburg's lake district has a number of tiny ski areas that are easy to get to (nearest little more than 30 min.). Wolfgangsee has a couple of tiny areas,

notably St. Gilgen, where the Zwölferhorn slopes are reached by a tiny cable car and have lake views. Other options include Faistenau, Hintersee, and Koppl. The biggest area is Postalm with 18km (12 miles) of slopes. This is also an area for **cross-country skiing,** with lakeside trails in Wolfgangsee, a high-mountain trail on the Postalm, and more than 45km (30 miles) around Faistenau. ☎ *0662/668844. www. salzburgerland.com.*

The lakeside ski area of Zell am See.

Thursday

5 ★ **Dachstein Glacier.** Year-round snow, skiing up to 2,700m (8,858 ft.), and wondrous views make this glacier near Schladming (and above the village ski resort of Ramsau) a place to visit. There's a goodly assortment of well-groomed pistes for all levels. It also has the glass-floored **Sky Walk** at 2,700m (8,858 ft.), high on a 250-m (820-ft.) vertical rock face. The 360°-panorama takes in Slovenia and the Czech Republic. ☎ *03687/81833. www.skiamade.com.*

Friday

6 ★ **Tennengebirge.** A small area near Werfen and the Hohenwerfen Fortress. There might only be 24km (15 miles) of runs but the close scenery of the Tennengebirge Mountains is wonderful. There are also 38km (25 miles) of cross-country skiing, 56km (35 miles) of winter hiking paths, ice-skating, sledding, and horse-drawn sleigh rides, making it an all-round family day out. ☎ *06466/420. www.werfen weng.org.*

Saturday

7 ★ **Grossarltal.** A small area in the beautiful Hohe Tauern National Park, which connects the village skiing of Grossarl with that of Dorfgastein at the head of the Gastein valley. There are 80km (50 miles) of slopes—not huge but attractive, with mostly easy to medium runs. And there are free ski buses to other resorts in the Gastein valley—Bad Gastein and Bad Hofgastein. ☎ *06414/281. www.grossarltal.info/ ew_home.html.*

Sunday

8 ★ **The Untersberg.** The mountain on the outskirts of Salzburg has a cable car and an 8-km (5-mile) off-piste run, which starts with a 20-minute hike from the top station. This isn't a place for beginners and you only get one run for your money, 9.50 €. Have lunch in the Hochalm, on the mountain by the lift, a traditional place stuffed with animal heads. *Bus: 25 from the city; 21, 28, 35 from other areas. For mountain info: www.untersberg.net. See p 84.* ●

Dining Best Bets

Coffee at Café Tomaselli.

Best **Gourmet Treat**
★★ Restaurant Goldener Hirsch
$$$ *Getreidegasse 37 (p 105)*

Best **Coffee Shop**
★★ Café Tomaselli $$ *Alter Markt 9*
(p 102)

Best **Views**
★★ Restaurant M32 $$ *Mönchs-
berg 32 (p 105)*

Best **Indoor Views**
★★★ Ikarus $$ *Wilhelm-Spazier-
Strasse 7a (p 103)*

Best **Secret**
★★ Auerhahn $$ *Bahnhofstrasse 15*
(p 101)

Best **Traditional Food**
★★ Restaurant s'Herzl $$
Getreidegasse 37 (p 105)

Best **Beer Garden**
★★ Augustiner Bräustübl $
Augustinergasse 4 (p 101)

Best for **Lording It**
★★ Festungrestaurant $$$
Mönchsberg 34 (p 103)

Best for **Style**
★★ Magazin $$ *Augustinergasse 13*
(p 104)

Best **Madly Modern**
★ Carpe Diem Finest Fingerfood $
Getreidegasse 50 (p 102)

Best **Value**
★ Wilder Mann $ *Getreidegasse 20*
(p 107)

Best for **History**
★★ Stiftskeller St. Peter $$$
St. Peter Bezirk 1/4 (p 107)

Best **Dessert**
★ Café Sacher $$ *Schwarzstrasse*
5–7 (p 102)

Best **Fast Food**
★ Balkan Grill $ *Getreidegasse 33*
(p 47)

Best for **Families**
★ Sternbräu Gastronomie World
$$ *Griesgasse 23–25 (p 106)*

Best for **Romance**
★★ Restaurant Schloss Mönchstein
$$ *Mönchsberg Park 26 (p 105)*

Previous page: A cafe seen from Mozart's Birthplace.

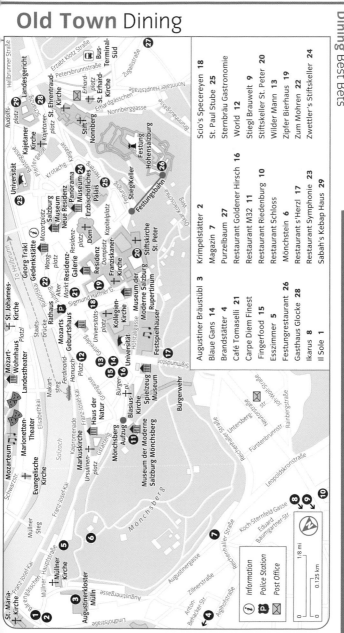

Old Town Dining

Augustiner Bräustübl **3**
Blaue Gans **14**
Brandstätter **4**
Café Tomaselli **21**
Carpe Diem Finest
Esszimmer **5**
Festungsrestaurant **26**
Gasthaus Glocke **28**
Ikarus **8**
Il Sole **1**

Krimpelstätter **2**
Magazin **7**
Purzelbaum **27**
Restaurant Goldener Hirsch **16**
Restaurant M32 **11**
Restaurant Riedenburg **10**
Restaurant Schloss
Mönchstein **6**
Restaurant s'Herzl **17**
Restaurant Symphonie **23**
Sabah's Kebap Haus **29**

Scio's Specereyen **18**
St. Paul Stube **25**
Sternbräu Gastronomie
World **12**
Stiegl Brauwelt **9**
Stiftskeller St. Peter **20**
Wilder Mann **13**
Zipfer Bierhaus **19**
Zum Mohren **22**
Zwettler's Stiftskeller **24**

Carpe Diem Finest
Fingerfood **15**

_i_ Information
🅟 Police Station
☒ Post Office

0   1/8 mi
0   0.125 km

New Town Dining

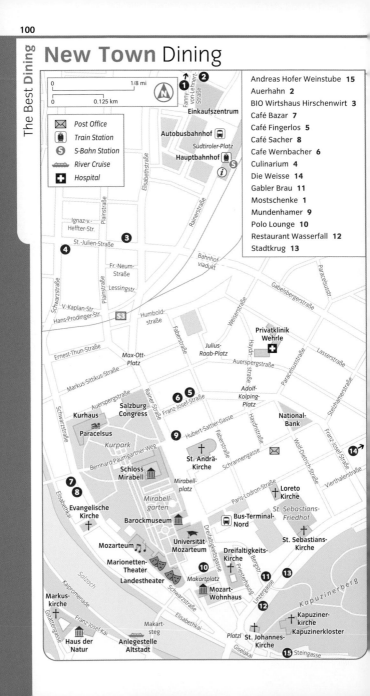

Andreas Hofer Weinstube **15**
Auerhahn **2**
BIO Wirtshaus Hirschenwirt **3**
Café Bazar **7**
Café Fingerlos **5**
Café Sacher **8**
Cafe Wernbacher **6**
Culinarium **4**
Die Weisse **14**
Gabler Brau **11**
Mostschenke **1**
Mundenhamer **9**
Polo Lounge **10**
Restaurant Wasserfall **12**
Stadtkrug **13**

Post Office
Train Station
S-Bahn Station
River Cruise
Hospital

Salzburg Dining **A to Z**

★★ **Andreas Hofer Weinstube**
NEW TOWN *AUSTRIAN* A wine bar-cum-restaurant that has a resolutely old-school charm. Here, lots of people meet to quaff (beer as well as wine), laugh, and knock back a bargain spag bol or Wiener schnitzel (thinly sliced veal or pork, breaded and fried) in quiet moments. *Steingasse 65.* ☎ *0662/882200. www. dieweinstube.at. Entrees 7€–12€. AE, DC, MC, V. Dinner Mon–Sat. Map p 100.*

★★ **Auerhahn** NEW TOWN *AUSTRIAN* To the delight of those in the know, this small, relaxing place in the self-named *gasthof* (guesthouse) produces award-winning modern food mixed with regional dishes—clams in a frothy lime sauce, dumplings made from soya, lots of game, and river fish. *Bahnhofstrasse 15.* ☎ *0662/451052. www.auerhahn-salzburg.at. Entrees 14€–21.50€. AE, DC, V. Lunch & dinner Tues–Sun; lunch & dinner daily Aug. Map p 100.*

★★ **Augustiner Bräustübl** OLD TOWN *BEER HALL* One of Austria's biggest beer halls (and biggest beer garden) also has a string of deli booths that make it a place for casual eating, with everything from radishes to grilled chicken, pickled fish to sausages. *Augustinergasse 4.* ☎ *0662/ 4312460. www.augustinerbier.at. Food 3€–15€. No credit cards. Lunch & dinner daily. Map p 99.*

★★ **BIO Wirtshaus Hirschenwirt** NEW TOWN *AUSTRIAN* Everything here is organic, from hearty vegetarian fare (think dumplings), to heartier meat (the Hirsch plate features venison and blood sausages). The setting is a quartet of historic rooms in the Hotel zum Hirschen. *St. Julien-Strasse 23.* ☎ *0662/881335.*

www.biowirtshaus.at. Entrees 8€–20€. AE, DC, MC, V. Dinner Mon–Sat. Map p 100.

Blaue Gans OLD TOWN *AUSTRIAN* Ancient vaulted ceilings soar over a heavenly mix of white walls and even whiter linen in this lovely, quiet hotel restaurant. Try timeless dishes such as Wiener schnitzel, or local Danube salmon and Tauern lamb. *Getreidegasse 43.* ☎ *0662/841317. www. blauegans.at. Entrees 15€–22€. AE, DC, MC, V. Lunch & dinner Wed–Mon. Map p 99.*

★ **Brandstätter** OUTSKIRTS *AUSTRIAN* Hidden in an out-of-town *gasthof*, this unassuming place has a Michelin star and serves exquisite takes on traditional food—brawn with pumpkin seed oil, for instance. *Münchner Bundesstrasse 69.* ☎ *0662/434535. www.hotel-brandstaetter.com. Entrees 15€– 30€. AE, MC, V. Lunch & dinner Tues–Fri. Bus: 4, 24. Map p 99.*

★★ **Café Bazar** NEW TOWN *COFFEE HOUSE* Opened in 1884, this is a cozy, riverside place, heavy with wood and chandeliers. Stop for coffee and cakes, or meals such as truffle tortellini, steaks, and casseroles. *Schwarzstrasse 3.* ☎ *0662/874278. www.cafe-bazar.at. Entrees 10€– 18€. AE, MC, V. Breakfast, lunch & dinner Mon–Sat; breakfast & lunch Sun. Map p 100.*

★★ **Café Fingerlos** NEW TOWN *COFFEE HOUSE* There's almost a French feel here in the big, airy salon and at the tables out on the terrace. The cakes are luscious, but many come for the elegant desserts featuring ice cream, fresh fruit, and even champagne. *Franz-Josef-Strasse 9.* ☎ *0662/874213. Entrees 5€–11€. AE, MC, V. Breakfast & lunch daily. Map p 100.*

Café Sacher is home of the chocolate and apricot Sachertorte.

★★ **Café Sacher** NEW TOWN *COFFEE HOUSE* This place exudes a classic riverside elegance as you nibble the chocolate-apricot Sachertorte (the iconic creation of Vienna's sister hotel). *Schwarzstrasse 5–7.* ☎ *0662/889770. www.sacher. com. Entrees 10€–20€. AE, MC, V. Breakfast, lunch & dinner daily. Map p 100.*

★★★ **Café Tomaselli** OLD TOWN *COFFEE HOUSE* This is a must— the city's oldest coffee house dating from 1705, where Mozart relaxed amid the marble tables, balcony, and garden. Enough coffee choices should keep you awake forever. *Alter Markt 9.* ☎ *0662/844488. www.tomaselli.at. Entrees 8€–16€. No credit cards. Breakfast, lunch & dinner daily. Map p 99.*

★★ **Cafe Wernbacher** NEW TOWN *COFFEE HOUSE* Around only since 1936, but it has its own history as home of Salzburg's first disco, the raffish Scotch Club, in the '60s. Coffee, snacks, and hot dishes are served in a grand European setting. *Franz Josef-Strasse 5.* ☎ *0662/ 881099. www.cafewernbacher.at. Entrees 7€–10€. MC, V. Breakfast, lunch & dinner Mon–Sat. Map p 100.*

★ **Carpe Diem Finest Fingerfood** OLD TOWN *MODERN INTERNATIONAL* This place is the wacky brainchild of Red Bull drinks creator Dietrich Mateschitz, with two floors of cafe, bar, and takeout serving inventive tapas-style food in cones. *Getreidegasse 50.* ☎ *0662/848800. www.finestfingerfood.com. Two courses 15€–30€. AE, DC, MC, V. Breakfast, lunch & dinner daily. Map p 99.*

★ **Culinarium** NEW TOWN *FRENCH-ITALIAN* The rustic decor is wedged beneath a modern high-rise, and the food is the kind of rustic menu you might find in Provence or Puglia rather than a small Alpine city, with lots of fish soup and risottos along with meat dishes. *St. Julien-Strasse 2.* ☎ *0662/878885. 16€–30€. DC, MC, V. Lunch & dinner Mon–Sat. Map p 100.*

Die Weisse NEW TOWN *AUSTRIAN* Popular with a younger party set, this microbrewery can be busy, so you may struggle to find a seat or at least a quiet one. Expect exceptional *weisse* (wheat) beers, which are a meal in themselves, plus original cuisine (wheat beer soup, Bavarian veal sausage). *Rupertgasse 10.* ☎ *0662/872246. www.dieweisse.at. Entrees 10€–16€.*

MC, V. Breakfast, lunch & dinner Mon–Sat. Map p 100.

Esszimmer OLD TOWN CONTEM-PORARY AUSTRIAN   A hip meeting of cuisines thanks to renowned local chef Andreas Kaiblinger, with dishes such as marinated trout with pumpkin rösti and pumpkin vinegar, and saddle of venison with red cabbage and polenta. The bright, modern decor with video screens is perhaps a tad too hip, although the view of the river running underneath adds a timeless touch. *Müllner Hauptstrasse 3.* ☎ *0662/870899. www.esszimmer. com. Entrees 25€–30€. AE, DC, MC, V. Lunch & dinner Tues–Sat. Map p 99.*

★ **Festungrestaurant** OLD TOWN AUSTRIAN   This is the restaurant high in the medieval fortress (at the top of the funicular), but the touristy setting belies the fine food, which includes game and *Salzburger bauernschmaus* (meat, sausage, and dumpling stew). *Mönchsberg 34.* ☎ *0662/841780. www.salzburg highlights.at. Entrees 11€–21€. MC, V. Dinner daily. Map p 99.*

Gabler Brau NEW TOWN AUSTRIAN   A locals' meeting place since 1429 and still serving reasonably priced fare, from *grill-würstl* (grilled sausage) to fish. There's an excellent happy hour antipasti buffet (4–5pm, 10:30–11pm) where you can escape the crowds. *Linzergasse 9.* ☎ *0662/88965. www.gablerbrau.com. Entrees 6.50€–15.50€. MC, V. Lunch & dinner Mon–Sat. Map p 100.*

Gasthaus Glocke OLD TOWN AUSTRIAN   Deep in the Old Town, this small restaurant seems to escape the attention of the tourist hordes. Local dishes include a selection of sugary pancakes, plus a changing daily menu. There's also a small garden. *Schanzlgasse 2.* ☎ *0662/8453910. Entrees 6€–13€. AE, DC, MC, V. Lunch & dinner Mon–Fri; lunch only Sat. Map p 99.*

★★★ **Ikarus** OUTSKIRTS MODERN INTERNATIONAL   This is perhaps Salzburg's sleekest restaurant, overlooking the aircraft collection at modernistic Hangar-7 (p 20, ❸). Each month a different chef is flown in from around the world, creating a new menu. The food is as modern (and attractive) as the surroundings. *Wilhelm-Spazier-Strasse 7a.* ☎ *0662/219777. www.hangar-7.com. Entrees 28€–35€. AE, DC, MC, V. Lunch & dinner daily. Map p 99.*

Café Tomaselli, one of Salzburg's most historic coffee houses.

Tradition . . . and Much More

Austrian food was long known for its heavy, meat tradition. However, what to the casual onlooker might have seemed to be a slab of pork with dumplings was often much more. Now the traditions have been refined and you can find old recipes with a modern touch as well as plenty of places where you'll find more varieties of dumpling—both as a main course and laden with sweet sauces—than you'd think possible. Combine that with the rest of the world catching up with Austria in the use of local, organic produce and you have some wonderful dishes you have to try.

Il Sole OLD TOWN *ITALIAN*   If you want an authentic Italian restaurant, this is the place, right by the Mönchsberg elevator. The relaxed room downstairs and the more refined upstairs are decorated with Italiana, down to the giant pepper mills. Top pizza, pasta, and a little bit more at rustic prices. *Gstättengasse 15.* ☎ *0662/843284. Entrees 13€– 18€. AE, DC, MC, V. Lunch & dinner daily. Map p 99.*

★★ **Krimpelstätter** OLD TOWN *AUSTRIAN*   To experience a real locals' hangout, you'll do well to head to this old *braugasthof* (an inn that brewed its own beer) off the tourist trail near the river, for schnitzel and much more, with a gastronomic touch. *Müllner Hauptstrasse 31.* ☎ *0662/432274. www. krimpelstaetter.at. Entrees 10€– 18€. MC, V. Lunch & dinner Mon– Sat. Map p 99.*

★★ **Magazin** OLD TOWN *CONTEMPORARY AUSTRIAN*   Within a modern complex (including a wine bar, wine shop, and kitchen store) behind the Mönchsberg, you'll discover a Michelin-starred restaurant where Austrian classics are reinvented and paired with local wines. *Augustinergasse 13.* ☎ *0662/841584. www. magazin.co.at. Three-course menu*

Carpe Diem Finest Fingerfood.

Expect classic Austrian cuisine at the Michelin starred Magazin.

around 50€. AE, MC, V. Lunch & dinner Mon–Sat. Bus 4, 21. Map p 99.

Mostschenke OUTSKIRTS *AUSTRIAN* Traditional food (much homebred pork) is served in the garden in summer or the homely kitchen in winter at the Rauchenbichlgut farm/guesthouse. Don't plan on driving home after tasting one of the homemade schnapps. *Rauchenbichlerstrasse 23. ☎ 0662/458048. www.rauchenbichlgut.at. Entrees 15€–20€. MC, V. Dinner Tues–Fri. Bus 3, 5, 23. Map p 100.*

Mundenhamer NEW TOWN *AUSTRIAN* Simple, traditional food is offered at bargain prices in this unassuming place across the road from the Mirabell Palace. Themed, seasonal weeks involve asparagus, not to mention dumplings and strudel. *Rainerstrasse 2. ☎ 0662/875693. www.mundenhamer.at. Entrees 7€–16€. AE, DC, MC, V. Lunch & dinner Mon–Sat. Map p 100.*

Polo Lounge NEW TOWN *AUSTRIAN* A rich and stylish place in the Hotel Bristol (p 135), rated alongside the Goldener Hirsch for sheer class (although the dress code for both is smart casual). It features an inspired take on Austrian cuisine, plus cross-border Italian dishes, in a

dreamy setting. *Makartplatz 4. ☎ 0662/8873557. www.bristol-salzburg.at. Entrees 18€–28€. AE, DC, MC, V. Lunch & dinner Mon–Sat. Map p 100.*

★ **Purzelbaum** OLD TOWN *BISTRO* Austria meets France on the sunny side of the Mönchsberg. Art Nouveau ceilings and marble tables are a charming foil to the Med-tinged cuisine, in what is a boisterous Festival crowd hangout. *Zugallistrasse 7. ☎ 0662/848843. www.purzelbaum. at. Entrees 22€–30 €. AE, MC, V. Lunch & dinner Mon–Sat. Map p 99.*

★★ **Restaurant Goldener Hirsch** OLD TOWN *AUSTRIAN* A Salzburg classic serving Austrian and Salzburg creations (often venison) in sumptuous 'rustic' surroundings. Ask for the Karajan-Table, composer Herbert von Karajan's regular spot. *Getreidegasse 37. ☎ 0662/8084861. www.goldenerhirsch.com. Entrees 18€–30€. AE, DC, MC, V. Lunch & dinner. Map p 99.*

★★ **Restaurant M32** OLD TOWN *MODERN INTERNATIONAL* A smart eatery in the Museum der Moderne (p 40, ❶) on the Mönchsberg with glorious city views. Snacks and coffee are served all day, there's a good-value business lunch, then candlelit dining takes over in the evening. *Mönchsberg 32.* ☎ *0662/ 841000. www.m32.at. Entrees 9.50€–29€. AE, DC, MC, V. Breakfast, lunch & dinner Tues–Sat; breakfast & lunch Sun. Map p 99.*

★★ Restaurant Riedenburg

OUTSKIRTS *MODERN AUSTRIAN* Head out of town for a sophisticated dining experience in a creampainted, suburban villa. Local fare such as venison and trout is served in imaginative ways with a country feel. *Neutorstrasse 31.* ☎ *0662/ 830815. www.riedenburg.at. Entrees 30€–35€. MC, V. Lunch & dinner Tues–Sat. Bus: 1, 22. Map p 99.*

★★ Restaurant Schloss Mönchstein OLD TOWN *CONTEMPORARY AUSTRIAN*

In the hotel atop the Mönchsberg, this eatery (sometimes referred to as Restaurant Paris Lodron) has city views and a terrace. It's modern cuisine with Austrian heritage (butter-fried pike/perch on a bed of celery purée, roast loin of lamb dredged in pumpkin seeds) and nods to a conservative international clientele (king prawns with sesame oil and ginger). *Mönchsberg Park 26.* ☎ *0662/ 8485550. www.monchstein.at. Entrees 25€–50€. AE, DC, MC, V. Lunch & dinner daily. Map p 99.*

★★ Restaurant s'Herzl OLD

TOWN *AUSTRIAN* The casual sister to Restaurant Goldener Hirsch is loved by the Festival types, not least Leonard Bernstein (his photo is on the wall). Try the *Nürnberger Bratwürstl* (small, roast sausages with sauerkraut). *Getreidegasse 37.* ☎ *0662/8084889. www.goldener hirsch.com. Entrees 7€–22€. AE, DC, MC, V. Lunch & dinner daily. Map p 99.*

★ Restaurant Symphonie OLD

TOWN *AUSTRIAN* Book a table here if you want a good excuse to get into the Altstadt SAS Radisson (p 132),

one of the most classic buildings in the Old Town. The country-baroque interior is the perfect setting for lighter Austrian fare including fried chicken and various fish dishes. *Rudolfskai 28.* ☎ *0662/84857155. www.austria-trend.at. Entrees 18€– 27€. AE, DC, MC, V. Lunch & dinner Mon–Sat. Map p 99.*

★★ Restaurant Wasserfall NEW

TOWN *ITALIAN* A temple of northern Italian cuisine, with dishes in rich sauces, simply grilled fish, and classic pasta. A small waterfall tumbles out of the Kapuzinerberg rock that forms the rear of the restaurant and runs through the dining area in a trough. *Linzergasse 10.* ☎ *0662/ 873331. www.restaurant-wasserfall. at. Entrees 8€–20€. AE, MC, V. Dinner Mon–Sat. Map p 100.*

Sabah's Kebap Haus OLD TOWN

TURKISH Much-loved by students and all lovers of kebab, this shack by the river serves up bargain doner and shish kebabs as well as other snacks. Sit on the riverbank or at one of the few tree-shaded tables. *Rudolfsplatz 1a.* ☎ *0662/844272. Entrees 3€–6€. No credit cards. Lunch & dinner Mon–Sat. Map p 99.*

★★ Scio's Specereyen OLD

TOWN *AUSTRIAN* Tempt the tastebuds at this cafe-bistro with tapasstyle dishes (oysters, ragout patties) and Austrian and Mediterranean dishes, followed by *Capezzoli di Venere* (Nipples of Venus), chocolatedipped chestnut and nougat truffles. *Sigmund Haffnergasse 16.* ☎ *0662/ 841638. www.venusbruestchen.at. Entrees 7€–21.50€. AE, MC, V. Breakfast, lunch & early dinner Tues–Sat. Map p 99.*

★★ St. Paul Stube OLD TOWN

AUSTRIAN A charmingly discreet, wood-paneled place in the shadow of the Mönchsberg. The menu is awash with hearty soups, dumplings, and meat, and more dumplings for dessert, all turned out with style. The place is packed with students and locals thanks to its reasonable prices, so a reservation is recommended. There's also a garden that can be so busy it's cozy. *Herrengasse 16.* ☎ *0662/843220. www.paul-stube.at. Entrees 8€–20€. AE, MC, V. Dinner Mon–Sat. Map p 99.*

Stadtkrug NEW TOWN *AUSTRIAN* In the traditional hotel of the same name, the restaurant serves fish from mountain lakes and beef from its own country estate, all with an Austrian flair. The room is stylishly rustic, while the roof garden offers a candlelit delight. *Linzergasse 20.* ☎ *0662/8735450. Entrees 18€–26€. AE, DC, MC, V. Lunch & dinner Wed–Mon. Map p 100.*

★ kids Sternbräu Gastronomie World OLD TOWN *AUSTRIAN* A 'food and drink world' on an historic

Historic cafe signs fill the streets.

brewery site—five restaurants and several beer gardens include the Braumeister brewpub and Trattoria La Stella. There's also a playroom and a good children's menu. *Griesgasse 23–25.* ☎ *0662/84214080. www.sternbrau.com. Entrees 8€–18€. AE, MC, V. Breakfast, lunch & dinner daily. Map p 99.*

★★ Stiegl Brauwelt OUTSKIRTS *BEER GARDEN* At the Stiegl brewery (p 47), where tours are followed by tastings, you'll find the brewer's buffet features meaty local dishes. You can also sample upmarket Austrian food in the Braustube tavern. *Bräuhausstrasse 9.* ☎ *0662/83871492. www.brauwelt.at. Entrees 11€–22€. AE, MC, V. Lunch & dinner daily. Bus 1. Map p 99.*

Coffee Culture

There are probably more flamboyant, elegant coffee houses crammed into a tiny area of Salzburg than just about any other city, and that's saying something for Austria, a place where thick, foamy, black coffee is its lifeblood. No Starbucks and muffins here. Aside from the simple black stuff we're talking extraordinary concoctions laced (well, perhaps a bit more than laced) with exotic liqueurs and topped with dramatic cream, served by waiters who look like they've stepped out of the Ritz, and cakes so rich they should be driving a Rolls Royce.

Yet cafes here aren't just places for a caffeine hit and a treat, they're extravagant all-day (and often all-evening) places, generally offering hot dishes or at least something real to eat. They should be visited every bit as much as a museum or castle, packed with history and culture. Maybe cut out the cakes every now and then.

Sternbräu.

★★ **Stiftskeller St. Peter** OLD TOWN *AUSTRIAN*   Europe's oldest restaurant was established by Benedictine monks in A.D. 803, in a warren of rooms and a vaulted cellar. Expect pork, sauerkraut, dumplings, and other staples, well done. *St. Peter Bezirk 1/4.* ☎ *0662/8412680. www. haslauer.at. Entrees 12€–20€. MC, V. Lunch & dinner daily. Map p 99.*

★★ **Wilder Mann** OLD TOWN *AUSTRIAN*   Try the piled-high farmer's plate of pork, sausage, veal, cabbage, and dumplings in this cheery old inn with a hunting lodge feel, yet right in the heart of town. *Getreidegasse 20.* ☎ *0662/841787. Entrees 8€–15€. No credit cards. Lunch & dinner Mon–Sat. Map p 100.*

★★ **Zipfer Bierhaus** OLD TOWN *AUSTRIAN*   Simple Austrian dishes—goulash, cheese-covered noodles—at a good price. The pub is divided into two rooms with simple wooden tables: one for drinkers, another for those who want to eat. In the summer, there are tables out on Universitätsplatz. *Sigmund-Haffner-Gasse 12.* ☎ *0662/840745. Entrees 8€–17€. DC, MC, V. Lunch & dinner Mon–Sat. Map p 99.*

★★ **Zum Mohren** OLD TOWN *AUSTRIAN*   Built into the 13th-century city walls, this historic restaurant has welcomed Mozart and Schubert. The menu is made up of innovative local food, particularly venison in winter. *Judengasse 9.* ☎ *0662/840680. www. restaurant-zummohren.at. Entrees 12€–25€. AE, DC, MC, V. Lunch & dinner Mon–Sat. Map p 99.*

kids **Zwettler's Stiftskeller** OLD TOWN *AUSTRIAN*   Austrian classics are served alongside more straightforward fare in this pub, beer garden, and restaurant open from late morning until 1am. The garden is also very family-friendly and is an ideal place to bring the kids. *Kaigasse 3.* ☎ *0662/844055. www. stiftskeller-zwettler.com. Entrees 8€–17€. AE, MC, V. Lunch & dinner daily. Map p 99.* ●

Nightlife Best Bets

Steinterrasse at night.

Best **Old-World Atmosphere**
★★★ Bar Goldener Hirsch,
Getreidegasse 37 (p 113)

Best **Views**
★★★ Steinterrasse, *Giselakai 3-5*
(p 114)

Best **Dance Club**
★★ Cave Club, *Leopoldskronstrasse*
5 (p 116)

Best **Open-Air Bar**
★ StieglKeller, *Festungsgasse*
10 (p 115)

Best **Beer Hall**
★★★ Augustiner Bräustübl,
Augustinergasse 4 (p 115)

Best **Riverside Garden Bar**
with Music
Baboon Bar, *Imbergstrasse 11*
(p 113)

Hippest **Cave**
★★★ Bar Saitensprung, *Steingasse*
11 (p 114)

Best **Champagne Skybar**
★★★ Threesixty Bar, *Hangar-7,*
Wilhelm-Spazier-Strasse 7A (p 113)

Best **Irish Bar**
O'Malley's, *Rudolfskai 16 (p 114)*

Best **Gay Bar**
Diva, *Priesterhausgasse 22 (p 116)*

Previous page: Nightlife in the Old Town.

Old Town Nightlife

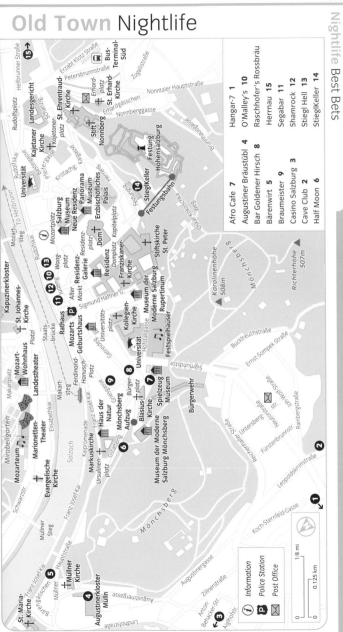

New Town Nightlife

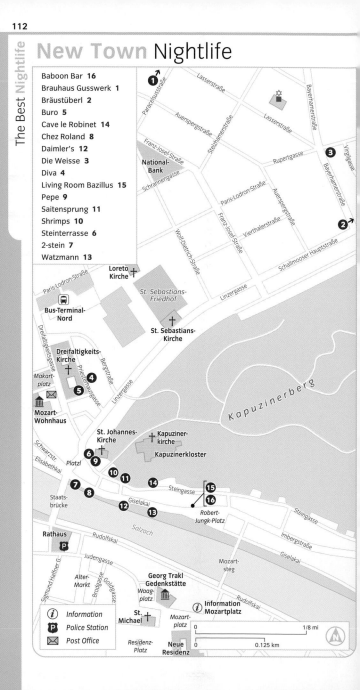

Baboon Bar **16**
Brauhaus Gusswerk **1**
Bräustüberl **2**
Buro **5**
Cave le Robinet **14**
Chez Roland **8**
Daimler's **12**
Die Weisse **3**
Diva **4**
Living Room Bazillus **15**
Pepe **9**
Saitensprung **11**
Shrimps **10**
Steinterrasse **6**
2-stein **7**
Watzmann **13**

(i) Information
(P) Police Station
(✉) Post Office

0 _____ 1/8 mi
0 _____ 0.125 km

Salzburg Nightlife A to Z

Bars

Afro Cafe OLD TOWN A strange, yet entrancing place that's good for daytime coffee, then Afro-inspired food such as curry and couscous in the early evening, before becoming a cool nighttime hangout until late. *Bürgerspitalplatz 5.* ☎ *0662/844888. www.afrocoffee.com. Map p 111.*

Baboon Bar NEW TOWN This lively spot with a garden, down by the river, is fun for all ages, as long as you can deal with the large music collection that focuses on the '70s, '80s, and, of course, disco. *Imbergstrasse 11.* ☎ *0662/885932. Map p 112.*

★★★ Bar Goldener Hirsch OLD TOWN The inner courtyard at one of the ancient hotels is now an irresistible bar, all stags' heads and arches. It's a Salzburg classic. Try the signature cocktail, the *Suzanne*—vodka, cassis, orange juice, and tonic. *Getreidegasse 37.* ☎ *0662/8084824. www.goldenerhirsch.com. Map p 111.*

Buro NEW TOWN American-themed cellar bar and pizzeria with arched brick ceilings, down an alley off Makartplatz. Free live jazz, blues, and soul music Wednesday to Saturday. *Richard Mayr Gasse 1.* ☎ *0662/8772970. www.buero-salzburg.at. Map p 112.*

Cave le Robinet NEW TOWN This wine merchant bridges the gap with a tasting cellar and tavern. You'll find the best of Austrian wines along with many others. *Steingasse 43.* ☎ *0662/5591237. www.amphora-ttgc.com. Closed evenings. Map p 112.*

★ Chez Roland NEW TOWN For more than 30 years, the Festival crowd has headed to this arty bar. It occupies an old salt storage cellar with its vaulted ceiling, yet natural light filters in. Choose from a large selection of Austrian wines. Usually open until at least 4am. *Giselakai 15.* ☎ *0662/874335. Map p 112.*

Daimler's NEW TOWN A lively riverbank bar and club that is also popular with the gay crowd, although it's not strictly a gay bar. *Giselakai 17.* ☎ *0662/890989. Map p 112.*

★★ Hangar-7 OUTSKIRTS Near the airport, this futuristic hangar has two bars, gourmet restaurant, Ikarus, and lots of planes. The **Threesixty Bar** hanging from the

Red Bull Hangar-7.

Steinterrasse, the spectacular roof top cafe-bar.

roof has views through its glass floor. The Mayday Bar serves Smart Food—dishes created by a nutritionist to supposedly make you look, feel, and act smarter. *Wilhelm-Spazier-Strasse 7A.* ☎ *0662/21970. www.hangar-7.com. Bus: 2. See p 20,* **3**. *Map p 111.*

Living Room Bazillus NEW TOWN   A small but busy and trendy bar. Relax in the small garden with city and river views. *Imbergstrasse 2a.* ☎ *0662/81631. Map p 112.*

O'Malley's OLD TOWN   On most days, this Irish-themed pub is pleasantly low key (avoid Thursday karaoke) in a pubby way with Guinness and Irish(ish) food. Its livelier sister, the Shamrock, is just down the street. *Rudolfskai 16.* ☎ *0662/84965. www.omalleyssalzburg.com. Map p 111.*

Pepe NEW TOWN   It's always fiesta time at this cocktail bar with a Mexican touch, hence margaritas, lots of tequila, and piles of nachos. *Steingasse 3.* ☎ *0662/873652. www.pepe-cocktailbar.at. Map p 112.*

★ **Saitensprung** NEW TOWN   A very trendy bar-cum-disco with a hip crowd and hip music. The setting is suitably inspiring—a cave dug into the Kapuzinerberg several centuries back. *Steingasse 11.* ☎ *0662/881377. Daily 9pm–4am. Map p 112.*

Segabar OLD TOWN   Noisy and generally packed, this club-style bar stays open until 4am Monday to Sunday. Music, TVs, and moderately priced drinks. *Rudolfskai 18.* ☎ *0662/846898. www.segabar.at. Map p 111.*

Shamrock OLD TOWN   While this Irish bar may lack Euro chic, it does have Guinness, pizza, burgers, a pool table, sports TV, and live music. *Rudolfskai 12/Judengasse 1.* ☎ *0662/841610. www.shamrocksalzburg.com. Daily midnight–3am, Thurs–Sat to 4am, Sun to 2am. Map p 111.*

Shrimps NEW TOWN   Cocktails and seafood go hand-in-hand at this bright and lively bar, not least the shrimp roll—an irresistible baguette oozing sauce and shrimps. *Steingasse 5.* ☎ *0662/874484. www.shrimps.at. Map p 112.*

★★★ **Steinterrasse** NEW TOWN   This spectacular roof terrace cafe-bar tops the stylish Hotel Stein (p 137) on the riverbank with views of the Mönchsberg. *Giselakai 3–5. www.hotelstein.at.* ☎ *0662/8743460. Map p 112.*

Watzmann NEW TOWN   'Cultbar-lounge-garden' as the place, next to the Hotel Stein, describes itself. The lively place, generally throbbing to disco and club music by the river, overflows with a young crowd until 4am. *Giselakai 17a.* ☎ *0662/877237. Map p 112.*

Brewpubs

★★★ **Augustiner Bräustübl** OLD TOWN   On a chilly winter Sunday evening when the city seems aslumber, there's still life in this old beer hall. Grab a stone mug of the in-house brew and everything's right with the world. It also has Austria's biggest beer garden. *Augustinergasse 4.* ☎ *0662/431246. www.augustiner bier.at. Daily 3–11pm. Map p 111.*

★ **Bärenwirt** OLD TOWN   An excellent pub with terrace down by the river at the foot of the Mönchsberg that manages to be both modern and traditional. Not strictly a brewpub, but it serves beer from the Augustiner brewery. Popular with students. *Müllner Hauptstrasse 8.* ☎ *0662/422404. www.baerenwirt-salzburg.at. Map p 111.*

★ **Brauhaus Gusswerk** OUTSKIRTS   A bit out of town, but worth the trek. This award-winning organic brewery serves up special beers (try the dark, herby Black Betty). The modern bar in an old warehouse also serves organic food. *Söllheimerstrasse 16.* ☎ *0662/243279. www.brauhaus-gusswerk.at. Bus: 21. Map p 112.*

★ **Braumeister** OLD TOWN   Part of the gigantic food and drink complex in the old Sternbrau brewery (p 106), yet with the feel of a tiny, hidden bar, this claims to be Salzburg's oldest pub. It's dark, fun, and has a goodly array of beer. Wednesday is students' night. *Griesgasse 23.* ☎ *0662/84214080. www.sternbrau. com. Map p 111.*

★★ **Bräustüberl** OUTSKIRTS   At Stiegl Brauwelt (p 106), a museum complex, this lively bar is open daily until midnight. There is also a bustling beer garden and a selection of simple Austrian food to soak up the ale brewed on the premises. *Bräuhausstrasse 9.* ☎ *0662/83871492. www.brauwelt.at. Bus: 1. Map p 112.*

Die Weisse NEW TOWN   Various rich *weisse* (wheat) beers—such as the wonderful dark *bock*, brewed before Easter and Advent—are created in this hugely popular microbrewery and bar tucked away in the backstreets. It's small, but only by comparison to the likes of the Augustiner. *Rupertgasse 10.* ☎ *0662/872246. www.dieweisse.at. Map p 112.*

Raschhofer's Rossbräu Herrnau OUTSKIRTS   Enjoy the atmosphere and jolly after-work clientele at this big, bustling, modern brewpub and beer garden by a shopping mall just off the busy Alpenstrasse. *Alpenstrasse 4/Zentrum Herrnau.* ☎ *0662/626444. www.rossbraeu.at. Map p 111.*

★ **Stiegl Hell** OLD TOWN   A dark, warm brewpub on the banks of the Salzach, with a selection of Stiegl beers—one of the liveliest small bars in town. *Rudolfskai 25.* ☎ *0662/ 843498. Map p 111.*

★★★ **StieglKeller** OLD TOWN   This is *the* place to go for a feel of Salzburg. Several beer halls are set into the rock beneath the Hohensalzburg Fortress, with terraces overlooking town. It's the perfect spot as the sun sets. *Festungsgasse 10.* ☎ *0662/ 842681. May–Sept. Map p 111.*

The StieglKeller is a massive beer hall cut into the face of the Mönchsberg here.

Beer Hall or Beer Garden?

Salzburg has cavernous beer halls and it has relaxing beer gardens. How do you choose? Well, beer gardens are perfect for a cooling daytime tipple, while a beer hall is a place where time stands still as you pass the evening. The city's two beer icons have them both. The **Augustiner Bräustübl** (p 115) is a huge place that serves just *beer*—one kind, out of one tap after you've paid the one lady for a ticket. Indoors is a series of rooms, all filled with tables and beer drinkers; outside is another world, even in the evening, with children playing and families enjoying themselves. The **StieglKeller** (p 115), serves a selection of the fabled Stiegl brew along with wine and waitress-service meals. Inside has a calming, restaurant air while outside the beer garden (actually a massive beer terrace) overlooks the city and is a place of nighttime partying.

There are plenty of other places where you can sit out with a beer, often a beer brewed on the premises, although not on the same scale. Many bars, especially by the river, have gardens.

Casino

Casino Salzburg OUTSKIRTS Expect the sort of casino you might see in a James Bond movie, set in a former prince archbishop's palace with a design based on Versailles palace. Roulette, poker, blackjack, stud poker, and slot machines. Jackets required. *Schloss Klessheim, Wals-Siezenheim.* ☎ *0662/8544550. www.casinos.at. Map p 111.*

Dance Clubs

★★ **Cave Club** OUTSKIRTS This famed spot with top-quality DJs and cutting-edge techno and house music is a world away from mainstream clubbing. Regular dub reggae nights too. And it really is a cave of sorts, built into the Rainberg mountain. *Leopoldskronstrasse 5.* ☎ *0662/840026. www.cave-club.at. Cover charge 5€–10€. Map p 111.*

Half Moon OLD TOWN A popular and sophisticated club and lounge where the lights combine with the arched ceilings to create a swirling scene that could be from a '60s pop-art movie. *Gstättengasse 4–6.* ☎ *0676/670407. www.half moon.at. Thurs–Sat 10pm–5am. Cover around 5€. Map p 111.*

Gay & Lesbian Bars

Diva NEW TOWN One of the city's two hottest gay bars, along with 2-stein. They're just around the corner from each other in the old, riverbank part of the New Town. *Priesterhausgasse 22.* ☎ *0662/ 832680502. Map p 112.*

2-stein NEW TOWN Smart bar (you might also see it called Zweistein) with modern art on the walls and occasional live entertainment. Fills up as the night goes on—which is until 4am in the week, 5am at weekends. The crowd moves in waves between here and Diva. *Giselakai 9.* ☎ *0662/877179. www. zweistein.at. Map p 112.*

Arts & Entertainment Best Bets

Mozart Dinner Concert at St. Peter's Monastery during the Salzburg Festival.

Best **Classical Concert**
★★★ Salzburger Schlosskonzerte, *Schloss Mirabell (p 121)*

Best **Festival**
★★★ Salzburg Festival, *various venues (p 122)*

Best **Concert Hall**
★★ Large Festival Hall, *Hofstallgasse 1, (p 24)*

Best **Sporting Event**
★★ FC Red Bull Salzburg, *Stadionstrasse 2, 5071 Siezenheim, Wals-Siezenheim (p 126)*

Best **Puppet Experience**
★★★ Salzburg Marionette Theater, *Schwarzstrasse 24 (p 121)*

Best for **Rock 'n' Roll**
Rockhouse, *Schallmooser Hauptstrasse 46 (p 125)*

Best **Dinner Show**
★★ Mozart Dinner Concert, *Stiftskeller St. Peter (p 122)*

Best for **Dance**
★★ Sommerszene, *various venues (p 124)*

Previous page: The Salzburg Festival is one of the world's most important arts festivals.

Old Town Arts & Entertainment

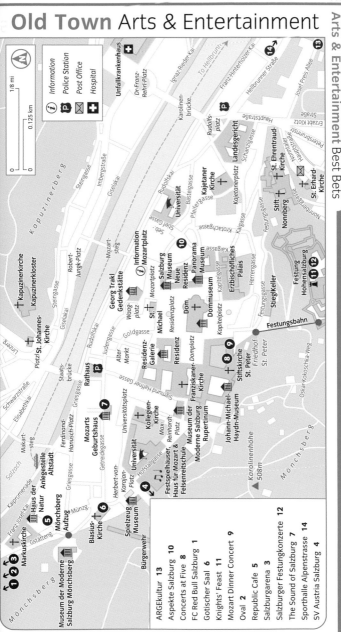

Map legend:

- *i* Information
- Police Station
- Post Office
- Hospital

Scale: 0 — 1/8 mi / 0 — 0.125 km

Labels on map:

Unfallkrankenhaus
Dr-Franz-Rehrl-Platz
Ignaz-Rieder-Kai
To Helbrunn
Franz-Hinterholzer-Kai
Karolinen-brücke
Rudolfskai
Rudolfs-platz
Hauptstraße
Josef Preis Allee
Erzabt Klotz Straße
Landesgericht
Schanzlgasse
Nonntaler Brücke
St. Ehrentraud-Kirche
Stift Nonnberg
St. Erhard-Kirche
Festung Hohensalzburg
Festungsgasse
Herrengasse
Stieglkeller
Festungsbahn
Oskar-Kokoschka-Weg
Mönchsberg
Kajetanerplatz
Kajetaner Kirche
Krotachgasse
Pfeifergasse
Kaigasse
Kapitelgasse
Erzbischöfliches Palais
Dommuseum
Dom
Kapitelplatz
St. Peter Friedhof
Stiftskirche St. Peter
Johann-Michael-Haydn-Museum
Franziskaner-Kirche
Domplatz
Residenzplatz
Neue Residenz
Salzburg Museum
Panorama Museum
Universität
Seb. Stief-Gasse
Mozartplatz
i Information
Mozartsteg
Georg Trakl Gedenkstätte
Woag-platz
St. Michael
Residenz
Residenz-Galerie
Alter Markt
Goldgasse
Judengasse
Rudolfskai
Mozart-steg
Robert-Jungk-Platz
Kapuzinerberg
Kapuzinerkloster
Kapuzinerkirche
St. Johannes-Kirche
Platz
Imbergstraße
Giselakai
Steingasse
Linzergasse
Schwarzstraße
Elisabethkai
Makart-steg
Makartplatz
Kapromenade
Franz-Josef-Kai
Haus der Natur
Markuskirche
Museum der Moderne Salzburg Mönchsberg
Mönchsberg Aufzug
Blasius-Kirche
Bürgerwehr
Karolinenhöhe 508m
Spielzeug Museum
Münzg.
Herbert-von-Karajan-Platz
Festspielhäuser, Haus für Mozart & Felsenreitschule
Museum der Moderne Salzburg Rupertinum
Kollegien-Kirche
Universität
Getreidegasse
Hofstallgasse
Max-Reinhardt-Platz
Universitätsplatz
Sigmund Haffner Gasse
Mozarts Geburtshaus
Rathaus
Staats-brücke
Ferdinand-Hanusch-Platz
Griesgasse
Gstättengasse
Anlegestelle Altstadt
Salzach
Mönchsberg

Best Bets list:

ARGEkultur **13**
Aspekte Salzburg **10**
Concerts at Five **8**
FC Red Bull Salzburg **1**
Gotischer Saal **6**
Knights' Feast **11**
Mozart Dinner Concert **9**
Oval **2**
Republic Cafe **5**
Salzburgarena **3**
Salzburger Festungskonzerte **12**
The Sound of Salzburg **7**
Sporthalle Alpenstrasse **14**
SV Austria Salzburg **4**

Hauptbahnhof

✉	Post Office
🚉	Train Station
Ⓢ	S-Bahn Station
⛴	River Cruise
✚	Hospital

0 _____ 1/8 mi
0 _____ 0.125 km

Ignaz-v.-Heffter-Str.
St.-Julien-Straße
Plainstraße
Elisabethstraße
Rainerstraße
Lasterstraße
Paracelsusstr.

1

Fr.-Neum-Straße
Lessingstr.
V.-Kaplan-Str
Hans-Prodinger-Str.
Schwarzstraße
Plainstraße

S3

Humbold-straße
Bahnhof-viadukt
Gabelsbergerstraße
Weiserstraße

Ernest-Thun-Straße
Max-Ott-Platz
Julius-Raab-Platz
Privatklinik Wehrle ✚
Lasserstraße
Paracelsusstraße
Steinbruchstraße

Markus-Sittikus-Straße
Auerspergstraße
Auerspergstraße
Adolf-Kolping-Platz

Kurhaus
Salzburg Congress
Paracelsus
National-Bank

Kurpark
Franz-Josef-Straße
Rainer-Straße
Schwarzstraße

Bernhard-Paumgartner-Weg
Hubert-Sattler-Gasse
Faberstraße
Haydnstraße
Wolf-Dietrich-Straße
Franz-Josef-Straße
Vierthalerstraße

Schloss Mirabell 🏛 **2**
St. Andrä-Kirche ✝
✉

Mirabell-platz
Schrannengasse
Paris-Lodron-Straße
Loreto Kirche ✝

Mirabell-garten
St. Sebastians-Friedhof

Evangelische Kirche ✝
Barockmuseum 🏛 **3**
4
Bus-Terminal-Nord 🚌
10 →
11 →
12 →

Mozarteum
5
Universität Mozarteum
Dreialtigkeitsgasse
Dreifaltigkeits-Kirche
St. Sebastians-Kirche ✝

Marionetten-Theater **6**
Landestheater **7**
Makartplatz
Bergstraße
Priesterhausg.
Linzergasse

Salzach
Mozart-Wohnhaus 🏛
Kapuzinerberg

Markus-kirche ✝
Kapromenade
Gstättengasse
Franz-Josef-Kai
Makart-steg
Elisabethkai
St. Johannes-Kirche ✝
8
9
Kapuziner-kirche ✝
Kapuzinerkloster

Haus der Natur 🏛
Anlegestelle Altstadt ⛴
Platzl

Museum der Moderne 🏛
Ferdinand-Hanusch-Platz
Griegasse
Staats-brücke
Giselakai
Steingasse
13 →
14 →

Das Kino **8**	Mozart Week **3**
Dialoge **4**	Rockhouse **12**
EC Red Bull Salzburg **13**	Salzburg Marionette Theater **6**
Encounter Festival **5**	Salzburger Landestheater **7**
Jazzclub Life **10**	Salzburger Schlosskonzerte **2**
Jazzit **1**	Summer Theater **11**
Mountain Film Festival **9**	Winterfest **14**

Arts & Entertainment **A to Z**

Cinema

Das Kino NEW TOWN   The city's arts cinema shows movies from around the world in their original language with German subtitles. *Giselakai 11.* ☎ *0662/873100. www. daskino.at. Ticket prices vary. Map p 120.*

Classical & Opera

★★ Concerts at Five OLD TOWN Enjoy charming hour-long summer concerts at the Haydn Museum, with varied composers celebrated by young musicians on original instruments. *Johann-Michael-Haydn-Museum, Courtyard, St. Peter's Abbey.* ☎ *0662/84457619. www. concerts-at-five.com. July–Sept Thurs–Tues 5pm. Tickets 15€ adults, 12€ children 6–15. Map p 119.*

Gotischer Saal OLD TOWN   The Gothic Hall in the Church of St. Blasius (also confusingly known as the Civic Hospital Church and Church of the Holy Spirit) snuggles up to the Mönchsberg. It provides a smart setting, with a ribbed ceiling, for classical recitals and Advent concerts (www.adventserenaden. at). *Bürgerspitalgasse 2. Ticket prices vary. Map p 119.*

Salzburg Marionette Theater NEW TOWN   Going strong since 1913, the puppets act out opera, mostly Mozart. Then there's *The Sound of Music* in English with *Thunderbirds*-like characters and a classy U.S.-recorded score. *Schwarzstrasse 24.* ☎ *0662/8724060. www. marionetten.at. Tickets 22€–35€ adults, 14€ children 11 and under. Map p 120.*

Salzburger Landestheater NEW TOWN   This beautiful auditorium dates back to 1775, and has been recently revamped. There's a wide selection of ballet, dance, opera, and classical operettas, along with plays and children's theater, but mostly in German. *Schwarzstrasse 22.* ☎ *0662/871512222. www.salzburger-landestheater.at. Tickets 5€–49.50€. Map p 120.*

★★★ Salzburger Schlosskonzerte NEW TOWN   The best regular music in Salzburg. Near-daily

Advance Tickets

The Mozarteum not only puts together Mozart Week, but also the Dialogues Festival and around 20 major concerts throughout the year. Its website (www.mozarteum.at) is a good place to buy these, but while Mozart Week operates at 95% capacity, there are still tickets available near the time. In Mozart Week, the Mozarteum ticket office is open daily 9am to 6pm. The Salzburg Festival has its own year-round shop and box office at the Festival Halls, while its website (www.salzburgerfestspiele.at) gives all sorts of ticket permutations. **Salzburg Ticket Service** (Mozartplatz 5; ☎ 0662/ 840310, www.salzburgticket.com) has tickets for most things. **Kartenbüro Arena** (Alpenstrasse 119; ☎ 0662/6232330, www. arena.at) has tickets for events in Salzburg and other cities.

The Salzburg Festival

The Salzburg Festival is the world's biggest arts festival with more than 200 concerts, plays, and operas in more than a dozen venues, from cathedral to theater. It's been going since 1920 and runs from late July until the end of August, paying tribute to Mozart and many other composers, with exciting new productions. The city comes alive and gets packed, so advance booking of hotels is essential. Moreover, despite there being more than 220,000 tickets on offer, most go swiftly. You can order tickets from the website (www.salzburgfestival.at), either individual tickets or one of many combinations, which give you performances on consecutive days. Either way, you should have your request (possibly appeal) in by mid-January. Don't simply plan to arrive in town and decide on a show; this has to be sorted out in advance. However, even if you're not planning on a show, the Festival weeks are a spectacle in themselves—the streets are full of beautiful gowns and dinner suits as people make their way to performances, restaurants are alive with arty visitors, and upmarket hotel bars are deep in excited discussions. On the other hand, if you like it quiet, stay away.

concerts by small ensembles in the Mirabell Palace's Marble Hall are arranged by, and often feature, Salzburg violinist Luz Leskowitz. Splendid music played with no costumes or fuss. *Schloss Mirabell, Mirabellplatz.* ☎ *0662/848586. www. salzburger-schlosskonzerte.at. Tickets 29€–35€ adults, 10€ children. Bus: 3, 5, or 6. Map p 120.*

Dinner Shows

★ **kids Knights' Feast** OLD TOWN Combination of medieval entertainment and traditional Austrian dinner in the Hohensalzburg fortress. Quaff beer from tankards, eat suckling pig, pitch horseshoes, and fire crossbows. Great family fun with a children's menu. *Mönchsberg 34.* ☎ *0662/825859. www.salzburg highlights.at. Tickets 32€ adults, 14€ children 11 and under. Map p 119.*

★★ **Mozart Dinner Concert** OLD TOWN   Musicians in period costume play and sing classics, including

opera, as you eat in a hall in the oldest restaurant in central Europe. This may be a tourist must, but is impressive nonetheless. *Stiftskeller St. Peter, St. Peter Bezirk 1/4.* ☎ *0662/ 828695. www.skg.co.at. Daily at 8pm. Tickets 48€ adults, 28€ children 13 and under. Map p 119.*

Knights' Feast takes place at the Hohensalzburg Fortress.

The ornate setting of the Mozart Dinner Concert, the oldest restaurant in Europe.

★ **Salzburger Festungkonzerte**
OLD TOWN   The **Mozart Ensemble Salzburg** perform Mozart, Haydn, and more high in the Golden Hall of the fortress. Dinner is served before the concert in the restaurant at the top of the funicular. *Hohensalzburg Festung.* ☎ *0662/825858. www.mozartfestival.at. Daily Apr–Oct; regularly for rest of year. Tickets 47/51€ with dinner; 31/38€ concert only. Map p 119.*

The Sound of Salzburg OLD TOWN   An evening of songs that made the city famous, largely from *The Sound of Music*, although you'll also find folk, operettas, Mozart, and the Trapp Family Folk Music Revival. There's a choice of three-course menus. *Sternbräu Dinner Theatre, Griesgasse 23.* ☎ *0662/826617. www.soundofsalzburgshow.com. Mid-May–Oct daily dinner 7:30pm, show 8:30pm; year-round for groups by arrangement. Tickets 46€ with dinner & drink; 32€ with drink only. Map p 119.*

Festivals
Aspekte Salzburg OLD TOWN   A celebration of modern classical music (with premieres) with the focus on the Austrian Ensemble for New Music, performing both as an

ensemble and as a chamber music orchestra. *Pfeifergasse 10.* ☎ *0662/881547. www.aspekte-salzburg.at. Early Mar. Ticket prices vary. Map p 119.*

★ **Culture Days** OLD TOWN   Classical performances, operas, and a wealth of local and international performers, ensembles, choirs, and orchestras. *Various venues.* ☎ *0662/845346. www.salzburg.com/kulturvereinigung. Two weeks in Oct. Ticket prices vary.*

Dialoge NEW TOWN   An event exploring Mozart's works through contemporary music, dance, film, and literature. Mahler, Schönberg, and John Cage have all been featured in the innovative selections. *Mozarteum, Theatergasse 2.* ☎ *0662/83154. www.dialoge-festival.at. Nov–Dec. Tickets 20€–25€. Map p 120.*

★★ **Easter Festival** OLD TOWN   Classical music, usually revolving around a major opera (Sir Simon Rattle conducted Richard Wagner's *Ring* cycle over several seasons). *Various venues.* ☎ *0662/8045361. www.osterfestspiele-salzburg.at. Week before Easter. Ticket prices vary.*

★ **Encounter Festival** NEW TOWN   Orchestral works, chamber music (played by the distinguished

Opera performed in the fantastical setting of the Felsenreitschule during the Salzburg Festival.

Camerata Salzburg group), and solo compositions with a theme such as 'Nature' held over a weekend in mid-May. *Mozarteum, Theatergasse 2. ☎ 0662/873154. www.mozarteum. at. Mid-May. Ticket prices vary. Map p 120.*

★ **Jazz Festival** CITYWIDE Expect everything jazz from the avant-garde to the traditional in locations as diverse as the University Auditorium and Stiegl's Brauwelt. Top international names as well as upcoming delights. *Various venues. ☎ 01/5048500. www.jazz4you.at. Late Oct–early Nov. Ticket prices vary.*

Literature Festival OLD TOWN A celebration of the written word with readings and discussions in various languages. Everything from Greek mythology marathons to poetry shows make this a true cross-border festival. *Various venues. ☎ 0662/885048. www.literaturfest-salzburg.at. Late May. Ticket prices vary.*

Mountain Film Festival NEW TOWN The world's leading climbers descend on the city for vertigo-inducing movies, talks, and discussions. *Das Kino, Giselakai 11.*

☎ 0662/873100. www.daskino.at. Late Nov–early Dec. Ticket prices vary. Map p 120.

★★★ **Mozart Week** NEW TOWN Winter's musical highlight is this expansive selection of popular classics combined with lesser-known works, plus contemporary composers, performed by world-renowned string quartets and orchestras. *Mozarteum, Theatergasse 2. ☎ 0662/873154. www.mozarteum.at. Late Jan. Ticket prices vary. Map p 120.*

★★★ **Salzburg Festival** CITYWIDE The world's leading classical, opera, and drama festival across 5 weeks (see p 122). *Various venues. ☎ 0662/873100. www.salzburg festival.at. Late July–Aug. Ticket prices vary.*

Sommerszene CITYWIDE Dance celebration—from hip-hop to ballet—involving world-renowned choreographers, plus theater, music, and art. Locations vary from the arts group Szene's Republic Theatre to the Museum der Moderne. *Various venues. ☎ 0662/843448. www.sommerszene.net. Mid-July. Ticket prices vary.*

★ **Whitsuntide Festival** CITYWIDE Music and opera festival that focuses on Neapolitan baroque and the links between Austria and Italy. Venues include the Mozarteum and Collegiate Church. *Various venues. ☎ 0662/8045500. www.salzburg festival.at. Mid-May. Ticket prices vary.*

★ **Winterfest** NEW TOWN A circus festival in a big top in a park near the river. Ensembles from various countries put on high-wire displays, as well as tumbling, clowning, and all the classics, yet with an upmarket air. *Volksgarten. ☎ 0662/887580. www.winterfest.at. Dec. Ticket prices vary. Map p 120.*

Live Music

★ Jazzclub Life NEW

TOWN   Popular jazz club with regular live acts, and some big-name Friday guests. Reasonably priced drinks. *Schallmooser Hauptstrasse 50. ☎ 0664/2134548. www.jazzclublife.at. Ticket prices vary. Bus: 4. Map p 120.*

★★ Jazzit NEW TOWN

Trendy club near the station featuring live acts from jazz to drum 'n' bass and more esoteric musical cousins. *Elisabethstrasse 11. ☎ 0662/875996. www.jazzit.at. Ticket prices vary. Map p 120.*

Oval OUTSKIRTS   Europark is apparently Europe's first shopping mall to have an arts and concert venue. The Oval puts on jazz, folk, and other music along with cabaret, dance, and movies each evening. Away from town but trains and buses stop outside. *Europastrasse 1. ☎ 0662/44202131. www.oval.at. Ticket prices vary. Bus: 1, 20, 28; S-bahn: S3. Map p 119.*

★★ Republic Cafe OLD TOWN

Hang out with musicians and rock fans in an artfully unkempt bar, performance areas, and club at the bottom of the Mönchsberg elevator.

Regular live music and other events. *Anton Neymayr Platz 2. ☎ 0662/841613. www.republic-cafe.at. Ticket prices vary. Map p 119.*

★★ Rockhouse NEW TOWN

A great rock venue set in a 19th-century wine cellar and ice store backing onto the Kapuzinerberg where you can catch well-known British and U.S. bands alongside a wide range of European acts. *Schallmooser Hauptstrasse 46. ☎ 0662/884914. www.rockhouse.at. Ticket prices vary. Bus: 4. Map p 120.*

Salzburgarena OUTSKIRTS   This large, 21st-century venue in the grounds of Salzburg's exhibition complex is a spectacular place combining a wooden dome with state-of-the-art equipment and stunning interior design. It stages major concerts and shows from chart acts to Bob Dylan to Michael Flatley's *Lord of the Dance. Am Messezentrum 1. ☎ 0662/24040. www.salzburgarena. at. Ticket prices vary. Bus: 1. Map p 119.*

Sporthalle Alpenstrasse OUTSKIRTS   Sports venue which is also used for pop concerts. *Otto-Holzbauer-Strasse 5. ☎ 0662/623344. Bus: 3, 8. Map p 119.*

The Mozarteum is home to the Mozart Festival and many other concerts.

Street musician performing outside the Cathedral.

Performance

ARGEkultur OLD TOWN   An independent arts complex that puts on avant-garde shows involving DJs, dance, modern music, cabaret, multimedia presentations, and even children's festivals. *Josef-Preis-Allee 16.* ☎ *0662/848784. www.argekultur.at. Ticket prices vary. Map p 119.*

Spectator Sports

EC Red Bull Salzburg OUTSKIRTS   One of Austria's leading ice-hockey teams, with games played throughout the winter at the Eisarena, a short walk from the Kapuzinerberg, near the river. *Salzburger Eisarena, Hermann Bahr-Promenade 2.* ☎ *0662/630752. http://ecredbulls.seso.at/2006/news. php. Ticket prices vary. Bus: 6, 7, 20. Map p 120.*

FC Red Bull Salzburg OUTSKIRTS   Watch the regular Bundesliga soccer champions in action against the likes of Rapid Vienna late summer to spring. There are tours of the modern, architecturally striking stadium on Saturdays (not matchdays) 10am to 1pm, free admission but must be booked via website. *Stadionstrasse 2, Wals-Siezenheim.* ☎ *0662/433332. www. redbulls.com. Tickets 11€–23€ adults, 2€–7€ children. Bus: 1, 20, 28; S-Bahn train to Europark/Taxham. Map p 119.*

Salzburg AMREF Marathon CITYWIDE   More than 4,000 runners take to the streets the first Saturday of May, starting and finishing on Residence Square, taking in Mozart Square, Hellbrunn, and Leopoldskron. Thousands more take part in a half-marathon, fun run, children's, and team races. *www. salzburg-marathon.at.*

SV Austria Salzburg OUTSKIRTS The soccer team was set up by fans after Salzburg's original soccer team was taken over and rebranded FC Red Bull Salzburg. SV are currently moving up through the divisions. *Eichetstrasse 31.* ☎ *0664/73631040. Tickets 5€. www.austria-salzburg.at. Bus: 27. Map p 119.*

Theater

Summer Theater NEW TOWN Summer sees an eclectic season of productions with everything from classics to Woody Allen's *Midsummer Night's Sex Comedy*. Mostly in German, though. *Kleines Theater Schallmoos, Schallmooser Hauptstrasse 50.* ☎ *0664/3021746. www. salzburger-sommertheater.at. Tickets 10€–20€. Map p 120.* ●

Lodging Best Bets

The Old Town has plenty of stylish hotels.

Best **Romantic Hotel**
★★★ Schloss Mönchstein $$$$
Mönchsberg Park 26 (p 139)

Best **Luxury Hotel**
★★★ Hotel Bristol $$$$ *Makart-platz 4 (p 135)*

Best **Budget Hotel**
★★ Hotel Schwarzes Rössl $
Priesterhausgasse 6 (p 137)

Best **Old Town Location**
★★★ Altstadt Radisson SAS $$$
Rudolfskai 28 (p 132)

Best **Country Retreat**
★★★ Schloss Leopoldskron $$
Leopoldskronstrasse 56 (p 139)

Best **Restaurant**
★★ Hotel Sacher $$$ *Schwarz-strasse 5–7 (p 137)*

Best **Boutique Hotel**
★★★ Arte Vida $$ *Dreifaltigkeits-gasse 9 (p 133)*

Best **Affordable Design**
★★ Hotel Evido Salzburg City $$
Rainerstrasse 25 (p 135)

Best for **History**
★★★ Arthotel Blaue Gans $$
Getreidegasse 43 (p 133)

Best **Views**
★★★ Hotel Stein $$ *Giselakai 3–5
(p 137)*

Best for **Families**
★★ Jedermann Design-hotel $$
Rupertgasse 25 (p 138)

Best for **Spa**
★★ Wolf-Dietrich $$ *Wolf-Dietrich-Strasse 7 (p 140)*

Best for *The Sound of Music*
Fans
★★ Villa Trapp $$$ *Traunstrasse
34 (p 140)*

Best **Business Hotel**
★ NH Hotel Salzburg $$ *Franz-Josef-Strasse 26 (p 138)*

Best **Low-Cost
Accommodation**
★★ Institut St. Sebastian $ *Linzer
Gasse 41 (p 138)*

Previous page: Schloss Leopoldskron.

Old Town Lodging

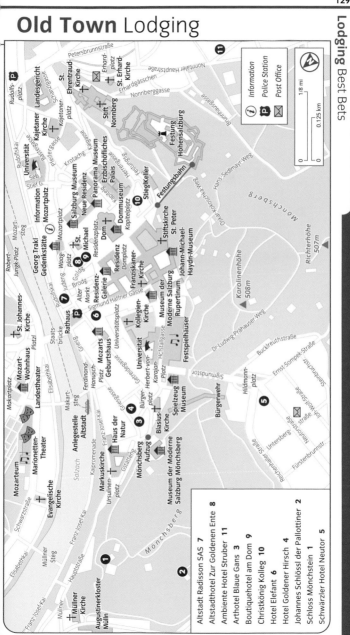

Altstadt Radisson SAS **7**

Altstadthotel Zur Goldenen Ente **8**

Ambiente Hotel Struber **11**

Arthotel Blaue Gans **3**

Boutiquehotel am Dom **9**

Christkönig Kolleg **10**

Hotel Elefant **6**

Hotel Goldener Hirsch **4**

Johannes Schlössl der Pallottiner **2**

Schloss Mönchstein **1**

Schwärzler Hotel Neutor **5**

New Town Lodging

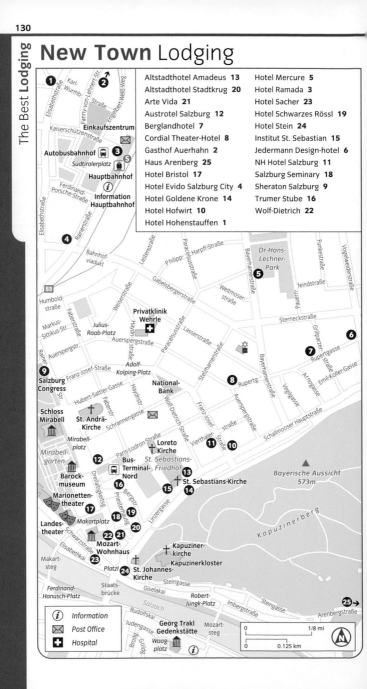

Altstadthotel Amadeus **13**	Hotel Mercure **5**
Altstadthotel Stadtkrug **20**	Hotel Ramada **3**
Arte Vida **21**	Hotel Sacher **23**
Austrotel Salzburg **12**	Hotel Schwarzes Rössl **19**
Berglandhotel **7**	Hotel Stein **24**
Cordial Theater-Hotel **8**	Institut St. Sebastian **15**
Gasthof Auerhahn **2**	Jedermann Design-hotel **6**
Haus Arenberg **25**	NH Hotel Salzburg **11**
Hotel Bristol **17**	Salzburg Seminary **18**
Hotel Evido Salzburg City **4**	Sheraton Salzburg **9**
Hotel Goldene Krone **14**	Trumer Stube **16**
Hotel Hofwirt **10**	Wolf-Dietrich **22**
Hotel Hohenstauffen **1**	

(ℹ) Information

✉ Post Office

✚ Hospital

Southern Outskirts Lodging

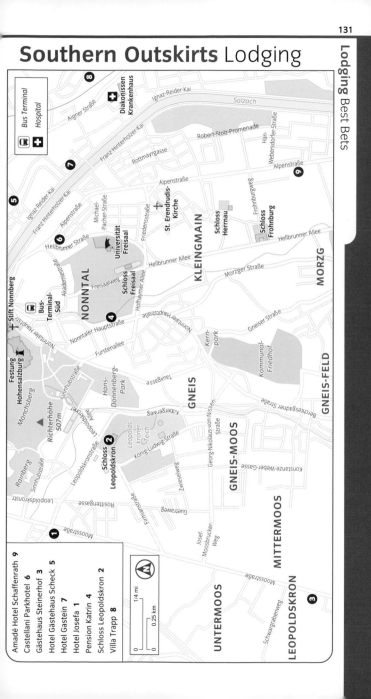

Amadé Hotel Schaffenrath 9
Castellani Parkhotel 6
Gästehaus Steinerhof 3
Hotel Gästehaus Scheck 5
Hotel Gastein 7
Hotel Josefa 1
Pension Katrin 4
Schloss Leopoldskron 2
Villa Trapp 8

Bus Terminal
Hospital

1/4 mi
0.25 km

Salzburg Lodging **A to Z**

Altstadthotel Amadeus.

www.austria-trend.at. *62 units. Doubles 245€–600€ w/breakfast. AE, DC, MC, V. Map p 129.*

★★ **Altstadthotel Amadeus** NEW TOWN I just love the views over the cemetery of St. Sebastian, where Mozart's father lies. Evocative corridors give way to modern rooms, some with four-posters, some six-bed family apartments. Good breakfast, and free afternoon coffee. *Linzergasse 43.* ☎ *0662/871401. www.hotel amadeus.at. 26 units. Doubles 100€– 180€ w/breakfast. AE, DC, MC, V. Map p 130.*

★★ **Altstadthotel Stadtkrug** NEW TOWN This is *so* Salzburg—a burgher's house snuggling against the Kapuzinerberg rock. The comfortable, modern rooms provide an agreeable contrast with the romantic setting. *Linzergasse 20.* ☎ *0662/ 873545. www.stadtkrug.at. 35 units. Doubles 135€–200€. AE, DC, MC, V. Map p 130.*

★★★ **Altstadt Radisson SAS** OLD TOWN It might sound like something big and modern, but this is a pink-washed inn dating back to 1377. Now a five-star hotel, its location is perfect. Some rooms have wooden beams, and there's a courtyard. *Rudolfskai 28.* ☎ *0662/8485710.*

Where to Stay

Where should you stay? Well, Salzburg's Old Town is the hub with some of the most classic, historic hotels. By and large, the price reflects this, but don't fear if they're out of your price range. The Old Town is also the busiest area and can be a little overwhelming. Head across the river and, as well as the biggest, swishest hotels (the Bristol (p 135) and Sacher (p 137)), you'll find many more reasonable properties. In the streets opposite the Mirabell Gardens, there are friendly, historic places like the Austrotel (p 133) and the smart, bright NH Hotel (p 138). Not only are prices more reasonable but you can enjoy a pleasing walk to and from the sights. Generally, the hotels around the station are cheaper but the surroundings are blandly European, you have none of the feel of staying in a classic city, and it's a goodly walk (or bus ride) from where you want to be. Hotels in treelined outskirts can be a good choice, offering a countryside air while rarely being far from bus or train stations, or even a pretty hike or bike ride from town.

★ Altstadthotel Zur Goldenen Ente

OLD TOWN   Sitting on the picturesque Goldgasse in the heart of the Old Town, the hotel dates back to the 14th century and offers style at a moderate price. Don't miss the roof terrace at happy hour. *Goldgasse 10.* ☎ *0662/845622. www.ente.at. 17 units. Doubles 110€–160€. AE, DC, MC, V. Map p 129.*

Amadé Hotel Schaffenrath

OUTSKIRTS   This is an excellent business base: eight meeting rooms, and apartments each with meeting space, kitchenette, extra beds, and connecting doors. It's also a good base for exploring the city and countryside. *Alpenstrasse 115–117.* ☎ *0662/639000. www.amadehotel.at. 48 units, 28 apartments. Doubles 128€–218€ w/breakfast. AE, DC, MC, V. Bus: 3, 8, 28, 840. Map p 131.*

★★ Ambiente Hotel Struber

OLD TOWN   A good-value place with a family atmosphere on the sunny plain beneath the Hohenfestung. Rooms are cozy and traditional; some have a balcony and a view of the fortress. It's a 10-minute walk, passing the Nonnberg Convent, into the Old Town, and a pretty stroll out to the Leopoldskron Palace. *Nonntaler Hauptstrasse 35.* ☎ *0662/843728. www.struber.at. 14 units. Doubles 90€–168€ w/breakfast. AE, MC, V. Map p 129.*

★★★ Arte Vida

NEW TOWN   This is a bizarre Moroccan-themed retreat with individually designed rooms, satellite TV, and free Wi-Fi, along with a courtyard garden (shared with the Mozart Residence, p 16, ➎). There's a communal kitchen or you can buy breakfast. *Dreifaltigkeitsgasse 9.* ☎ *0662/873185. www.artevida.at. 5 units. Doubles 70€–120€. AE, MC, V. Map p 130.*

★★ Arthotel Blaue Gans

OLD TOWN   Claiming to be Salzburg's oldest inn (650 years old), the 'Blue Goose' has undergone a 21st-century rebirth. Cool decor and original art in rooms are in contrast to the ancient stone vaults housing the restaurant. *Getreidegasse 43.* ☎ *0662/84219150. www.blauegans.at. 40 units. Doubles 130€–250€ w/breakfast. AE, DC, MC, V. Map p 129.*

★★★ Austrotel Salzburg

NEW TOWN   The former palace of Archbishop Paris Lodron, this is now a smart place to stay opposite the Mirabell Gardens (p 12, ➓). My children loved the free soft drinks and free Internet in the lobby, while we relaxed with a free coffee. *Paris-Lodron-Strasse 1.* ☎ *0662/8816880. www.austrotel.at. 73 units. Doubles 210€ w/breakfast. AE, DC, MC, V. Map p 130.*

Many of Salzburg's best hotels are close to the river.

Salzburg Card Packages

The local tourist board (www.salzburg.info) puts together reasonably priced packages for 2 or 3 nights in conjunction with its Salzburg Card (p 165). The packages give accommodation in a selection of three- and four-star hotels and a Salzburg Card, which gives entry to all attractions and use of public transport during the period. Prices depend on the season, and vary from around 100€ to 190€ per break. There are small discounts for children. The website also offers a general booking service for most hotels in Salzburg.

★★ **Berglandhotel** NEW TOWN
A small, well-priced hotel that combines Austrian warmth with modern simplicity. It's in a quiet street away from the tourist trail (although just along from the Die Weisse brewpub). It boasts a solarium and a delightful roof terrace. *Rupertgasse 15.* ☎ *0662/ 872318. www.berglandhotel.at. 18 units. Doubles 95€–108€ w/breakfast. AE, MC, V. Map p 130.*

★★ **Boutiquehotel am Dom**
OLD TOWN   On the outside, this

Berglandhotel.

hotel looks traditional; inside, it's been refurbed, so ancient stone steps and wooden ceilings complement white rooms, modern art, and soft lighting. *Goldgasse 17.* ☎ *0662/ 842765. www.hotelamdom.at. 15 units. Doubles 140€–220€. AE, DC, MC, V. Map p 129.*

Castellani Parkhotel OUTSKIRTS
This big hotel complex combines an old house and newer buildings that have been finished to a charming, if businesslike, effect in parklike gardens, with a baroque wedding chapel and an old priory. There are conference facilities and two restaurants. *Alpenstrasse 6.* ☎ *0662/ 20600. www.hotel-castellani.com. 151 units. Doubles 150€–230€. AE, DC, MC, V. Bus: 3, 8, 28, 840. Map p 131.*

★★ **Christkönig Kolleg** OLD
TOWN   A guesthouse at the foot of the Mönchsberg that's part of the Archbishopric Salzburg—during term time it also accommodates female students. The prices are very reasonable (singles from 36€) although some have shared showers and WC, but there's a decent breakfast buffet included. *Kapitelplatz 2A.* ☎ *0662/842627. www.christkoenig-kolleg.at. 20 units. Doubles 70€–84€ w/breakfast. MC, V. Map p 129.*

Hotel Bristol is one of Salzburg's best addresses, opposite Mozart's Residence.

Cordial Theater-Hotel NEW TOWN This historic building oozes Salzburg style with an attractive lobby bar, and a hidden garden. The Barcarole restaurant serves local and international cuisine while the Intermezzo cafe with its terrace is good for lighter fare. There's also massage, sauna, and solarium. *Schallmooser Hauptstrasse 13.* ☎ *0662/881681. www.cordial.at. 58 units. Doubles 139€–218€ w/breakfast. AE, DC, MC, V. Map p 130.*

★★ Gästehaus Steinerhof OUT-SKIRTS It's difficult to resist the red deer and the lush grounds of this charming guesthouse. Resident chickens provide breakfast, and there are pretty, traditional rooms. Town is a short bus ride away. *Moosstrasse 138.* ☎ *0662/826280. www.gaestehaus-steinerhof.at. 8 units. Doubles 60€ w/breakfast. AE, MC, V. Bus: 60. Map p 130.*

Gasthof Auerhahn NEW TOWN Families would do well to seek out this guesthouse past the station but only a bus hop (most lines) or mostly riverside stroll from the sights. It comes complete with a great breakfast buffet in an award-winning restaurant. *Bahnhofstrasse 15.* ☎ *0662/451052. www.auerhahn-salzburg.at. 15 units. Doubles 72€–85€ w/breakfast. AE, MC, V. Map p 130.*

★★ Haus Arenberg NEW TOWN A B&B on the slopes of the Kapuzinerberg. It's just away from the river in pretty gardens (and a garden room for the big buffet breakfast) with gorgeous views of the city and mountains from most rooms. *Blumensteinstrasse 8.* ☎ *0662/640097. www.arenberg-salzburg.at. 13 units. Doubles 125€–160€ w/breakfast. AE, MC, V. Map p 130.*

★★★ Hotel Bristol NEW TOWN A classic grand European affair on a square facing Mozart's Residence. Gloriously over-the-top rooms are decorated in the style of historical eras. The Polo Lounge restaurant (p 104) creates seasonal Austrian and Italian specialties. *Makartplatz 4.* ☎ *0662/8735570. www.bristol-salzburg.at. 60 units. Doubles 215€–670€ w/breakfast. AE, DC, MC, V. Map p 130.*

★★★ Hotel Elefant OLD TOWN Tucked away down a small street in the heart of the city you'll find this 700-year-old palace. It's a Best Western hotel but retains all its Austrian character, including a restaurant with vaulted ceilings and local dishes with an international touch. *Sigmund-Haffner-Gasse 4.* ☎ *0662/843397. www.elefant.at. 60 units.*

Doubles from 210€ w/breakfast. AE, DC, MC, V. Map p 129.

Hotel Evido Salzburg City NEW TOWN   This small but stylish hotel has simple yet sophisticated rooms including flatscreen TVs. It's a few minutes' walk in from the station, and near the river. Good breakfast buffet. Free laptop rental. *Rainerstrasse 25.* ☎ *0662/875400. www. evido.at. 20 units. Doubles 86€–138€ w/breakfast. AE, MC, V. Map p 130.*

★★ Hotel Gästehaus Scheck OUTSKIRTS   The feel of a chateau—white rooms and dark furniture, set in a country garden—makes this a splendid getaway. Yet it's just off the river past the Kapuzinerberg. *Rennbahnstrasse 11.* ☎ *0662/623268. www.hotel-scheck.com. 10 units. Doubles 90€–110€ w/breakfast. AE, MC, V. Map p 131.*

★★ Hotel Gastein OUTSKIRTS The 15-minute walk to the sights from this villa on the Salzach is stunning. You can sit and enjoy the views of the mountains and fortress from the lounge in the garden. Inside the hotel, the hand-carved stairs lead to traditionally furnished rooms. *Ignaz*

Rieder Kai 25.* ☎ *0662/622565. www.hotel-gastein.at. 14 units. Doubles 118€–168€ w/breakfast. AE, MC, V. Map p 131.*

Hotel Goldene Krone NEW TOWN   A great setting—backing onto the Kapuzinerberg with a courtyard set into the rock—makes this 15th-century family-run hotel a joy. Great views across the city skyline. *Linzergasse 48.* ☎ *0662/872300. www.hotel-goldenekrone.com. 24 units. Doubles 84€–130€ w/breakfast. AE, DC, MC, V. Map p 130.*

★★★ Hotel Goldener Hirsch OLD TOWN   A star in Salzburg's crown, this is a 15th-century inn turned sleek international property (part of the Starwood Luxury Collection), which has all the flair and style you'd hope for from the city. It's the discreet home to musical stars during the Festival. *Getreidegasse 37.* ☎ *0662/80840. www.goldener hirsch.com. 69 units. Doubles 170€–615€. AE, DC, MC, V. Map p 129.*

Hotel Hofwirt NEW TOWN   An 1898 property given a modernistic makeover with bright rooms and a smart bar. It's just off Linzergasse at

Let's Go Camping

Salzburg might not seem like a city for campsites, but there are several within easy reach of the center. **Camping Nord-Sam** (www.camping-nord-sam.com) is just north of the New Town and on the no. 23 bus route. Set in a pine forest, there's a big open-air pool and rentable cycles for a streamside trail into the city. **Panorama Camping Stadblick** (www.panorama-camping.at) is close by (near the nos. 3, 5, and 23 bus routes) and is more open with big city and mountain views. **Camping Kasern** (www.camping-kasern-salzburg. com) is the wrong side of the A1 autoroute, but the no. 21 bus stops outside, and there are big, ready-pitched tents to rent. **Camping Schloss Aigen** (www.campingaigen.com) is to the south of the city, in a nice spot at the foot of the Gaisberg mountain, but a bit of a walk from transport (bus no. 7/Salzberg Aigen station).

Hotel Sacher, seen from across the river.

the end of the traffic-free thorough-fare, so quiet while still only a short stroll to the river. *Schallmooser Hauptstrasse 1. ☎ 0662/8721720. www.hofwirt.net. 15 units. Doubles 82€–125€ w/breakfast. AE, MC, V. Map p 130.*

Hotel Hohenstauffen NEW TOWN Built when the trains arrived (1860) and run by the same family for a cen-tury, this is perfect for the station area. There are four-poster beds, a baroque lounge, and a cycle room. *Elisabethstrasse 19. ☎ 0662/ 872193. www.hotel-hohenstauffen.at. 31 units. Doubles 95€–145€ w/break-fast. AE, MC, V. Map p 130.*

Hotel Josefa OUTSKIRTS A cen-tury-old hotel in a country setting with a secluded garden between the Old Town and Leopoldskron Palace. The city's attractions are walkable, or it's 5 minutes by bus. Reasonable prices and away from the hustle-bus-tle. *Nussdorferstrasse 5. ☎ 0662/ 825586. www.hotel-josefa.at. 15 rooms. Doubles 85€–125€ w/break-fast. AE, MC, V. Bus: 21, 22. Map p 131.*

kids Hotel Mercure NEW TOWN The Mercure is a modern chain hotel in a quiet street 10 minutes' walk from the river. Ideal for families, chil-dren can stay free in the parents' room and there's a children's menu in the restaurant. *Bayerhamerstrasse 14. ☎ 0662/ 8814380. www.mercure. at. 121 units. Doubles 115€–175€. AE, MC, V. Bus: 2. Map p 130.*

★ Hotel Ramada NEW TOWN Chain hotel right by the station but with a touch of flair—a sixth-floor restaurant, smart roof terrace, and two-floor spa. *Südtiroler Platz 13. ☎ 0662/22850. www.ramada.de. 120 units. Doubles 75€–200€. AE, MC, V. Map p 130.*

★★★ Hotel Sacher NEW TOWN Along with the Bristol (p 135), this is Salzburg's five-star height, on the river, awash with antiques and run by the family of the Sachertorte dessert

The Hotel Stein's roof terrace offers wonderful views of the city.

The beautiful Schloss Leopoldskron, formerly an archbishop's palace.

creator. The Zirbelzimmer, with river terrace and original wood ceiling, is one of four places to dine. *Schwarzstrasse 5–7.* ☎ *0662/889770. www.sacher.com. 112 units. Doubles 276€–980€ w/breakfast. AE, DC, MC, V. Map p 130.*

★★★ Hotel Schwarzes Rössl
NEW TOWN   Tucked away in a little street off Linzergasse, this 15th-century building makes a pleasing hideaway, full of wood and white walls. The rooms are charmingly traditional, even if many lack en-suite facilities. *Priesterhausgasse 6.* ☎ *0662/84426. www.academiahotels.at. 50 units. Doubles 50€–66€. AE, DC, MC, V. Map p 130.*

★★★ Hotel Stein NEW TOWN
Wedged between the river and Kapuzinerburg, the views—particularly from the rooftop cafe-bar, one

of my favorite Salzburg spots—are stupendous. The Stein opened in 1399, and was turned into a design icon in 2003. *Giselakai 3–5.* ☎ *0662/8743460. www.hotelstein.at. 17 units. Doubles 169€–219€ w/breakfast. AE, DC, MC, V. Map p 130.*

★ Institut St. Sebastian NEW
TOWN   A guesthouse, youth hostel, and student dorm at St. Sebastian Church. There's no age limit, but it's for the young-at-heart with communal lounges, kitchens, and laundry in an ancient setting. It has regular en-suite rooms as well as dorms (beds around 20€). *Linzer Gasse 41.* ☎ *0662/871386. www.st-sebastian-salzburg.at. 110 beds incl. 3 10-bed dorms. Doubles 55€–70€. MC, V. Map p 130.*

★ Jedermann Design-hotel
NEW TOWN   A grandiose 1830s

Religious Rooms

Several places linked to the city's religious orders offer simple and very reasonably priced lodging. The **Christkönig Kolleg** (p 134) has an enviably central position and rooms with breakfast from 35€ per person. Nearby is the **Seminary Guesthouse** (p 139) where other people staying will be candidates to the priesthood of the diocese. **Johannes Schlössl der Pallottiner** (above) is high on the Mönchsberg while the **Institut St. Sebastian** (above) offers rooms and dormitories in Linzergasse on the other side of the river.

building with cool, modern rooms and family apartments, some with a garden. Breakfast in the hidden garden is a treat. The atmosphere might be sleek, but the place is friendly and family-run. A good family choice. *Rupertgasse 25.* ☎ *0662/ 873240. www.hotel-jedermann.com. 15 units. Doubles 95€–160€ w/ breakfast. AE, MC, V. Map p 130.*

★★ Johannes Schlössl der Pallottiner OLD TOWN Atop the

Mönchsberg is the religious retreat of the Pallottiner monks amid trees and gardens, with stunning views, and only a stroll from the Augustiner beer hall (p 115). Guest rooms are light and simple; breakfast and dinner is served in the hall for 7.50€. *Mönchsberg 24.* ☎ *0662/846543. http://pallottiner.szg.at. 55 units. Doubles 80€–100€. No credit cards. Map p 129.*

★★ NH Hotel Salzburg NEW

TOWN A bright chain hotel, used by tourists and businessmen alike, in a quiet spot just off historic Linzergasse with a relaxed bar and sauna. Special packages have extras such as bike hire. *Franz-Josef-Strasse 26.* ☎ *0662/ 8820410. www.nh-hotels.com. 140 units. Doubles 110€–210€ w/breakfast. AE, DC, MC, V. Map p 130.*

Schloss Mönchstein, atop the Mönchsberg.

Pension Katrin OUTSKIRTS If you enjoy cycling, this unassuming *pension* (small, family-run hotel) with sunny patio in a green and pleasant area south of the Old Town is handy for various cycle paths as well as Hellbrunn and Leopoldskron. *Nonntaler Hauptstrasse 49.* ☎ *0662/ 830860. www.members.aon.at/ pensionkatrin.at. 12 units. Doubles 90€–125€ w/breakfast. DC, MC, V. Bus: 5, 22, 25. Map p 131.*

Salzburg Seminary NEW TOWN A simple guesthouse that is home to trainee priests, but also open to the public. Breakfast, all organic or FairTrade, is 6€. Cheap and central. *Dreifaltigkeitsgasse 14.* ☎ *0662/ 87749545. www.kirchen.net/priester seminar. 60 units in July–Aug, 22 from Oct–June. Doubles 46€–78€. No credit cards. Map p 130.*

★★★ Schloss Leopoldskron

OUTSKIRTS An absurdly beautiful former archbishop's palace renovated by Salzburg Festival founder Max Reinhardt, and famed for its role as the lakeside Trapp mansion in *The Sound of Music*. It has been owned by a private foundation since 1947 but is now opening rooms to outside guests. There are palace suites (the Reinhardt Suite has a secret passage to the library) and rooms in the adjoining Meierhof building. You're likely to mix with visitors here for seminars, but you have the run of the palace and grounds, and get breakfast in the Marble Hall or in the mirrored Venetian Room, recreated by Hollywood for the film. Dinner is served for group bookings. If you're not a guest, you won't get to see any of this—it's behind locked gates. *Leopoldskronstrasse 56.* ☎ *0662/ 839830. www.schloss-leopoldskron. com. 66 units. Doubles 98€–145€; Reinhardt Suite 350€ w/breakfast. AE, DC, MC, V. Bus: 22. Map p 131.*

★★★ **Schloss Mönchstein** OLD TOWN Atop the Mönchsberg with city views and treelined walks, this is boutique luxury. Rooms and suites are individually furnished in Vienna Workshop style or in castle character. You can borrow a laptop, and eat in the glass-fronted restaurant. *Mönchsberg Park 26.* ☎ *0662/ 8485550. www.monchstein.at. 24 units. Doubles 240€–1,200€ w/breakfast. AE, DC, MC, V. Bus: 25. Map p 129.*

Schwärzler Hotel Neutor OLD TOWN Behind the Mönchsberg, just a short walk through the mountain parking cave to the sights, this hotel brands itself as the 'meeting place for artists' and features work by local and international artists. *Neutorstrasse 8.* ☎ *0662/8441540. www.s-hotels.com. 89 units. Doubles 85€–186€ w/breakfast. AE, MC, V. Map p 129.*

★★ **Sheraton Salzburg** NEW TOWN You know what you're getting at this glossy international luxury hotel, with a gourmet restaurant serving international cuisine and Austrian favorites. *Auerspergstrasse 4.*

☎ *0662/889990. www.sheraton.com/ salzburg. 162 units. Doubles 125€– 450€. AE, DC, MC, V. Map p 130.*

Trumer Stube NEW TOWN The flower-bedecked windows draw you to this pink-painted hotel tucked away between Mirabell Gardens and Linzergasse. Simple, baroque-tinged rooms make this a pleasant retreat. *Bergstrasse 6.* ☎ *0662/84776. www. trumer-stube.at. 20 units. Doubles 89€–135€ w/breakfast. AE, MC, V. Map p 130.*

★★★ **Villa Trapp** OUTSKIRTS This is the real Trapp home (not the one in The Sound of Music movie), a country mansion set in parkland. The family lived here from 1923 to 1938 (when they fled the Nazis) and it was owned by a religious order until 2008. It's now a sophisticated B&B with simple, dark furniture, and a private chapel where you can get married. There's also an exhibition on the history of the house and the Trapps' fate, and a Sound of Music theme in the park. Although there's a country feel, you're only minutes from the station (which is minutes from the city) and bus stop. *Traunstrasse 34.* ☎ *0662/630860. www.villa-trapp. com. 14 units. Doubles 105€–225€ w/breakfast. AE, DC, MC, V. Train: Bahnhof Aigen; Bus: 7. Map p 131.*

★ **Wolf-Dietrich** NEW TOWN A classic Austrian hotel with buildings on either side of the street. Smart decor and—a rarity here—a swimming pool and spa. The hotel's restaurant, Ährlich, claims to be Austria's first licensed organic restaurant. *Wolf-Dietrich-Strasse 7.* ☎ *0662/ 871275. www.salzburg-hotel.at. 40 units. Doubles 119€–199€ w/break-fast. AE, MC, V. Map p 130.* ●

10 The Best Day Trips & Excursions

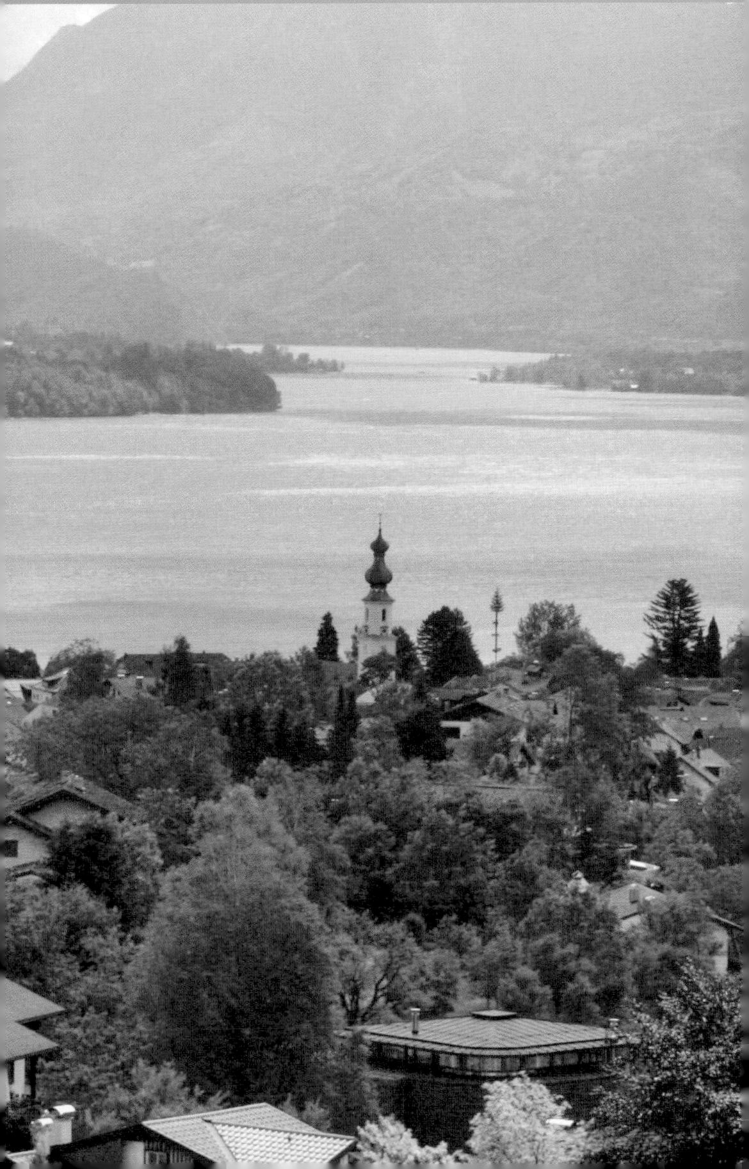

Salt, Rock & Ice

1. The road South
2. Salzwelten
3. Keltenmuseum
4. Gasthof Pass-Lueg-Hohe
5. Eisriesenwelt
6. Hohenwerfen Fortress

Mattsee

Mattsee

Straßwalchen

Neumarkt

Obertrum

Wallersee

Irrsee

Seekirchen

Henndorf

Kasten

Saaldorf

Eugendorf

Mondsee

Freilassing

Hallwang

A1

E55   E60

Bergheim

Thalgau

Mondsee

Plainfeld

Fuschlsee

Salzburg Airport
W.A. Mozart

Ebenau

Fuschl

Salzburg

A8

E52   E60

Glasenbach

Vordersee

St. Gilgen

Bad
Reichenhall

Anif

Wiestalstausee

Hintersee

▲
Zwölferhorn
1521m

Niederalm

Oberasch

Großmain

AUSTRIA

Hintersee

Marktschellenberg

1

Adnet

Hallein

20

Winkl

2   3

Vigaun

OSTERHORNGRUPPE

*Hoher
Zinken
1764m*
▲

Bischofswiesen

Berchtesgaden

305

Kuchl

GERMANY

*Watzmann
2713m*
▲

Königssee

Golling

Pichl

4

Oberscheffau

Königssee

Abtenau

NATIONALPARK
BERCHTESGADEN

Salet

Obersee

HAGENBIRGE

TENNENGEBIRGE

E55

5

*Bleikogel
2412m*
▲

STEINERNES   MEER

6

A10

Werfen

159

*Hochkönig
2940m*
▲

Hinterthal

| 0 | | 5 mi |
| 0 | | 5 km |

Previous page: Wolfgangsee.

This day out provides an overview of what the Salzburg region is all about, heading deep down into a salt mine and way up to a mountaintop castle, all within classic Alpine scenery. This is a great day for children, a roller-coaster ride of experiences. And all of it is an easy drive from Salzburg, whether you have a car or take a private taxi tour. START: **South down the A10 Tauern-Autobahn.**

1 The road South. The drive is a rather beautiful one. You're quickly clear of the city and you pass the craggy point of the Untersberg (p 84) off to the right, surging up from the flat surroundings. The valley passes between gradually rising mountains and follows the River Salzach until you reach the town of Hallein. 🕐 *30 min.*

Entering Hallein, follow signs to Salzwelten. After crossing the rail line, turn right at the roundabout, which takes you across the river before a sharp right onto Durnberg-Landestrasse, which passes Salzwelten 5 minutes up the mountain road.

2 ★★★ kids Salzwelten. A hole in the mountain that's fun for all the family. The experience starts when you put on a protective suit and continues on a train ride along a narrow tunnel. You'll creep along paths going back hundreds of years in a salt mine that only ceased production in 1989.

DER BERG, DER FÜRST UND SEINE STADT AUS SALZ

Sign in Hallein's Salzwelten.

You'll take two wooden slides (once used by miners hurrying to work), and a barge across a salt lake, all the while with an English-speaking guide, plus various film shows. For my children, the slides (one around 46m/150 ft.) that once rushed miners to work were a highlight of their time in Salzburg. Outside is a reconstructed village, on the same ticket, while entry here also gets you into the Keltenmuseum (**3**) in Hallein, 5 minutes down the mountain. 🕐 *1½ hr. Ramsaustrasse 3, Bad Dürrnberg.* ☎ *06132/ 2008511. www.salzwelten.at. Entry only on a tour. Admission 17€ adults, 10€ children 15 and under, 8€ children 6 and under. Daily Apr–Oct regular tours 9am–5pm, Nov–Mar hourly 10am–3pm.*

Retrace your steps, but just before crossing the river, turn right onto Brauerstrasse, then immediately left onto Colloredostrasse, and the museum is on your left.

A Land for Children

The SalzburgerLand is an ideal place to combine with the city if you have a family. The area has around 25 hotels dedicated to families, many with pools and playgrounds, as well as a number of farms that offer a true countryside experience. The latter work together (www.salzburg.farmholidays.com) and give youngsters the chance to get involved with animals, try out many kinds of adventure, and eat farm-fresh produce.

SalzburgerLand Card

What the Salzburg Card (p 165) does for the city, this does for the whole region. The SalzburgerLand Card includes admission to almost 200 sights and attractions across the area, from mountain lifts to mines, trains to lake cruises. The card costs 43€ for 6 days (and just 52€ for 12 days) with children half price. It also includes entry to most of Salzburg's attractions for a 24-hour period. www.salzburgerlandcard.com. See p 165 for more details. **Salzburger-Land Tourism** (☎ 0662/668866, www.salzburgerland.com) also has details of what to do and where to go in the region.

3 Keltenmuseum. In the middle of Hallein, this modern museum tells the history of the Celts who made their fortunes hundreds of years ago mining salt from the mountains. It occupies Hallein's largest non-religious building, what was for several centuries the HQ of the 'Salina' plant including salt-drying rooms. The stylish, fascinating exhibits, with English explanations, also detail how salt was mined. ⏱ *30 min. Pflegerplatz 5, Hallein.* ☎ *06245/80783. www.keltenmuseum.at. Admission 6€ adults, 2.50€ children 19 and under, free 6 and under. Daily 9am–5pm.*

Head south on the *autobahn* for a few minutes, take the Golling exit, then turn right and follow the old road a short distance up the Pass-Lueg-Hohe.

4 Gasthof Pass-Lueg-Hohe. Stop for lunch at this delightful hotel and restaurant on Pass Lueg, a little road bypassed by a tunnel near the A10 Tauern-Autobahn. Nestled in the mountains are views of mighty peaks almost close enough to touch from the picture windows and terrace. The menu is full of local produce including mountain fish as well as seasonal specialties such as asparagus (soup, risotto) in spring. The Tauernradweg cycle path passes the door. ☎ *06244/4280. www.pass-lueg-hoehe.com. $$.*

Hohenwerfen Fortress dominates the surrounding area.

Birds of prey display at Hohenwerfen Fortress.

Follow the pass, the B159, which soon dips under the *autobahn* and parallels it south for 10 minutes before you pass the Hohenwerfen Fortress car park, from where a shuttle bus runs to Eisriesenwelt along the road.

5 ★★ **kids** **Eisriesenwelt.** It brags of being the world's biggest ice cave and who could doubt it. You get to walk almost 1.5km (1 mile) through huge caverns where a sea of ice (which partially melts in summer) drifts and creates strange formations—and it's not hard to believe that there are another 40km (25 miles) beyond the boundaries of the guided tour. There's no electric light, just hand-held lamps. The whole place is an adventure with a 20-minute walk (it's not ideal for younger children) from the car park, a cable car ride, then another walk before the 70-minute tour. ⏱ 1½–2 hr. Wimstrasse 24, Werfen. ☎ 06468/5248. www.eisriesenwelt. at. Admission 19€ adults, 9.50€ children 14 and under. Daily May–Oct 9am, last tour at 3:30pm (4:30pm July–Aug).

6 ★★ **kids** **Hohenwerfen Fortress.** A mountaintop castle that has 900 years of history, yet which is best known as the setting of the classic war movie *Where Eagles Dare* starring Clint Eastwood and Richard Burton. The massive stone walls and circular turrets with pointy roofs flow down the ridgeline in fairy-tale fashion. You can hike up, but a new funicular (so steep it's almost an elevator) is easier, and included in the admission price. There are fabulous views up and down the valley and the whole place has the feel of an adventure playground with steep paths, steep lawns, and steep steps. Get here for 11am or 3pm when there's a free falconry demonstration (there are more in high summer) featuring eagles and vultures the size of Spitfires. ⏱ 1hr. ☎ 06468/7603. www. salzburg-burgen.at. Admission 14€ adults, 7.50€ children 15 and under. 10.50/5.50€ without elevator. Daily Apr–Oct 9am–4pm; May, June, Sept 5pm; July, Aug 6pm; closed Mon Apr.

The view from Hohenwerfen Fortress.

Salzkammergut

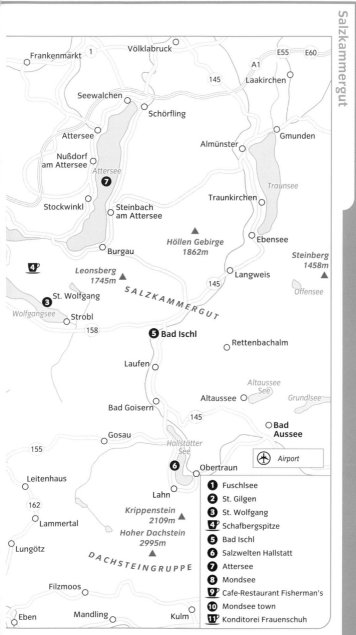

Frankenmarkt
Völklabruck
1
E55 E60
A1
Laakirchen
145
Seewalchen
Schörfling
Gmunden
Almünster
Attersee
Nußdorf
am Attersee
Attersee
7
Traunkirchen
Traunsee
Stockwinkl
Steinbach
am Attersee
Burgau
Ebensee
*Höllen Gebirge
1862m*
*Steinberg
1458m*
4
*Leonsberg
1745m*
Langweis
S A L Z K A M M E R G U T
145
Offensee
3 St. Wolfgang
Wolfgangsee
Strobl
158
5 Bad Ischl
Rettenbachalm
Laufen
*Altaussee
See*
Grundlsee
Altaussee
Bad Goisern
145
O**Bad
Aussee**
Gosau
*Hallstätter
See*
155
✈ Airport
Leitenhaus
6
Obertraun
162
Lahn
Lammertal
*Krippenstein
2109m*
Lungötz
*Hoher Dachstein
2995m*
D A C H S T E I N G R U P P E
Filzmoos
Eben
Mandling
Kulm

1 Fuschlsee
2 St. Gilgen
3 St. Wolfgang
4 Schafbergspitze
5 Bad Ischl
6 Salzwelten Hallstatt
7 Attersee
8 Mondsee
9 Cafe-Restaurant Fisherman's
10 Mondsee town
11 Konditorei Frauenschuh

This is Salzburg's lake district, only a half-hour drive yet a different world. It's a place that has long been wealthy through the salt mined here. The name means 'Estate of the Salt Chamber' and comes from the Imperial Salt Chamber, the authority that ran the salt mines during the Habsburg Empire between the 15th and 18th centuries. **START: East along Schallmooser Hauptstrasse.**

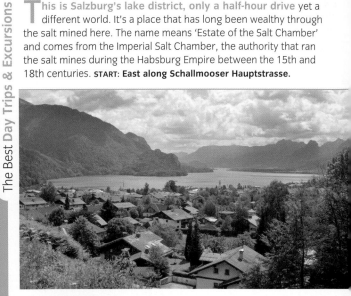

St. Gilgen and Wolfgangsee.

TRAVEL TIP

It is possible to get the no. 150 bus from Salzburg to Fuschl, St. Gilgen, and Bad Ischl, and then the no. 356 from St. Gilgen to Mondsee, but the tour really only works with a car.

Along Schallmooser Hauptstrasse, take a right onto Minnesheim-strasse, which twists back on itself for a moment as it climbs (offering a brief but beautiful cityscape). This road, the B158, takes you straight to the lake.

➊ ★ **Fuschlsee.** Drive along the length of the lake, about 6km (4 miles), then drop down into the village of Fuschl. It's a pretty place for a short stroll, or you can head off along the lakeside path for a longer hike. ⏱ *30 min.* ☎ *06626/83840. www.fuschlseeregion.com.*

Keep going along the B158 for 14km (8 miles) to:

➋ ★ **kids** **St. Gilgen.** After emerging from the hilltop forest, you'll be wowed by one of Austria's great views, looking down on the village of St. Gilgen with **Lake Wolfgang (Wolfgangsee)** stretching out before you, surrounded by hazy peaks. The village is a popular year-round holiday spot and you can sun yourself on the promenade, take a variety of boat trips, or ride the small **cable car** up the Zwölferhorn. St. Gilgen was the home of Mozart's mother, Anna Pertl, and the house where she was born is the **Mozart Haus St. Gilgen,** a small museum devoted to the composer's life. There are also walks up into the hills. ⏱ *1 hr.* ☎ *06138/8003. www.wolfgangsee.at. Cable car: Raiffeisen-strasse.* ☎ *06227/2350. www.12erhorn.at. Daily 8am–6pm. Return tickets 19€ adults, 13.50€ children 16 and under. Mozart Haus St. Gilgen:*

Ischlerstrasse 15. ☎ *06227/2348. www.mozartdorf.at. June–Sept Tues–Sun 10am–noon, 3–5pm. Admission 4€ adults, 2.50€ children 18 and under, free 5 and under.*

Follow the B158 down to the end of the lake then round to the other side, around 18km (12 miles).

❸ ★★ kids St. Wolfgang. On the other side of the lake you'll find the village of St. Wolfgang, a bustling, touristy hub although beautiful with it. There are lots of quaint buildings and the ornate, lakeside **Church of St. Wolfgang,** with its large gilded carved altar. A must-do attraction is the **SchafbergBahn,** a cog steam train which clacks up to the peak of the 1,783m (5,800 ft.) Schafberg, a dizzying, jagged ridge with views of Wolfgangsee in one direction, Attersee in the other. ⏱ *3 hr.* ☎ *06138/ 8003. www.wolfgangsee.at. SchafbergBahn: Markt 35.* ☎ *06138/2232. www.schafbergbahn.at. Daily May–Oct 9:15am–5pm. Return tickets 28.60€ adults, 14.30€ children 14 and under, free 5 and under.*

❹ Schafbergspitze. At the pinnacle of the Schafberg, this ludicrously sited hotel and restaurant has nevertheless been a success since 1862. The dark, traditional restaurant features traditional Austrian dishes,

although I'd suggest you go for a coffee on the terrace (taking a sweater as it's a breezy spot). *Ried 23, St. Wolfgang.* ☎ *06138/3542. www. schafberg.net. $$.*

Drive another 13km (8 miles) east along the B168 until you get to:

❺ ★★ Bad Ischl. This small town was a royals' spa resort in the days of the Austro-Hungarian empire. Here is the **Kaiservilla,** summer residence of Emperor Franz Josef. It is open daily for tours, which also include the English-Elizabethan-style cottage in the park the Emperor had built for his Empress Sissi. Sissi's private swimming pool is now open under the name **Bad Ischl Parkbad,** expanded with slide, whitewater canal, and children's pool. The small town has narrow streets and smart, yellow-painted buildings. ⏱ *1½–2 hr.* ☎ *06132/277570. www.badischl. com. Kaiservilla: Jainzen 38.* ☎ *06132/23241. www.kaiservilla.at. Daily Apr–Oct, varying times between 9:30am and 5pm, and Advent weekends 10am–4pm. Admission 4.50€ adults, 3.50€ children 16 and under, free 6 and under. Parkbad: Emperor Franz-Josef-Strasse 19.* ☎ *06132/ 26991. Daily May–Sept 9am–7pm. Admission varies on facilities used between 1.50€ and 5€.*

Boat trips on the Wolfgangsee.

SchafbergBahn.

Drive south along the B145 for around 12km (7 miles), turning right to follow the western side of Hallstättersee, the same distance again until you reach:

6 ★★ Salzwelten Hallstatt. This is a Salzwelten attraction linked to Salzwelten Hallein (p. 143, **2**), which involves tours with hard hats and lamps, deep inside the mountain, showing traces of 7,000 years of salt mining including wall markings and what is believed to be the oldest staircase in the world. About the same distance from Bad Ischl (just keep on the B145 rather than turning right) is **Salzwelten Altaussee,** which also involves an underground tour, past glistening, salt-packed rock walls and down to a subterranean lake. These, of course, involve at least

The Schafbergspitze tops the breath-taking Schafberg.

an extra hour if you're planning a visit. ⏱ *1½–2 hr. Hallstatt: Salt Bergstrasse 1. ☎ 06132/277570. www.salzwelten.at. Admission 15€ adults, 10€ children 15 and under, 8€ children 6 and under. Tours 9:30am–3/3:30/4pm, late Mar–late Oct: Altaussee: Lights Berg 25. ☎ 06132/2002400. Admission 14€ adults, 8.50€ children 15 and under, 7€ children 6 and under. Tours 9am–3/4pm, late Mar–late Oct.*

From Hallstatt, head north on the A145 for 16km (10 miles), passing Bad Ischl then turning left onto the A153 at Mitterweissenbach. From here, it's 11km (8 miles) to:

7 kids Attersee. This is the biggest lake in the area, 20km (12 miles) long and 4km (2 miles) wide. There are beaches and parking spots, while the main village, Attersee, is at the other end of the lake. ⏱ *30 min.*

As you reach the lake, turn left onto the B152 for an 8-km (5-mile) lakeside drive. Turn left onto the A151 for 3km (2 miles) and you reach:

8 ★ kids Mondsee. Another of the region's major and most picturesque lakes. You emerge on the north bank and the road hugs the shore for most of the way, around 11km (8 miles), to the pretty, lively resort town of Mondsee at the far tip. Start by the lakefront (near where there is a car park) with its breathtaking views of lapping water surrounded by peaks. There's a park that runs along the water's edge with jetties to walk out on and plenty of grass to lie down on as well as an adventure playground, cafe, and restaurant. 🕐 *1 hr.*

🏆 Cafe-Restaurant Fisherman's. This is a glorious place for lunch with its south-facing, railed waterfront terrace—you could almost be adrift on a boat. The place concentrates on fish, particularly those from the lake as well as the mountain rivers. *Robert-Baum-Promenade 1, Mondsee.* ☎ *06232/ 36479. www.fishermans.at.* $$.

🔟 ★★ Mondsee town. A treelined avenue, the haunt of happy cyclists, leads away from the lake for a short stroll into the middle of Mondsee. This is an upmarket town of smart hotels and cake shops, the stylishness countered only slightly by an abundance of souvenir stalls and *The Sound of Music* coach parties. Most tourists come here for *The Sound of Music* connections—the ornate **Church of St. Michael** with its twin towers was the setting for the wedding of Maria and Captain von Trapp. 🕐 *1½ hr.* ☎ *06132/ 26909. www.mondsee.at.*

The ancient gates at the Salzwelten Hallstatt.

🔟🏆 Konditorei Frauenschuh. This busy, classic Austrian cafe and cake emporium on the town square is just along from the church. This is touted as having the country's best apple strudel, and it's certainly good, especially with the rich vanilla sauce. Tour parties fill the place out, but you should find a seat for a late afternoon rest, a perfect way to end the day. *Marktplatz 8, Mondsee.* ☎ *06232/2312. www.konditorei-frauenschuh.at.* $$.

From Mondsee, there are many routes back to Salzburg through the countryside but the A1 *autobahn* runs nearby and takes you straight back to the city in less than half an hour.

Salzkammergut Adventure Card

Even if you're only planning to visit a couple of attractions, the Salzkammergut Card generally involves a saving. It gives up to 30% off public transport including lake ferries, mountain railways, and lifts, along with salt mines, ice caves, scenic roads, nature parks, museums, swimming, and other activities. The card costs 4.90€ a day; there's no card for children 15 and under, who simply benefit from child rates. The card is available from tourist offices, shops, and hotels. See www.salzkammergut.at for details.

Berchtesgaden

■	Place of Interest
✈	Airport

① Almbach Gorge
② Berchtesgaden
③ Obersalzberg Documentation Center
④ Eagle's Nest
⑤ Kehlsteinhaus
⑥ Königssee

Just across the border in Germany you'll find stirring Alpine scenery and one of the most important surviving relics of the Third Reich, the Eagle's Nest. You can combine 20th-century history with timeless beauty, all set around the picturesque Bavarian town of Berchtesgaden. START: **Alpenstrasse.**

Head south on this main road which passes under the A10 *autobahn*, past St. Leonhard and the Untersberg cable car, all the way, as the B305, to Berchtesgaden, around 24km (15 miles).

1 ★★ kids **Almbach Gorge.** The entrance to this hidden wonderland is the car park by the Kugel-mühle Inn and Marble Mill outside Berchtesgaden on the road from Salzburg. A path leads through the imposing gorge and takes you, via wooden bridges and even a tunnel through the rock, past crashing waterfalls and swirling pools. As the gorge opens out there's a path through the woods to the church of Ettenberg with its historic frescoes, and cafe next door. The hike takes you steeply upward to a point where you can turn back (around an 80-minute round trip) or you can carry on to Ettenberg (around 2 hr 20 min return). Longer hikes take you all the way to the town of Berchtesgaden. ⏱ 2–3 hr. ☎ 08652/

9670. www.berchtesgadener-land. info. Admission 2.50€ adults, 1.30€ children 18 and under. Daily May–Oct 7:30am–7pm.

Leaving the gorge, it is only about 1.5km (1 mile) into:

2 ★ **Berchtesgaden.** This pretty Bavarian town is on the other side of the mountains from the town of Hallein and shares an age-old interest in salt mining. It's the heart of **Berchtesgaden National Park** and offers countless opportunities for hiking and biking. The imposing **Royal Palace** is still home to descendants of Bavarian royalty and combines Romanesque cloisters with a stunning Gothic hall, Biedermeier, and baroque styles across the centuries. Don't miss the hunting halls filled with their trophies and guns, and the rose gardens with their views. The **Grassl Schnapps Distillery** is the oldest in Germany and gives free tours and tastings. ⏱ 1 hr. ☎ 08652/9670. www.berchtesgadener-land.info.

Berchtesgaden and Mt Watzmann.

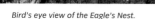

Bird's eye view of the Eagle's Nest.

*Royal Palace: Schlossplatz 2.
☎ 08652/947980. www.berchtes
gadener-land.info. Mid-May–mid-Oct
Sun–Fri, 10am–1pm, 2–5pm; Mon–
Fri 11am–2pm. Admission 7€ adults,
3€ children 17 and under. Grassl
Schnapps Distillery: Salzburger-
strasse 105. ☎ 08652/95360. www.
berchtesgadener-land.info. May–Oct
Mon–Fri 8am–6pm, Sat 9am–2pm;
Nov–Apr Mon–Fri 9am–6pm, Sat 9am–
4pm. Free admission.*

From town you can get a bus to
the Obersalzberg Documentation
Center. By car, it is about 2km
(1.5 miles) from the B305 (now
Berkwerkstrasse). Take the B319
Salzbergstrasse across the river
and you pass the Center as you
go up the hill.

❸ ★★★ Obersalzberg Docu-
mentation Center. The mountain
village of Obersalzberg, a holiday
retreat since the 1900s, is where
Adolf Hitler renovated a house to
live in and where he had his southern HQ, but pretty much anything
that wasn't obliterated by Allied
bombs was torn down after the war.
This smart museum (which opened
in 1999, part of Germany's Institute
of Contemporary History) sits on the
foundations of a former Nazi guesthouse, near the car park for Eagle's

Nest buses. It tells the chilling tale of
the Nazi regime and World War II
but also gets you into the vast, eerie
expanse of the underground bunker
system. ⏱ *1 hr. Obersalzberg-
strasse, Berchtesgaden. ☎ 08652/
947960. www.obersalzberg.de.
Admission 3€ adults, children free.
Apr–Oct, daily 9am–5pm; Nov–Mar
Tues–Sun 10am–3pm.*

Buses from the Center car park
are the only way up (apart from
walking) to:

❹ ★ **Eagle's Nest.** The bizarre
side of Nazi Germany. This lofty
retreat was Hitler's 50th birthday
present, masterminded by his right-
hand man, Martin Bormann, who
really should have known about the
Führer's dislike of heights. The
house, at 1,834m (6,017 ft.), was a
monumental statement, with a mar-
ble-lined tunnel leading from the car
park to an elevator with brass fit-
tings rising several hundred feet
through the rock of the Kehlstein
mountain, stopping within the
safety of the 1-m (3-ft.) thick walls.
Incredibly, it escaped Allied bombing and these features are still
there. The road especially built from
Obersalzberg was just as much a
feat of engineering. It's now closed
to public traffic and the only way to

A boat trip on Königssee.

visit is by a special bus from the Documentation Center car park, unless you fancy a 2- to 3-hour hike. The building has been a restaurant since 1952. ⏱ *2–3 hr.* ☎ *08652/ 9670. www.eagles-nest.de. Buses from Obersalzberg Documentation Center.* ☎ *08652/2029. www. berchtesgadener-land.info. Bus 15€ adults, 8.50€ children 14 and under. Daily mid-May–Oct. Obersalzberg parking 3€. Bus from Berchtesgaden to Obersalzberg*

(one way) 3€ adults, 1.50€ children 14 and under.

5 **Kehlsteinhaus.** The restaurant in the Eagle's Nest building is far from the iconic destination one might expect, but the setting of the granite-walled Grand Hall with its beams and chandeliers is worth a stop. The food is traditional Bavarian—sausages, sauerkraut, and schnitzel (the breadcrumbed and fried veal or pork dish)—and there's a terrace with phenomenal views if you just fancy a coffee or beer. ☎ *08652/61244. $$.*

Drive back into town and take the B20 south 6km (4 miles) to:

6 ★ **Königssee.** Germany's highest lake (603m/1,978 ft.) is only a short drive from Berchtesgaden, in Berchtesgadener National Park. It is 7.7km (5 miles) long, 190m (623 ft.) deep and framed by peaks such as Mt. Watzmann, the second highest in Bavaria. The best place to access it is the little town of **Schönau,** where there are electric boat rides across the incredibly clean waters to pretty **St. Bartholomä.** Often the guide plays a trumpet blast so you can hear the echoes as you sweep almost silently across. ⏱ *1 hr.* ●

Berchtesgaden Facts

Berchtesgaden is less than 24km (15 miles) from Salzburg, and the easiest way to explore the area is to hire a car (see 'Car Rentals,' p 159). Alternatively, take a train from Salzburg Hauptbahnhof to the town, a journey of around 45 minutes (departures around every 30 minutes). See www.bahn.de for details. There is also a bus (no. 840), which goes from the station as well as various spots in the city, including Rathausplatz on the Old Town riverbank.

The Savvy Traveler

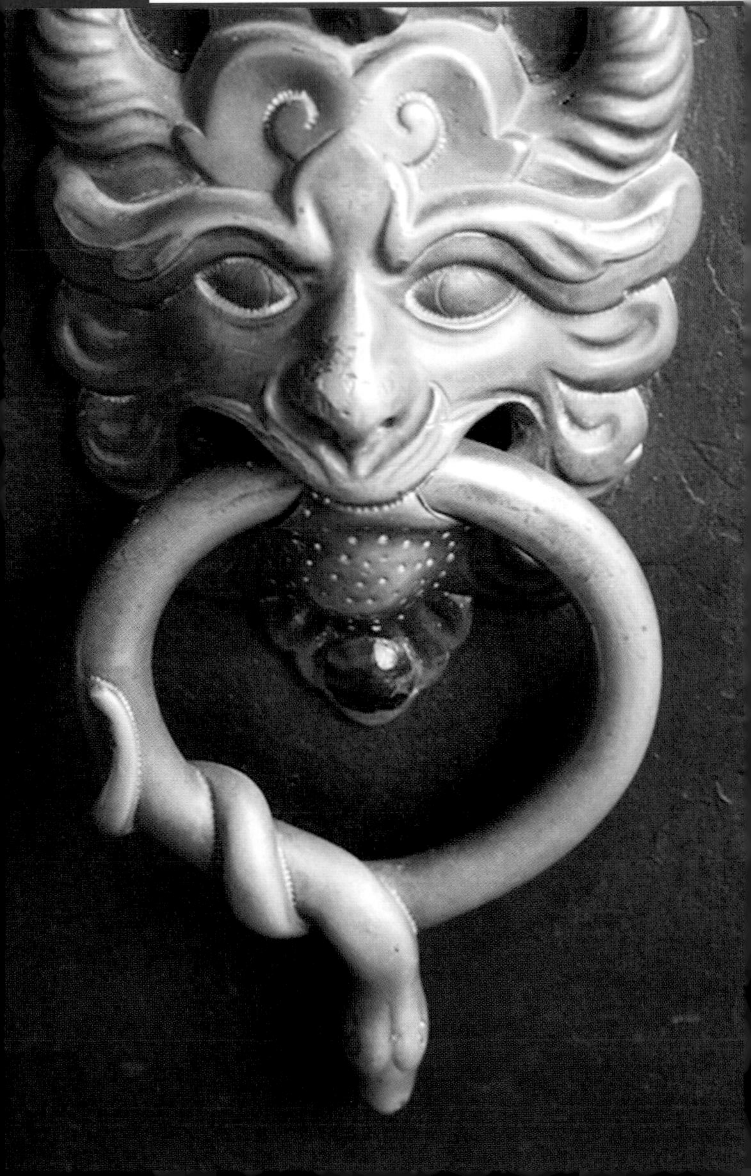

Before You Go

Government Tourist Offices

In the U.S.: 500 Fifth Avenue, Suite 800, New York NY 10103 (☎ 212/944-6885); 11601 Wilshire Boulevard, Los Angeles, CA 90049 (☎ 310/477-3332). **In Canada:** 2 Bloor Street East, Suite 3330, Toronto, Ontario M4W 1A8 (☎ 416/967-3381). **In the U.K. and Ireland:** 9–11 Richmond Buildings, London, W1D 3HF (☎ 020/7440-3830). **In Australia:** 1st Floor, 36 Carrington Street, Sydney, NSW 2000 (☎ 02/9299-3621).

The Best Times to Go

There isn't strictly a best time to visit Salzburg—it depends what you want from it. However, this is a stop-off on grand European bus tours, so high season is crowded. **May** to **September** is the best time to experience the cafe society and the walks, but this is also the busiest. More and more coach tours arrive and then there are the Salzburg Festival crowds from the last week in **July** until the end of **August. October** can be a nice mix of weather and uncrowded streets, and the Kapuzinerberg and Mönchsberg look beautiful as the leaves fall. By late **November,** Salzburg has turned into a fairy-tale winter city. Even if the streets aren't covered with snow, the surrounding peaks are. This is when the skiers start to arrive, and plenty more people start to arrive on short breaks for the Christmas markets. **January** can be a good time with bright, clear skies and the city stays lively with the Mozart Festival at the end of the month. **February** to **March** sees Salzburg as a ski town, while **April** can be snowy and wet.

Festivals & Special Events

SPRING. Easter is a big event in Salzburg, one which brings together two local high points—music and chocolate. While the shops are piled high with charming confections, emotive music fills places of worship, with the **Easter Festival**, 10 days from Palm Sunday, involving bigger concerts. May 1 brings parades while **Whitsun** (late May–early June) again unites a religious festival with music, the **Baroque Music Festival. Corpus Christi,** in the second week of June, brings many closures.

SUMMER. A season that simply gears itself up for the **Salzburg Festival,** the last week of July and the whole of August, when the city comes alive with the feeling of a carnival. Mid-August is the Feast of the Assumption, which can close shops and restaurants.

FALL. Austrian National Day (**Nationalfeiertag**), October 26, is the anniversary of the neutrality declaration after World War II. November 1 is All Saints Day while November 11 is **St. Martin's Day** when children flock from house to house collecting sweets and candy, a bit like trick or treating.

WINTER. From Advent, the last weekend in November, the city is alive with Christmas—markets, music, special events, and church services in churches. This is also the time for **Krampus and Perchten** runs, a Salzburg tradition. The hideous pair, said to dispel the evil spirits of winter, dash through the streets flailing with sticks and cows' tails amid

Previous page: A medieval door knocker.

SALZBURG'S AVERAGE DAILY TEMPERATURE & MONTHLY RAINFALL					
	JAN	FEB	MAR	APR	MAY	JUNE
TEMP (°F)	39	43	52	55	66	72
TEMP (°C)	4	6	11	13	19	22
RAINFALL (IN.)	2.2	2	1.6	2.1	3.1	4.4
	JULY	AUG	SEPT	OCT	NOV	DEC
TEMP (°F)	73	75	68	57	46	39
TEMP (°C)	23	24	20	14	8	4
RAINFALL (IN.)	5.6	4.3	3.2	2.7	2.1	1.8

screaming, cheering children—anyone hit is said to be blessed. Runs, which are a riot of laughter, take place in late afternoon and early evening. December 8 is the Feast of the Immaculate Conception, a day that can involve shop and restaurant closures.

The Weather

The weather's what it is, when it is. I've arrived in Salzburg in late May to 35°C (95°F) temperatures and the following day it's been cold with torrential rain. And I've been in January when I could comfortably wander the streets all day, lunching on a cheese roll by the river, finishing with a sunset walk on the Kapuzinerberg. This is mountain weather, temperamental and changeable by the minute. It's often much nicer than you might imagine . . . balmy, blue-skied, and beautiful. But it's also often rainy and dismally damp. And snow can be expected any time from November to April. Come prepared for the worst—but expect the best.

Useful Websites

- **www.austria.info** The worldwide site for the Austrian Tourist Board, with full information on travel and accommodations and links to all individual areas.

- **www.salzburg.info** Excellent official site with regularly updated and changing information.

- **www.visit-salzburg.net** Independent site with plenty of info to browse.

- **www.salzburg-airport.com** Airport information along with transport connections.

Cellphones

World phones—or GSM (Global System for Mobiles)—work in Austria. If your cellphone is on a GSM system, and you have a world-capable multiband phone, you can make and receive calls from Austria. Just call your wireless operator and ask for 'international roaming' to be activated. North Americans can rent a GSM phone before leaving home from **InTouch USA** (☎ 800/872-7626; www.intouchglobal.com) or **RoadPost** (☎ 888/290-1606 or 905/272-5665; www.roadpost.com).

Car Rentals

Driving in Austria is easy enough, but if you're simply visiting the city, you won't really need a car. If you're staying for a few days, though, you'll want to head into the beautiful surrounding countryside and mountains; it can be done with excursions, but a car gives you greater flexibility, if only for a day. A number of companies have offices here, with **Avis** (☎ 0662/877278; www.avis.at), **Hertz** (☎ 0662/852086; www.hertz.com), and **Budget** (☎ 0662/855038; www.budget.com) being the major names, along with **Europcar** (☎ 0662/850208; www.europcar. at) and **Sixt** (☎ 0662/856051; www. sixt.com). And if you fancy a Rolls Royce Phantom, Ferrari Spider, or Porsche Cayenne, there's luxury specialist **Blue Box** (☎ 0662/ 85809010; www.blueboxrent.com).

Getting **There**

By Plane

Salzburg's W.A. Mozart airport

(Innsbrucker Bundesstrasse 95; ☎ 0662/8580150; www.salzburg-airport.com) is on the edge of the city, a 15-minute drive from the center. The airport has a daily British Airways service from London Gatwick, as well as Frankfurt, Dusseldorf, Vienna, Zurich, and major cities in Russia, Finland, and Spain, amongst others.

Ryanair (www.ryanair.com), the low-cost operator, has a daily flight in summer with a second during the ski season from London Stansted. However, the year-round flight, at the crack of dawn, can be inconvenient. Flights aren't always cheap and the best prices only come to those who watch the website like a hawk . . . and then there are the notorious extra charges for luggage, booking, and more.

easyJet (www.easyjet.com), the other budget giant, has several flights a week from London Gatwick. Tour operator Thomson offers reasonably priced charter flights twice a week from London Gatwick, London Stansted, Belfast, Birmingham, Bournemouth, Bristol, Dublin, East Midlands, Glasgow, Luton, Manchester, and Newcastle (www.thomson lakes.co.uk/ www.thomsonski.co.uk).

From the airport: Bus 2 runs every 10 minutes (20 min. on Sundays and holidays) to Salzburg's main station, covering many of the city center streets, from around 5:30am to midnight. The journey takes around 20 minutes. A single ticket costs 2€ and is available (with change) from the driver. Tickets are also sold at the airport news kiosk, but when I've been there they've only had multi-tickets. The kiosk, however, does sell the Salzburg Card (p 165) that gives free bus travel. A taxi takes around 15 minutes to the city and costs around 12€.

By Car

The **A8** heads down from Munich in Germany, becoming the Tauern-Autobahn, the **A10,** just outside Salzburg. The Tauern-Autobahn runs almost the length of Austria, from Villach, prior to which it is the **A11** from Slovenia. From the east the A1 autobahn leads to Salzburg from Vienna, via Linz.

In Austria all vehicles using autobahns have to display a **toll sticker** from the moment they cross the border. Available from border control offices, a 10-day ticket is 7.50€. See www.asfinag.at for details.

By Train

The central train station in the New Town is a 20-minute walk from the Old Town. There are connections from London, the main one being the Eurostar from St. Pancras to Paris, followed by the German sleeper train to Munich, then a 2-hour journey to Salzburg the following morning. There are good connections with the rest of Austria along with Switzerland and Germany.

By Tour

A number of British companies offer package tours to the city and surrounding area, which can be a simple option if you are flying to London from the U.S. Leading summer operators **Thomson** (☎ 0871/230-8181; www.thomson lakes.co.uk), Crystal (☎ 0871/231-5661; www.crystallakes.co.uk) and **Inghams** (☎ 020/8780-4444; www.inghams.co.uk) feature the city in their Lakes and Mountains programs. For skiing, all of the above offer packages with the following having dedicated ski websites: **Crystal** (☎ 0871/231-2256; www.crystalski.co.uk) and

Thomson (☎ 0871/971-0578; www.thomsonski.co.uk). In addition to the above, you can also search for ski packages via the U.K. with **First Choice** (☎ 0871/664-0130; www.firstchoice-ski.co.uk) and **Neilson** (☎ 0845/070-3460; www.neilson.co.uk). Ski packages can include flights, transfers, hotels, and often food, sometimes for as little as 300€ per person all in.

Getting **Around**

On Foot
Salzburg is a small, compact city and most of the attractions are within walking distance of each other. Given the historic nature of the place, many of the narrow streets are traffic-free. For families, this is an ideal first city-break because of the ease in getting about.

By Bus
Salzburg's city bus network, the **Stadtbus** (www.stadtbus.at), operates with fine Austrian efficiency, and centers on the main bus station outside the Hauptbahnhof in the New Town. There are 10 bus routes and eight trolley-bus routes, almost all of which pass through the city center. Most make a loop—or at least part of the loop—which takes in the New Town, including the Mirabell Palace and the riverbank of the Old Town. They run every 10 minutes during the day. You're most likely to want to use the buses if you're staying near the station or in one of the rural hotels on the outskirts and want to cut out the long stroll to the Old Town.

Single tickets are 1.70€ if bought on board, 1.40€ from a ticket machine or newsstand. Books of five tickets, cheaper still, are available from tobacconists (see the Austria

Tabak sign). A 24-hour ticket is 4€, 2€ for children.

The Salzburg Card is valid for unlimited journeys on all buses. Night buses run until 12:45am on Friday and Saturday, connecting with Lokalbahn trains departing from the main station. Post Buses (tickets available from the driver) serve the countryside.

By Train
The **Lokalbahn,** from the main station, serves areas to the north of the city as well as some southern spots after curving around the Kapuzinerberg.

By Taxi
There is a taxi rank in front of the station, and taxi journeys are reasonably priced (rarely more than 10€), yet you don't really need one unless you're staying out of town. A novel late-night option is the bus-taxi, a service serving 12 routes, picking up at central spots on either side of the river. Each car carries up to four people, with additional cars called if more people are waiting. The service costs 3.50€ per person and operates Sunday to Thursday, 11:30pm to 1:30am, and 11:30pm to 3am on Friday and Saturday.

By Bike

Many hotels rent out bikes (generally less than 10€ a day) while others have them available for free. There are also rental shops at which hotels will often be able to gain you discounts. Bike lanes and paths throughout the city, including the riverbank, make cycling safe and easy. Salzburg can also be used as the starting point for a number of longer tours that pass along the river. The Tauern Cycle Path (**Tauernweg**) runs 282km (175 miles), reaching Krimml Falls in the southwest; the **Salzkammergut** Path covers 354km (220 miles) past 13 lakes; while the **Mozartweg** takes you 450km (280 miles), linking Mozart-related sites. rad.salzburgerland.com is the address for SalzburgerLand cycling queries. For a 40-mile route, along the River Salzach by bike, see p 80–83.

By Car

Assuming you don't arrive by car, there's no need to hire one unless you're planning repeated jaunts out into the countryside. There's nowhere to park for free and parking in the streets is generally limited to 3 hours. As a tourist there is something to be said for the **Altstadtgarage,** a car park carved from the interior of the Mönchsberg, but at 2.40€ an hour it's the cost of a tourist attraction (although Old Town shops and restaurants will stamp your ticket, giving a 3€ for 4 hours rate). It, like other car parks, accepts credit cards. Comprehensive car park information is on www.salzburg.info.

By Tour

There are various companies offering tours in Salzburg and the surrounding areas.

Salzburg Panorama Tours (☎ 0662/8832110; www.panoramatours.com) is the major operator with a variety of tours in the city and out, including the Original Sound of Music Tour, Christmas tours, and tours of mountains, salt mines, and lakes.

Salzburg Sightseeing Tours (☎ 0662/881616; www.salzburg-sightseeingtours.at) is the other main operator and was the first, in 1921. Coaches with multi-lingual guides offer general city and countryside tours along with specialist tours including those on Mozart and The Sound of Music. Some tours are combined with walks and river trips. The company's **Hop-on Hop-off** service is a way to combine a tour with doing your own thing. Luxury coaches that call at 12 stops are equipped with headphones, which have commentaries in seven languages. A 2-hour ticket costs 15€, while a 24-hour ticket is just 20€.

Austria Guides (☎ 0650/ 4566704; www.dididobrasil.com) is an innovative service offering independent options from simple city tours to gourmet tours and even arranging group escorted Harley Davidson tours. Boss Didi Niederkofler, an Austrian-Brazilian, is an engaging font of knowledge about Salzburg and the surrounding area.

Bob's Special Tours (☎ +43 662 849511; www.bobstours.com) offer personal, English-speaking tours by minibus, including one on The Sound of Music, in and around Salzburg. Private tours can also be arranged.

There are also peculiarly Austrian options such as **Fräulein Maria's Bicycle Tour** (☎ 0650/ 3426297; www.mariasbicycletours. com). The 3½ hour small group tours offer easy cycling around the sights for adults and children, and provide bikes, helmets, and child seats. Tours leave Mirabell Square at 9:30am daily, May to September, and reach the palaces of Leopoldskron and Hellbrunn through back roads and cycle paths. The cost is 24€ for adults, 15€ for children.

Equally gentle is a **horse-drawn carriage** from Residence Square, but with a 50-minute ride for four costing 72€ it is an expensive (and touristy) option. Various individual carriages have their own websites and phone numbers (www.salzburg.info has a list), but there are usually plenty waiting.

Fast **Facts**

APARTMENT RENTALS Salzburg Tourism (www.salzburg.info) has all the rentals you'll ever need. There's everything from simple apartments in private houses on the outskirts to city center delights with roof terraces.

AREA CODES Salzburg 0662.

ATMS/CASHPOINTS The easiest way to get euros is at an ATM with your credit card—but remember that credit card companies charge interest from the moment of transaction even if you pay your bill as soon as you receive it.

BIKE RENTALS There are various bike rental shops in Salzburg. **Top Bike Salzburg** (☎ 0676/4767259; www.topbike.at) has an excellent website in English and rates of 6€ for 2 hours, 15€ a day, and 45€ a week, with a 20% Salzburg Card discount (p 165). It has two central locations, in the Old Town by the river on Franz-Josef-Kai by the Staatsbrücke bridge, and in the New Town by the main station. It's also possible to book from hotels, with a 5€ delivery charge. **City Bike** also has a riverside Old Town shop on Hanuschplatz (☎ 0810 500500; www.citybikesalzburg.at). Try also **VELOactive** (Willibald-Hauthaler-Strasse 10; ☎ 0662/4355950).

BUSINESS HOURS Banks are open Monday through Friday from 8:30am to 2pm. Most offices are open Monday through Friday from 9am to 6 or 7pm. (In July, 8am–3pm). In August, businesses are on skeleton staff if not closed altogether. At restaurants, lunch is usually from 1:30 or 2 to 4pm and dinner from 9 to 11:30pm or midnight. Major stores are open Monday through Saturday from 9:30 or 10am to 8pm; staff at smaller establishments, however, often still close for siesta in the mid-afternoon, doing business from 9:30am to 2pm and 4:30pm to 8 or 8:30pm.

DRINKING LAWS The minimum drinking age is 16, when it is possible to buy beer and wine, and be served in a bar or restaurant—but if a person appears to be getting drunk he or she will be refused service. The legal age for buying and drinking spirits is 18. The drink-drive limit is 0.5 milligrams of alcohol per 100 milliliters of blood, stricter than the U.S. and U.K. (0.8 per 100).

DRIVING See 'Getting There.'

ELECTRICITY Hotels operate on the continental two-pin 220-volt AC system, but a simple plug adaptor is all that is needed to get connected.

EMBASSIES & CONSULATES U.K. Consulate, Altermarkt 4; ☎ 0662/848133. All others are in Vienna: **U.S. Embassy,** Boltzmanngasse 16; ☎ 01/313-390; **Canadian Embassy,** Laurenzerberg 2; ☎ 01/531-383-000; **Australian Embassy,** Mattiellistrasse 2-4; ☎:01/506-74-0; **Irish Embassy,** Rotenturmstrasse 16–18; ☎ 01/715-4246.

EMERGENCIES For police dial ☎ 133, or for general police enquiries ☎ 0591/33550. For an ambulance ☎ 144; for fire ☎ 122.

GAY & LESBIAN TRAVELERS For a small city Salzburg has a lively gay scene, focused on a small area in the riverside area of the New Town. **Diva** (p 116) in Priesterhausgasse and the **2-Stein** (p 116) on Giselakai are the main bars, while the restaurants in between are the places to eat. **HOSI** (the Salzburg Homosexual Initiative) is very active and holds a festival four times a year at the ARGEKultur arts complex (Josef-Preis-Allee 16; ☎ 0662/8487840; www.argekultur.at), a party that goes on until very late. HOSI has events dates on its website (www.hosi.or.at) but it is only in German.

GUIDES A good way to see Salzburg if you are on a tight schedule is with a walking guide. The **Salzburg Guide Service** (Linzergasse 22; ☎ 0662/840406; www.salzburg-guide.at) offers 2- to 3-hour tours.

HOLIDAYS Holidays observed are January 1 (New Year's Day), January 6 (Feast of the Epiphany), March/April (Good Friday and Easter Monday), May 1 (Labor Day), May/June (Whit Monday), June Corpus Christi, August 15 (Feast of the Assumption), October 26 (Austria's National Day), November 1 (All Saints' Day), December 8 (Feast of the Immaculate Conception), and December 25 (Christmas) and December 26 (Feast of St. Stephen).

HOSPITALS Salzburg's main hospital is Landeskrankenhaus, Müllner Hauptstrasse 48 (☎ 0662/4482, but 144 for an ambulance).

INSURANCE Check your existing insurance policies before you buy travel insurance to cover trip cancellation, lost luggage, medical expenses, or car rental insurance. For more information, contact one of the following recommended insurers: **Access America** (☎ 866/807-3982; www.accessamerica.com); **Travel Guard International** (☎ 800/826-4919; www.travelguard.com); **Travel Insured International** (☎ 800/243-3174; www.travelinsured.com); and **Travelex Insurance Services** (☎ 888/457-4602; www.travelex-insurance.com). For travel overseas, most U.S. health plans (including Medicare and Medicaid) do not provide coverage, and the ones that do often require payment for services upfront. If you require additional medical insurance, try **MEDEX Assistance** (☎ 410/453-6300; www.medexassist.com) or **Travel Assistance International** (☎ 800/821-2828; www.travelassistance.com; for general information on services call the company's Worldwide Assistance Services, Inc., at ☎ 800/777-8710).

For E.U. citizens, emergency health treatment is covered with the free **European Health Insurance Card** (www.ehic.uk.com or www.ehic.ie).

INTERNET ACCESS Most hotels now have Internet connections, whether via connection or Wi-Fi. Some charge, but some are free and even offer free computer terminals in reception. Internet cafes are becoming rarer but you can try the **Cybar** (Mozartplatz 5; ☎ 0662/844822; www.cybar.at) in the Old Town or **Isis** (Südtiroler Platz 1; ☎ 0699/12363717) by the station.

LANGUAGE English is spoken widely, and the Austrians have no problems with you not speaking their language, but it is wise to take a good phrasebook such as Frommer's *German PhraseFinder & Dictionary*. For useful terms and phrases see p 170.

Salzburg & SalzburgerLand Cards

The Salzburg Card is an excellent value card, making visiting Salzburg easy at reasonable cost. The card gives a single free entry to 25 attractions in Salzburg, including the Hohenfestung Fortess, Hellbrunn, a river cruise, and the Untersberg cable car. The card gives free bus travel throughout the city. There are also discounts on most regular concerts, coach tours, bike rental, dinner shows, and more, along with discounts on many attractions outside Salzburg such as salt mines and waterfalls. The card is available from most hotels, tourist offices, the airport newsstand, and some shops. In high season (May–Oct) it costs 24€ for 24 hours, 32€ for 48 hours, and 37€ for 72 hours. Children are half price. See www.salzburg.info for details.

The **SalzburgerLand Card** is similar to the Salzburg Card, but useful if you're planning a few days outside the city. It gives free entry to almost 200 sights and attractions including spas, mountain lifts, sports activities, and lakes. A 6-day card costs 43€, 12 days 52€ (children half price) with Salzburg city attractions covered for a 24-hour period. It is available at tourist offices, many hotels, shops, and from www.salzburgerlandcard.com.

LEGAL AID If you have a serious legal problem while in Austria, you should contact your embassy for advice (see p 163).

LOST PROPERTY Call credit card companies the minute you discover your wallet has been lost or stolen and file a report at the police HQ on Alpenstrasse. Your credit card company or insurer may require a police report number or record. The city's lost property office is on the ground floor of the Mirabell Palace (☎ 0662/80723580) and is open Monday to Thursday 7:30am to 4pm, and Friday 7:30am to 1pm.

MAIL & POSTAGE There are a number of post offices (with the sign of a yellow horn and the word *Postamt*) in the city, including in Residenzplatz and Makartplatz. Main offices are generally open from 8am to noon and 2pm to 6pm, Monday through Friday. There is a post office at the Hauptbahnhof open longer hours, including weekends.

MONEY The single European currency in Austria is the **euro.** At press time, the exchange rate was approximately 1€ = $1.40 (or 90p). For up-to-the-minute exchange rates, check the currency converter website www.xe.com/ucc. There are various currency exchange offices which take credit cards as well as cash. At the airport there's the **Salzburger Sparkasse** exchange, generally open 8am to 4pm, with an after-hours service (until around 11pm) at the airport information counter. **Interchange Austria** (Mozartplatz 5; ☎ 0662/84384045) is open Monday to Friday 9am to 5:30pm, Saturday 9am to noon. Banks will also exchange currency.

NEWSPAPERS & MAGAZINES English-language newspapers from both the

U.K. and the U.S. are available at a number of kiosks and shops, including the one at the Hauptbahnhof (the main station).

PASSPORTS If your passport is lost or stolen, contact your country's embassy or consulate immediately. See 'Embassies & Consulates' above. Make a copy of your passport's critical pages and keep it separate from your passport.

PHARMACIES Pharmacies (*apothekes*) operate during normal business hours, including Saturday mornings, and have a rota for night and holiday cover. The location and phone number of the duty pharmacy is posted on the door of all the other pharmacies.

POLICE For police dial ☎ 133, or for general police enquiries ☎ 0591/33550.

SMOKING Austria was one of the smokiest places on earth (I've been in smart hotels when someone has lit up at breakfast) but things are changing . . . up to a point. A law introduced on January 1, 2009, rules that bars, pubs, and restaurants with several rooms must offer separate non-smoking areas. But you need to look out for signs as smaller establishments can choose whether to be smoking or non-smoking.

TAXES If you are from outside the EU you can claim back VAT paid on most goods. A form must be obtained from the shop on purchase, then stamped at the airport or border. The form should be returned to the shop, which will credit the money to your account.

TELEPHONES Telephone boxes are a vanishing species but there are still a few around. Post offices have them, with instructions in English. To make an international call, dial ☎ 00, wait for the tone, and dial

the country code (1 for the U.S. and Canada, 44 for the U.K.) then the area code (omitting the first zero) and number. When dialing Austria from abroad, the international dialing code is 43.

TIME Austria is in the Central European Time zone, 1 hour ahead of Greenwich Mean Time and 6 hours ahead of Eastern Standard Time in the U.S. Summer time moves ahead 1 hour on the same dates as the U.K., but a few days out of sync with the U.S.

TIPPING While tipping is still expected in Salzburg, it is not an issue to the same extent as in some European destinations. Around 10% would be normal in a restaurant and simply rounding up in a bar or cafe. Tour guides and coach drivers expect tips and show it, in the nicest possible way.

TOILETS Here they're signed as WCs (*damen* for women, *herren* for men) and there are a few around the city, some with a .50€ charge. It is acceptable to use the facilities in restaurants and bars, but not always appreciated unless you place an order.

TOUR COMPANIES A number of companies offer escorted tours to Austria which take in Salzburg.

In the U.S.:

American Express Vacations (☎ 800/335-3342; www.american expressvacations.com).

Brendan Vacations (☎ 800/421-8446; www.brendanvacations.com).

Collette Vacations (☎ 800/340-5158; www.collettevacations.com).

Globus & Cosmos Tours (☎ 800/338-7092; www.globusandcosmos.com).

In the .U.K.:

Travelsphere (☎ 0800/567-7372; www.travelsphere.co.uk).

Archers Direct (☎ 0844/573-4806; www.archersdirect.co.uk).

Cox & Kings (☎ 020/7873-5000; www.coxandkings.co.uk).

TOURIST INFORMATION The main tourist office (☎ 0662/88987330) is on Mozartplatz. From May to September, plus Advent, Christmas, and New Year, it is open daily, 9am to 7pm. The rest of the year (9am to 6pm) it is closed Sundays.

There is a smaller office (☎ 0662/88987340) at the Hauptbahnhof, open daily year-round. In high season it is open 8:30am to 8pm, low season 9am to 6pm.

A further office is at the Park & Ride car park Salzburg-Süd, near Hellbrunn (Alpensiedlung-Süd, Alpenstrasse, ☎ 0662/88987360). It is open daily in July to August;

Monday to Saturday in September and Advent, Christmas, and New Year; Easter and May to June Thursday to Saturday.

TRAVELERS WITH DISABILITIES The bulk of Salzburg's buildings are very old so access might well have been a problem, but the problem has been tackled well. Salzburg Tourism (www.salzburg.info) has a comprehensive brochure, *Salzburg Without Barriers*, which can be downloaded in PDF format (click on *Service*, then *Salzburg for . . .*). It gives full information, including door widths, WC access, and height of any steps, for hundreds of attractions, hotels, restaurants, and bars. Travel is also taken care of, with special access on Salzburg's buses.

VISAS No visas are required for U.S. or Canadian visitors to Austria providing your stay does not exceed 90 days. British and Irish visitors need no visa.

Salzburg: **A Brief History**

4000 B.C. Stone Age settlement on the Rainberg mountain.

500 B.C. Celts invade the area and start to mine salt and build fortifications.

1ST–5TH C. B.C. The region becomes a trade hub, with salt transported along the river.

15 B.C. Romans conquer the Celts and create a town, Luvavum.

A.D. 45 Luvavum acquires *municipium* status, and becomes one of the largest administrations outside Rome.

500 Bavarian hordes drive out the Romans and set Luvavum ablaze.

700 Bishop Rupert von Worms arrives from Bavaria as a missionary and founds St. Peter's Abbey and the Nonnberg Convent.

719 Salzburg becomes a bishopric, and is later one of the most important areas outside the Vatican.

755 Name Salzburg is first documented.

774 Irish bishop Virgil consecrates the new cathedral.

798 City becomes an archbishopric.

803 St. Peter's restaurant opens.

1077 Archbishop Gebhard starts work on Hohensalzburg Fortress.

1167 German Emperor Barbarossa burns the city to the ground.

13TH C. Salt from Hallein brings glory days of archbishops' rule.

1322 Salzburg gains independence after civil war between Bavaria and Austria.

1328 Salzburg becomes an autonomous state.

1348 Plague kills almost half the population.

1492 Stiegl brewery is founded.

1495–1519 Fortress rebuilt by Archbishop Leonard von Keutschach into the form that exists today.

1525 Salzburg is occupied and the fortress besieged for three months during the Bauerkriege (Peasants' Revolt).

1578–1612 The reign of visionary Archbishop Wolf Dietrich von Raitenau, when the Baroque age began.

1612–19 Archbishop Markus Sittikus continues Salzburg's rebirth, and creates Hellbrunn Palace.

1619–53 Archbishop Paris Lodron continues the work while keeping Salzburg out of the 30 Years' War that devastated Europe.

1620–44 City fortifications built.

1653 Cathedral completed by Paris Count of Lodron.

1687–1709 Under the reign of Johann Ernst von Thun, Salzburg finally completes its Baroque makeover.

1731 Twenty thousand protestants banished from the province by Archbishop Leopold Anton von Firmian.

1756 Wolfgang Amadeus Mozart born.

1779–81 Mozart is organist at Salzburg Cathedral.

1803 Rule of the archbishops ends after defeat to Napoleon.

1805 Salzburg incorporated into Austria.

1809–10 Salzburg under French rule after second Napoleonic defeat.

1816 Salzburg becomes part of the Austrian Habsburg Empire.

1918 Austrian republic proclaimed.

1920 Salzburg Festival founded.

1938 Austria annexed by Nazi Germany. Book burnings are held on Residenzplatz and persecution of Jews begins.

1944–45 Fifteen Allied airstrikes destroy almost half of Salzburg's buildings, especially around the station.

1955 New Austrian republic declared.

1959 Restoration of the cathedral completed.

1964 *The Sound of Music* filmed.

1997 Salzburg becomes a UNESCO World Cultural Heritage site to honor its unique Baroque architecture.

Salzburg's **Architecture**

Renaissance (2nd century B.C.–4th century A.D.)
The early conquerors of Spain were extraordinary engineers. Relics of the Roman colony of Barcino can be seen in the surviving columns of the

Salzburg Cathedral.

Temple d'Augustus, originally part of the Roman forum, and gates and sections of the 3rd and 4th century walls that encircled the city. The finest Roman ruins are beneath **Plaça del Rei,** in the **Museu d'Història de la Ciutat.**

Romanesque (11th–12th century)

Salzburg, a city filled with churches in traditional style, started to change around now. Churches were remodeled in the fashionable Romanesque style. The nave of the Franciscan Church is a good example, the chunky simplicity and round arches a rebellion against the more joyous styles of earlier years.

Gothic (14th–16th century)

The more ornate style, with its pointed arches, also made its mark in Salzburg. The hall choir of the Franciscan Church is a beautiful example, the work of German master builder **Hans von Burghausen.** The earliest example is the chapel of St. Mary in St. Peter's Abbey, rebuilt in Gothic fashion in 1319.

Baroque (16th–18th century)

When the Romanesque cathedral was damaged by fire Archbishop Wolf Dietrich von Raitenau (related to the Pope and educated in Rome) had a vision. He brought in Vincenza architect **Vincenzo Scamozzi** to draw up plans for a new Salzburg, which involved razing the area around the cathedral. The result was a vast workforce of Italian stucco artists, painters, and architects building a new life for themselves in Salzburg creating the blueprint for the cathedral that exists today along with squares, Mirabell Palace, and more. Wolf Dietrich's imprisonment in a salt-related dispute didn't stop the work—his successor Marcus Sittikus had a similar vision, appointing Italian **Santino Solari** court architect, which yielded the cathedral and the Italianate Hellbrun summer palace. Archbishop Johann Ernst Thun along with respected architect **Johann Bernhard Fischer von Erlach** completed the picture, achieving his

Hangar-7.

dream of making Salzburg the 'German Rome' with buildings such as the Collegiate Church.

20th century

The Mozarteum, completed in 1914, was built in late Munich historical style with a touch of Baroque. In 1924 what is now the Festival Halls complex started taking shape under the guidance of architect Clemens Holzmeister. It brought together the ageless Mönchsberg rock with a simpler, modern approach, taking in set designer Benno von Arendt's Nazi-era Baroque touches. The halls have changed regularly, most recently the former royal stables being adapted by **Wilhelm Holzbauer,** one of Holzmeister's students, and Luxembourg architect **François Valentiny** as a House for

Mozart to celebrate the 250th anniversary of Mozart's birth in 2006.

Modern (21st century)

Austria has taken to stylish modernism in architecture with gusto, and generally gets it right. The Museum of Modern Art atop the Mönchsberg is a simple, marbled form, which can be appreciated from the Makartsteg footbridge with its vertical and horizontal curves. But with so much history in the Old Town, new building is rare and development (most of it very ordinary) takes place near the station or farther out. An exception is **Hangar-7,** the curved glass homage to food, drink, and historic planes near the airport, the work of Salzburg architect Volkmar Burgstaller.

Useful Phrases & Menu Terms

Useful Words & Phrases

ENGLISH	GERMAN	PRONUNCIATION
Good morning	Guten morgen	guu-ten morgen
Good evening	Guten abend	guuten-abend
Good night	Gute nacht	goot nacht
Thank you	Danke	dan-ke
You're welcome	Bitte sehr	bit-tuh zayr
Goodbye	Auf Wiedersehen	awf veed-er-shane
Please	Bitte	bit-tuh
Yes	Ja	yah
No	Nein	nine
Excuse me	Entschuldigen Sie	ent-shul-di-gen zee
Where?	Wo?	woah?
Where's the toilet?	Wo ist die toilette?	voh ist dee twah-let-uh?
How much?	Wieviel?	wee-veel?
When?	Wann?	one?
What?	Was?	woss?
Is/are there?	Gibt es?	gibb-et ess?
May I?	Darf ich?	darf-ikh
Is it near here?	Ist es ganz in der nähe?	Ist ez gans in der nye?
I'm sorry	Es tut mir leid	es toot meer lied
Do you speak English?	Sprechen sie Englisch?	shprekhen zee Eng-lish
Station	Bahnhof	ban-hof
Airport	Flughafen	floog-hafen

ENGLISH	GERMAN	PRONUNCIATION
Next week	Nächste Woche	nex-tuh voh-khuh
I need	Ich brauche...	ikh brow-khuh
Tomorrow morning	Morgen früh	mor-gen fruh
Today	Heute	hoy-tuh
Next week	Nächste Woche	nex-tuh voh-khuh
This week	Diese Woche	dee-zuh voh-khuh
I would like...	Ich möchte...	ikh mersh-ta
To eat	Essen	ess-en
A room	Ein Zimmer	ain tzim-mer
For one night	Für eine Nacht	feer ai-neh nakht

Emergencies

It's an emergency	Es ist ein Notfall	ess ist ighn noht-fahl
I'm sick	Ich bin krank	ikh bin krahnk
I'll call the police	Ich rufe die Polizei	ikh roo-fuh dee poh-lee-tsigh
I need your help	Ich brauche deine/ Ihre Hilfe	ikh brow-khuh digh-nuh/ee-ruh hill-fuh
I'm lost	Ich habe mich verirrt	ikh hah-buh mikh fer-irt
Help!	Hilfe!	hill-fuh!

Restaurants

Is service included?	Ist die Bedienung inbegriffen?	Ist dye bedden-ung inbe-griffen?
The check, please	Die Rechnung, bitte	die reck-nung, bit-tuh
Do you have a table?	Haben sie einen Tisch?	haben see I-nen tish?
Menu	Speisekarte	space-kart
Do you have...?	Haben sie?	haben see?

Food

Chicken	Huhn	hoon
Beef	Rindfleisch	rint-flighsh
Fish	Fisch	fish
Ham	Schinken	shink-en
Sausage	Wurst	vurst
Cheese	Käse	kay-zuh
Salad	Salat	zah-laht
Eggs	Eier	igh-er
Vegetables	Gemüse	guh-muu-zuh
Fruit	Obst	owpst
Bread	Brot	broht
Noodles	Nudeln	noo-deln
Rice	Reis	righzz
Beans	Bohnen	boh-nen
Tea	Tee	Tay
Coffee	Kaffee	kaff-ey
Juice	Saft	zahft
Mineral water	Mineralwasser	mineral-vasser
Tap water	Leitungswasser	ligh-toongs-vasser

ENGLISH	GERMAN	PRONUNCIATION
Meat		
Cold cuts	Aufschnitt	owf-shnitt
Roast chicken	Brathuhn	braht-hoon
Grilled sausage	Bratwurst	braht-vurst
Hamburger/ beefsteak	Hamburger/ Fleischleibchen	hamburger/ flighshlaib-chen
Duck	Ente	en-ter
Goose	Gans	ganz
Poultry	Geflügel	ge-floo-gel
Veal	Kalb	kalb
Pork chops	Kassler Rippchen	kass-ler rip-chen
Lamb	Lamm	lamm
Liver	Leber	lay-ber
Roast beef	Rinderbraten	rin-der-brah-ten
Roast pork	Schweinebraten	shwai-ner-brah-ten
Turkey	Truthahn	troot-hahn
Fish		
Eel	Aal	aahl
Trout	Forelle	for-ell
Pike	Hecht	hect
Carp	Karpfen	karp-fen
Crayfish	Kerbs	kerbs
Salmon	Lachs	lackhs
Mackerel	Makrele	mak-rel
Rhine salmon	Rheinsalm	rine-saahm
Haddock	Schellfisch	shel-feesh
Sole	Seezunge	see-zung-er
Vegetables		
Cauliflower	Blumenkohl	blue-men-kohl
Beans	Bohnen	bohr-non
Fried potatoes	Bratkartoffeln	braht-kart-off-eln
Peas	Erbsen	erb-sehn
String beans	Grüne Bohnen	groo-neh bohr-non
Cucumber	Gurken	gurr-ken
Carrots	Karotten	karr-o-ten
Mashed potatoes	Kartoffelnbrei	karr-toff-eln-brei
Potato salad	Kartoffelnsalat	karr-toff-eln-sal-aht
Cabbage	Kohl	kohl
Beets	Rote Rüben	roh-ter roo-ben
Red cabbage	Rotkraut	roht-rowt
Lettuce	Salat	sal-aht
Boiled potatoes	Salzkartoffeln	salz-karr-toff-eln
Asparagus	Spargel	spar-gel
Spinach	Spinat	spee-naht
Tomatoes	Tomaten	Tom-ah-ten

Beverages (Getränke)

Beer	Bier	beer
A dark beer	Ein dunkles	ein dun-kuls
A light beer	Ein helles	ein hels
Milk	Milch	milsh
Chocolate	Schokolade	shok-oh-laa-der
A cup of coffee	Eine Tasse Kaffee	ein-er tass-er kaff-ey
A cup of tea	Eine Tasse Tee	ein-er tass-er tay
Water	Wasser	vass-er

Cooking Terms

Rare	Blutig	blue-tig
Baked	Gebacken	ge-back-en
Fried	Gebraten	ge-brah-ten
Stuffed	Gefült	ge-fuult
Boiled	Gekocht	ge-coct
Roasted	Geröstet	ge-rerr-stet
Well done	Gut durchgebraten	goot dursh-ge-brah-ten
Hot	Heiss	hiyse
Cold	Kaltes	kal-tez

Condiments

Butter	Butter	butt-er
Ice	Eis	aiys
Vinegar	Eissig	aiy-sig
Dumplings	Knödel	nuuh-del
Pepper	Pfeffer	pheff-er
Rice	Reis	raiys
Cream	Sahne	sah-ner
Salt	Salz	salz
Mustard	Senf	senph
Sugar	Zucker	zoo-ker

Numbers

1	eins	(einz)
2	zwei	(z-vai)
3	drei	(dry)
4	vier	(veer)
5	fünf	(foonf)
6	sechs	(secks)
7	sieben	(see-ben)
8	acht	(act)
9	neun	(noon)
10	zehn	(zen)
11	elf	(elf)
12	zwölf	(z-wulf)
13	dreizehn	(dry-zen)
14	vierzehn	(veer-zen)
15	fünfzehn	(foonf-zen)
16	sechzehn	(seck-zen)

Numbers

17	siebzehn	(seeb-zen)
18	achtzehn	(act-zen)
19	neunzehn	(noon-zen)
20	zwanzig	(z-wan-zig)
30	dreißig	(dry-zig)
40	vierzig	(veer-zig)
50	fünfzig	(foonf-zig)
60	sechzig	(seck-zig)
70	siebzig	(seeb-zig)
80	achtzig	(act-zig)
90	neunzig	(noon-zig)
100	hundert	(hund-ert)

Days of the Week

Monday	Montag
Tuesday	Dienstag
Wednesday	Mittwoch
Thursday	Donnerstag
Friday	Freitag
Saturday	Samstag
Sunday	Sonntag

Toll-Free Numbers & Websites

AER LINGUS
☎ 15852100 in Austria
☎ 01/886-8844 in Ireland
☎ 0871 718 5000
in the U.K.
☎ 800/474-7424 in the
U.S. (NOT TOLL-FREE)
www.aerlingus.com

AUSTRIAN AIRLINES
☎ 051766 1002
in Austria
☎ 0870 1 24 26 25
in the U.K.
☎ 800/843-0002
in the U.S.
www.aua.com

BRITISH AIRWAYS
☎ 179 567 567 in Austria
☎ 0870 850 9850
in the U.K.
☎ 800/247-9297
in the U.S.
www.british-airways.com

EASYJET
☎ 0900 370120
in Austria
No U.S. number
☎ 0905 821 0905 in the
U.K. (NOT TOLL-FREE)
www.easyjet.com

FIRST CHOICE
☎ 0871 200 7799 in U.K.
(U.K.-based call center)
www.firstchoice.co.uk

KLM
☎ 0820 420 414
in Austria
☎ 0871 222 7740
in the U.K.
☎ 800/374-7747
in the U.S.
www.klm.nl

LUFTHANSA
☎ 0810 1025 8080
in Austria
☎ 0871 945 9747
in the U.K.
☎ 800/645-3880
in the U.S.
www.lufthansa.com

THOMAS COOK
☎ 0871 895 0060
in the U.K. (U.K.-based
call center)
www.thomascook.com

Index

See also Accommodations and Restaurant indexes, below.

Accommodations

Photo **Credits**

Front Matter Credits: i: © Shutterstock; © Leonid Serebrennikov / Alamy; © Pictorium / Alamy

All images: © Nick Dalton with the following exceptions:

© Berchtesgadener Land Tourismus: p154-156.

© F1online digitale Bildagentur GmbH / Alamy: p94.

© Foto Herbert Raffalt: p93.

© Helge Kirchberger / Red Bull Photofiles: p113.

© Hotelstein Salzburg: p114.

© Leonid Serebrennikov / Alamy: p42.

© Ski amadé/Leo Himsl/Salburg Tourism: p89.

© Tourismus Salzburg: p50, p52, p53, p81, p82, p86, p87, p95, p98, p109, p110, p117, p118, p124, p148, p149, p150.

© Ulrich Grill / Red Bull Photofiles: p20.

Courtesy Berglandhotel, Salzburg: p134.

Courtesy of Carpe Diem and Afro Coffee, Salzburg: p104 bottom.

Courtesy Hotelstein: p137 bottom.

Courtesy of Magazin Restaurant, Salzburg: p105.

Notes

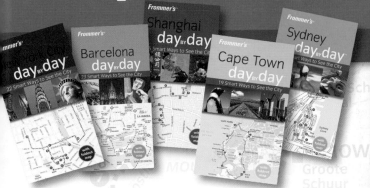

Explore over 3,500 destinations.

TOKYO — 7766 miles

LONDON — 3818 miles

TORONTO — 4682 miles

SYDNEY — 5087 miles

NEW YORK — 4947 miles

LOS ANGELES — 2556 miles

HONG KONG — 5638 miles

Frommers.com makes it easy.

Find a destination. ✓ Book a trip. ✓ Get hot travel deals.
Buy a guidebook. ✓ Enter to win vacations. ✓ Listen to podcas
Check out the latest travel news. ✓ Share trip photos and memories.
And much more.

Frommers.com